T0073759

Internet Law in China

CHANDOS
ASIAN STUDIES SERIES:
CONTEMPORARY ISSUES AND TRENDS

Series Editor: Professor Chris Rowley,
Centre for Research on Asian Management, Cass Business School,
City University, UK; HEAD Foundation, Singapore
(email: c.rowley@city.ac.uk)

Chandos Publishing is pleased to publish this major Series of books entitled *Asian Studies: Contemporary Issues and Trends*. The Series Editor is Professor Chris Rowley, Director, Centre for Research on Asian Management, City University, UK and Director, Research and Publications, HEAD Foundation, Singapore.

Asia has clearly undergone some major transformations in recent years and books in the Series examine this transformation from a number of perspectives: economic, management, social, political and cultural. We seek authors from a broad range of areas and disciplinary interests: covering, for example, business/management, political science, social science, history, sociology, gender studies, ethnography, economics and international relations, etc.

Importantly, the Series examines both current developments and possible future trends. The Series is aimed at an international market of academics and professionals working in the area. The books have been specially commissioned from leading authors. The objective is to provide the reader with an authoritative view of current thinking.

New authors: we would be delighted to hear from you if you have an idea for a book. We are interested in both shorter, practically orientated publications (45,000+ words) and longer, theoretical monographs (75,000–100,000 words). Our books can be single, joint or multi-author volumes. If you have an idea for a book, please contact the publishers or Professor Chris Rowley, the Series Editor.

Dr Glyn Jones
Chandos Publishing
Email: gjones@chandospublishing.com
www.chandospublishing.com

Professor Chris Rowley
Cass Business School, City University
Email: c.rowley@city.ac.uk
www.cass.city.ac.uk/faculty/c.rowley

Chandos Publishing: Chandos Publishing is an imprint of Woodhead Publishing Limited. The aim of Chandos Publishing is to publish books of the highest possible standard: books that are both intellectually stimulating and innovative.

We are delighted and proud to count our authors from such well known international organisations as the Asian Institute of Technology, Tsinghua University, Kookmin University, Kobe University, Kyoto Sangyo University, London School of Economics, University of Oxford, Michigan State University, Getty Research Library, University of Texas at Austin, University of South Australia, University of Newcastle, Australia, University of Melbourne, ILO, Max-Planck Institute, Duke University and the leading law firm Clifford Chance.

A key feature of Chandos Publishing's activities is the service it offers its authors and customers. Chandos Publishing recognises that its authors are at the core of its publishing ethos, and authors are treated in a friendly, efficient and timely manner. Chandos Publishing's books are marketed on an international basis, via its range of overseas agents and representatives.

Professor Chris Rowley: Dr Rowley, BA, MA (Warwick), DPhil (Nuffield College, Oxford) is Subject Group leader and the inaugural Professor of Human Resource Management at Cass Business School, City University, London, UK and Director of Research and Publications for the HEAD Foundation, Singapore. He is the founding Director of the multi-disciplinary and internationally networked Centre for Research on Asian Management (http://www.cass.city.ac.uk/cram/index.html) and Editor of the leading journal *Asia Pacific Business Review* (www.tandf.co.uk/journals/titles/13602381.asp). He is well known and highly regarded in the area, with visiting appointments at leading Asian universities and top journal Editorial Boards in the UK, Asia and the US. He has given a range of talks and lectures to universities, companies and organisations internationally with research and consultancy experience with unions, business and government and his previous employment includes varied work in both the public and private sectors. Professor Rowley researches in a range of areas, including international and comparative human resource management and Asia Pacific management and business. He has been awarded grants from the British Academy, an ESRC AIM International Study Fellowship and gained a 5-year RCUK Fellowship in Asian Business and Management. He acts as a reviewer for many funding bodies, as well as for numerous journals and publishers. Professor Rowley publishes very widely, including in leading US and UK journals, with over 370 articles, books, chapters and other contributions.

Bulk orders: some organisations buy a number of copies of our books. If you are interested in doing this, we would be pleased to discuss a discount. Please email wp@woodheadpublishing.com or telephone +44 (0) 1223 499140.

Internet Law in China

GUOSONG SHAO

CHANDOS
PUBLISHING

Oxford Cambridge Philadelphia New Delhi

Chandos Publishing
Hexagon House
Avenue 4
Station Lane
Witney
Oxford OX28 4BN
UK
Tel: +44 (0) 1993 848726
Email: info@chandospublishing.com
www.chandospublishing.com

Chandos Publishing is an imprint of Woodhead Publishing Limited

Woodhead Publishing Limited
80 High Street
Sawston
Cambridge CB22 3HJ
UK
Tel: +44 (0) 1223 499140
Fax: +44 (0) 1223 832819
www.woodheadpublishing.com

First published in 2012

ISBN 978-0-08-101677-0 (Chandos Publishing print)
ISBN 978-0-85709-159-8 (Woodhead Publishing print)
ISBN 978-1-78063-337-4 (online)

© G. Shao, 2012

Typeset by Domex e-Data Pvt. Ltd.
Printed in the UK and USA.

Dedicated to the memory of my mother, CHEN Heying,
for her boundless love and care;
to my father, SHAO Tongxiang, who always
encourages me to strive for glory;
to my wife ZHANG Ying,
for her infinite love and support;
and to my angel daughter, SHAO Meishi,
who is a source of joy and meaning in my life.

Contents

List of cases

List of abbreviations

CCTV	China Central Television
CD	compact disc
CNNIC	China Internet Network Information Center
CPC	Communist Party of China
DNS	Domain Name System
DVD	digital video disc
FTP	File Transfer Protocol
GAPP	General Administration of Press and Publication
Gb	gigabyte
Gbps	gigabytes per second
HTTP	Hypertext Transfer Protocol
ICANN	Internet Corporation for Assigned Names and Numbers
ID	identity
IMAP	Internet Message Access Protocol
IP	Internet Protocol
ISC	Internet Society of China
ISP	Internet service provider
MIIT	Ministry of Industry and Information Technology
NPC	National People's Congress
POP	Post Office Protocol
PRC	People's Republic of China

PSN	processor serial number
RMB	renminbi
SAIC	State Administration of Industry and Commerce
SARFT	State Administration of Radio, Film and Television
SCIO	State Council Information Office
SMT	Surface Mount Technology
SPC	Supreme People's Court
TCP	Transmission Control Protocol
TRIPS	Trade-Related Intellectual Property Rights
URL	Uniform Resource Locator
VCD	video compact disc
WIPO	World Intellectual Property Organization
WTO	World Trade Organization

Preface

By the nature of the subject, any study of Internet law is a formidable task. Why go through all the trouble of writing a book on a subject that is constantly evolving and remarkably complicated? I can offer a brief answer: because I could and because I should. During the past decade, China has built up a relatively complete system of laws and regulations governing the Internet; and it is now possible to write a whole book on China's Internet law relatively easily. That is why I say I could. The reason I should do it is twofold: first, China's Internet industry has experienced dramatic growth, and China's regulation of the Internet has become the focus of public discussion, but internationally, there is no book that comprehensively explores the legal doctrines and principles that apply to the Internet and related activities in China. As an academic person, I think I should fill this gap; and second, I have a more ambitious goal, that is, through clarifying the principles of China's Internet law, I hope I can contribute to the development of China's regulation of the Internet and eventually the improvement of China's rule of law system. I am not sure that I can achieve this, but I think I should have a try.

The book provides a structured and up-to-date introduction to the law governing the dissemination of information in a computer-mediated world in China. It stresses the practical applications of the law that are encountered by all individuals and organizations in Chinese cyberspace, but always in the light of theoretical and jurisprudential underpinnings. Specifically, the book comprises five chapters. Chapter 1 introduces the legal system in China. Chapter 2 starts by providing basic information on the Internet, and then discusses how the Internet is controlled in China. Chapter 3 focuses on how China regulates Internet speech that may harm national security, social order, and personal reputations. Chapter 4 examines how China protects online privacy, especially how it deals with such issues as online data collection, online profiling, and online data protection that are unique to the Internet. Chapter 5 investigates how China protects copyright, trademarks, and patents in the context of the Internet, especially how various intellectual property infringements have emerged in cyberspace and how they have been addressed by China's existing and new laws and regulations. It should be noted that the book focuses mainly on Internet law in mainland China. Areas including Hong Kong, Macau, and Taiwan are part of China, but they have a different legal system. Internet-related laws in such areas are thus not covered in the book.

As the first text on Chinese Internet law, this book will be particularly valuable for legal, business, and communication professionals, academics, and students who are concerned with the regulation of the Internet and related activities in China.

Acknowledgments

I want to thank the following people at Chandos Publishing: Dr. Glyn Jones (Publisher), Jonathan Davis (Commissioning Editor), Vicki Hart (Production Editor), George Knott (Editorial Assistant), Emma Whitford (Editorial Assistant), and Judith Oppenheimer (Copy Editor). Without their initiation and valuable support, this book would not have been published.

I am also indebted to the following legal scholars, whose classic works have deeply affected my thinking and writing about communication law: C. Edwin Baker, University of Pennsylvania; Eric Barendt, University College London; Erwin Chemerinsky, University of California, Irvine; Lawrence M. Friedman, Stanford University; Richard A. Posner, the United States Court of Appeals for the Seventh Circuit; Paul Siegel, University of Hartford; Don R. Pember, University of Washington; and Robert Trager, University of Colorado.

About the author

Dr. Guosong Shao is Dean and Professor of the Journalism School at Nanjing University of Finance and Economics, China. He obtained his PhD in mass communication from The University of Alabama, USA. His research interests include media law and policy, media economics and management, new media, and political communication. He has published more than 15 journal articles in these areas during the past three years. Prior to joining Nanjing University of Finance and Economics in 2011, Dr. Shao was Assistant Professor of Communication at Pittsburg State University, USA.

The Chinese legal system

Abstract: This chapter provides an introduction and overview of China's legal system, including the sources of law, the court system, and legal procedure. The sources of law include constitutional law, statutory law, administrative law, local law, and international law. The court system consists of the local courts, the special courts, and the Supreme Court. Legal procedure involves criminal procedure, civil procedure, and administrative procedure. In addition, this chapter provides a guide to finding Chinese law, both offline and online.

Key words: Chinese legal system, sources of law, court system, legal procedure

To understand a particular area of law, such as Internet law, we may need an introduction to the law in general. By definition, law refers to a set of rules that guide human conduct in order to protect the rights of individuals as well as to ensure public order. Although Chinese law is a complicated subject, this chapter describes its basics so that we will have a framework within which to place and understand Chinese Internet law. Specifically, this chapter explains the sources of law, the court system, and legal procedure in China. It also provides a guide to finding Chinese law both offline and online.

The sources of law

China is one of the world's oldest civilizations and is also regarded as the oldest continuous civilization. For most of its history, China adopted a legal system that combined the Confucian philosophy of social control through moral education with the Legalist emphasis on codified law and criminal sanction. Following the revolution of 1911, which led to the overthrow of imperial rule, the Republic of China (ROC) brought in a largely German-influenced civil law system.[1] When the People's Republic of China (PRC) was established in 1949, it abolished the ROC's legal codes and introduced a more Soviet-influenced legal system. The current legal system dates from the early 1980s, a few years after the end of the Cultural Revolution. A mix of Chinese traditions and Western influences, this system has grown in size and complexity over the past decades. This is particularly reflected in the development of Internet law, which originates from five sources: constitutional law, statutory law, administrative law, local law, and international law.

Constitutional law

The current Constitution of the PRC, adopted in 1982, establishes the framework and principles of government and enumerates the fundamental rights and duties of Chinese citizens. It is the fundamental law of the state and has supreme legal authority, and no laws and regulations may contravene it. Three prior constitutions from 1954, 1975 and 1978 have partially contributed to the formation of the current Constitution.

Article 1 of the current Constitution prescribes that the PRC is a socialist state. Article 2 prescribes that all power in the country belongs to the people, and the National People's Congress (NPC) and the local people's congresses at various levels are the organs through which the people exercise state power. Article 3 prescribes that all administrative, judicial, and procuratorial organs of the state are created by, responsible for, and supervised by the people's congresses, thus fundamentally differing from the separation of executive, legislative, and judicial powers in many Western countries. Article 3 also indicates that all power comes from the central government, and local governments have only such power as the central government chooses to delegate to them.

Important to understanding Chinese constitutional law is the concept of the NPC as the supreme organ of state power. The Constitution stipulates that the NPC has power to amend the Constitution by a two-thirds majority, supervise the enforcement of the Constitution, enact and amend basic laws, determine the budget, control social and economic planning, and decide on matters of war and peace. It also stipulates that the NPC has power to elect and remove highest-level officials, including the President and Vice-President of the State, Premier and Vice-Premier of the State Council, the Chairman of the Central Military Commission, and the Presidents of the Supreme People's Court and the Supreme

People's Procuratorate. When the NPC is not in session, many of its functions and powers are delegated to and exercised by its Standing Committee.

The Constitution establishes that the NPC sits at the apex in the hierarchy of Chinese government structure. This national level is followed in descending order by the provincial, city, county, and township levels. At the county and township levels, the delegates to the people's congresses are directly elected by their constituencies. At national, provincial, and municipal levels, however, delegates are elected by the people's congresses at the next lower level. People's congresses at all levels have a term of five years and hold a meeting annually.

The Constitution also lists the fundamental rights and duties of Chinese citizens. The rights include equality before the law; equality of all nationalities; freedom of speech, the press, religion, assembly, and petition; freedom and privacy of personal correspondence; the right to personal dignity; the right to criticize state organs; social and economic rights; cultural and education rights; and familial rights. However, these rights are connected to social duties, such as paying tax, serving in the military, observing the law and social ethics, and safeguarding the unity, security, honor, and interests of the country. Many of these provisions have a direct or indirect impact on the Internet activities of individuals and organizations.

Statutory law

The Chinese Constitution explicitly delegates the power to enact statutory laws to the NPC, the highest level of legislative authority in the country. First of all, the NPC has power to enact major legal codes, often referred to as "basic laws," for the purpose of predicting or responding to problems affecting society at large. There are currently three sets of basic laws: the *Criminal Law and the Criminal Procedure Law*; the *General Principles of Civil Law and the Civil Procedure Law*; and the *Administrative Procedure Law and the Administrative Penalty Law*. Many provisions of these laws are closely related to the regulation of mediated communication and Internet activities. Taking the *Criminal Law* as an example, more than 20 criminal actions in this law can apply to speech and other activities in cyberspace, such as crimes of endangering national security, crimes of endangering public security, crimes of disrupting the order of the socialist market, and crimes of infringing upon citizens' democratic and personal rights. Similarly, the *General*

Principles of Civil Law can also apply to Internet activities, especially its provisions relating to defamation and intellectual property.

The Standing Committee of the NPC has power to enact and amend laws and regulations apart from basic laws. Compared to basic laws, these laws and regulations are more limited in scope, mainly responding to or predicting specific problems in society. The laws related to journalism and communication activities in general include the *National Security Law*, the *Law on Guarding State Secrets*, the *Advertising Law*, the *Copyright Law*, the *Patent Law*, the *Trademark Law*, the *Minor Protection Law*, the *Consumer Protection Law*, the *Law against Unfair Competition*, etc.[2] A considerable proportion of these laws can apply to Internet regulation. In addition, since the popularization of the Internet in 1994, the NPC has enacted a few laws that specifically address Internet problems, such as the *Electronic Signature Law* and the *Decision of the NPC Standing Committee on Safeguarding Internet Security*. However, so far there is no single statutory law that attempts to address Internet problems comprehensively.

Pursuant to the *Legislation Law of the PRC*,[3] a legislative bill submitted to the NPC or its Standing Committee should go through repeated deliberation in the group discussions and plenary meetings of the NPC or its Standing Committee, respectively; if a consensus is reached at this stage, the bill will then be submitted to the NPC or its Standing Committee for a final vote at a plenary meeting, and will be publicized via the order of the President of the PRC when it has been adopted by more than a simple majority of the deputies. In addition, to enhance transparency and public participation, the NPC tries to legislate in an open fashion and has established some good practices. For example, during the law-making process it may distribute the bill to central and local government departments to solicit written opinions.[4] It may also solicit opinions from society at large, through such means as holding public forums, expert panel meetings, and hearings.

Finally, according to the *Decision of the NPC Standing Committee on the Strengthening of Legal Interpretation Work*,[5] the Supreme People's Court has the right to make judicial interpretations on questions concerning the specific applications of laws and decrees in trial proceedings. Due to such delegation from the legislation, judicial interpretations by the Supreme Court may thus function as statutory laws. In practice, judicial interpretations have applied to both civil law and criminal law. In the field of civil law, there are at least two important judicial interpretations that may apply to Internet and other communication activities. They are the *Interpretation of the Supreme*

People's Court on Several Issues about the Trial of Cases Concerning the Right of Reputation and the *Interpretation of the Supreme People's Court on Several Issues on the Ascertainment of Compensation Liability for Emotional Damage in Civil Torts.* In the field of criminal law, the Supreme Court and the Supreme Procuratorate jointly issued a judicial interpretation on crimes of spreading obscene content via the Internet, mobile WAP sites, or telephone information services in 2010, when China intensified its crackdown on online pornography. This judicial interpretation clarified crimes involving producing, replicating, publishing, selling, and spreading pornographic and vulgar information via or on the Internet.

Administrative law

The next tier of the Chinese legislative hierarchy is the State Council, the supreme administrative organ. It is empowered under Article 89 of the Constitution to "adopt administrative measures, enact administrative regulations, and issue decisions and orders in accordance with the Constitution and other statutes." In addition, the ministries and commissions directly under the State Council are empowered under Article 90 of the Constitution to "issue orders, directives and regulations within the jurisdiction of their respective departments and in accordance with law and the administrative regulations, decisions and orders issued by the State Council." As such, both the State Council and its departments possess inherent power to make legislation. This makes a stark contrast to the common law systems in the United States and England, where administrative authorities possess substantive power only by delegation from the legislation.[6] By virtue of inherent power principle, the State Council and its departments possess both legislative and executive powers within their own jurisdictional authority. But there are some limits to their law-making power: they can neither change the nature of rights and obligations in the higher law nor create rights and obligations that have not been recognized by higher laws. If administrative bodies plan to create new regulations that involve rights or obligations that have never previously been touched upon by higher laws, they are required to seek the approval of and then report back to the NPC or its Standing Committee. In this case, the law-making power of administrative bodies can be viewed as conferred by higher state power organs.

As implied in the Constitution, there are two types of administrative law in China: one is enacted by the State Council and the other by the ministries and commissions directly under the State Council. The regulations by the State Council respond to problems that are fundamental and commonplace in certain administrative jurisdictions. These regulations are important legal resources for the courts in handling administrative trials. In terms of the Internet, the major administrative regulations include the *Telecommunications Regulation*, the *Regulation on the Protection of the Right to Network Dissemination of Information*, the *Administrative Measures for Internet Information Service*, the *Regulation for Safety Protection of Computer Information Systems*, the *Interim Provisions on the Administration of International Connection of Computer Information Network*, and the *Administrative Provisions on Foreign-Funded Telecommunications Enterprises*.[7]

The regulations and rules enacted by the departments directly under the State Council mainly respond to specific problems in certain administrative jurisdictions. The regulations enacted by the departments have lower legal authority than those enacted by the State Council, and are used only as a reference in administrative trials by the courts. Among numerous Internet regulations enacted by the departments of the State Council, the major ones include the *Administrative Provisions on Electronic Bulletin Services on the Internet* (by the Ministry of Industry and Information Technology), the *Interim Provisions on the Administration of the Engagement of Internet Sites in the Business of News Publication* (jointly by the State Council Information Office and the Ministry of Industry and Information Technology), the *Interim Provisions on the Administration of Internet Publication* (by the General Administration of Press and Publication), the *Administrative Provisions on Internet Audio-Visual Program Service* (jointly by the State Administration of Radio Film and Television and the Ministry of Industry and Information Technology), etc. These regulations and rules play a critical role in the administration of various cyberspace problems in China.

Local law

Used as a broad term in this book, local law refers to all regulations and rules established by local people's congresses and local people's governments. In China, there are four levels of local administration—provincial, city, county, and township. Only the people's congresses and people's governments of provinces, provincial capitals, and quite large cities possess powers to enact their own local regulations, which, however, must not contravene the Constitution and statutory laws or the administrative regulations promulgated by the State Council and its departments. Also, the provincial regulations have higher legal authority than the regulations of the provincial capital and of the quite large cities in the province. The regulations of the local people's congress have higher legal authority than the regulations of the local people's government at the same level.

Local regulations generally fall into three categories—regulations to implement the laws of the central government; regulations promulgated to supplement broad national laws that lack detail; and regulations that deal strictly with local issues not covered by national legislation.[8] All must be enacted in the light of the specific conditions and actual needs of the local administrative jurisdiction, and in most cases they are valid only in that jurisdiction. In the case of local Internet regulations, most of them emerged after 1998, when the Internet began to expand around the country. Exemplary local regulations include the *Interim Measures of Beijing Municipality for the Administration of Internet Advertising*, the *Regulation of Hangzhou Municipality for Safety Protection of Computer Information Networks*, and the *Regulation of Shandong Province for Safety Protection of Computer Information Networks*.

International law

International law refers to treaties and agreements that govern formal relationships between independent nations, establishing policies for how states can interact with each other politically and economically. Under the Chinese Constitution, the State Council exercises the power to conclude treaties and agreements with foreign states, the NPC Standing Committee exercises the power to decide on the ratification or abrogation of such treaties and agreements, and the President of the PRC, pursuant to the decisions of the Standing Committee of the NPC, exercises the power to ratify or abrogate such treaties and agreements. Furthermore, the *Law of the PRC on the Procedure for the Conclusion of Treaties* specifies that there are six types of treaties and agreements that shall go through the above concluding procedure. They include: (1) treaties of friendship and cooperation, treaties of peace, and other treaties of a political nature; (2) treaties and agreements concerning territory and the delimitation of boundary lines; (3) treaties and agreements relating to judicial assistance and extradition; (4) treaties and agreements which contain stipulations inconsistent with Chinese laws; (5) treaties and agreements which are subject to ratification as agreed by the contracting parties; and (6) other treaties and agreements subject to ratification.

One critical issue regarding international treaties is how the member state applies or implements a treaty at the domestic level. In China, many signed international treaties have been automatically incorporated into Chinese domestic law, and they are superior to the relevant stipulations of the latter. This is reflected particularly in Article 142 of the *General Principles of the Civil Law*, which clearly stipulates that if any international treaty concluded or acceded to by China contains provisions differing from those in Chinese domestic law, the provisions of the international treaty shall apply, unless the provisions are ones on which China has announced reservations. For instance, when joining the WIPO[9] *Performances and Phonograms Treaty* in 2006, China announced that the country is specifically exempt from restrictions of Article 15(1) of the treaty.[10] In cases of this kind, international treaties are directly incorporated into domestic law, even though the country applies reservations to certain provisions of a treaty. In some cases, however, China may adopt an indirect application approach to international treaties. For example, responding to the *Vienna Convention on Diplomatic Relations*, China enacted the *Regulation on Diplomatic Privileges and Immunities* to transform the Vienna Convention into domestic law for enforcement purposes. Another example is that, in order to facilitate China's entry into the World Trade Organization (WTO), the country has fundamentally changed its commercial legal system through such measures as invalidation, amendment, and enactment of relevant laws.

The court system

According to the Chinese Constitution, the people's courts represent the judicial organs of the state. The task of the people's courts is to try criminal and civil cases and to punish criminals and settle civil disputes through judicial means. Specifically, the judicial authority of the state is exercised by the following types of courts: local people's courts at various levels, military courts and other special people's courts, and the Supreme People's Court (SPC). Local people's courts are set up in accordance with the administrative jurisdictions, while special people's courts are established out of necessity. Both local courts and special courts are subject to the supervision of the Supreme Court.

Local people's courts

Under the *Law on the Organization of the People's Courts*, local people's courts are divided into three levels: primary, intermediate, and higher. Primary people's courts consist of tribunals in counties/autonomous counties, the administrative districts of cities, and cities without administrative districts. The main responsibility of primary courts is to adjudicate criminal and civil cases of first instance, except where otherwise provided for by law. If a primary court deems the case to be of major importance, it may request the transfer of the case to a higher court. Besides trying cases, a primary court also handles civil disputes and misdemeanors that do not need trials, and directs the work of people's mediation committees. To facilitate lawsuits, primary people's courts may set up a number of tribunals according to the conditions of the locality, population, and cases involved.[11] Although these tribunals are not trial units, they are responsible for hearing general civil cases and misdemeanors. The judgments and orders of the tribunals represent those of the primary people's courts.

Intermediate people's courts are established in the prefectures of a province or autonomous region, cities directly under the jurisdiction of a province or autonomous region, and districts in the four municipalities directly under the central government. Their responsibilities include trying criminal, civil, and administrative cases of first instance assigned by law to their jurisdiction, cases of first instance transferred by primary courts, and cases appealing or protesting the verdicts and decisions of primary courts. First-hearing criminal cases under the jurisdiction of intermediate courts include those involving national security, life imprisonment, the death penalty, foreign citizens, or Chinese citizens violating the legal rights and interests of foreigners. Civil cases heard by intermediate courts include those related to foreign people or organizations, those that have a major impact on the area under their jurisdiction, and those as determined by the Supreme Court to be under the jurisdiction of intermediate courts. In addition, intermediate courts have the right to hear the following administrative cases: confirmation of patent rights, cases handled by the customs, suits against administrative actions undertaken by the departments under the State Council or by provincial-level governments, and other grave and complicated cases. When an intermediate court considers that the criminal or civil case it is handling is of major importance, it may request that the case be transferred to a superior court for trial.

Higher people's courts are established in provinces, autonomous regions, and municipalities directly under the central government. They are responsible for handling cases of first instance assigned by laws and decrees to their jurisdiction, cases of first instance transferred from lower courts, appeals and protests lodged against judgments and orders of lower courts, and protests lodged by prosecutors in accordance with trial-monitoring procedures. The first type of case may need to be further clarified: it refers to a situation in which a higher court functions as the court of first instance over criminal, civil, and administrative cases that have a major impact on its jurisdiction, though the cases of major importance are not specifically enumerated. In addition, for verdicts or judgments passed by lower courts that have been found to contain errors, higher courts are authorized to hear or to ask lower courts to re-examine the case.

The presidents of local people's courts at all levels are elected by the local people's congresses at their corresponding levels. The vice-presidents, chief judges, associate chief judges, and judges of all local courts are appointed and removed by the standing committees of the local people's congresses at their corresponding levels.

Special people's courts

Article 28 of the *Law on the Organization of the People's Courts* stipulates that the organization, functions, and powers of special people's courts be prescribed separately by the NPC Standing Committee. In practice, special courts are established for trying special cases wherever necessary, pursuant to the approval of the NPC Standing Committee. China has so far set up special courts for handling military, maritime, and railway cases. Military courts make up the largest group of special courts. Established within the People's Liberation Army, they are in charge of hearing criminal cases involving servicemen, including trying all cases of treason and espionage. Military courts are basically independent of civilian courts and directly subordinate to the Ministry of National Defense, but their judicial decisions are reviewed by the Chinese Supreme Court. Maritime courts are special courts established to handle first-hearing maritime or commercial cases between Chinese legal persons/citizens, between Chinese legal persons/citizens and foreign legal persons/citizens, and between foreign legal persons/citizens. In addition, railway transportation tribunals are special courts set up along railways that try cases involving economic disputes, as well as criminal cases investigated by the railway public-security authorities and filed by railway prosecutors.

The Supreme People's Court

Located in Beijing, the Supreme People's Court is the highest judicial organ of the state. It has jurisdiction over all local and special courts, for which it serves as the ultimate appellate court. The SPC is composed of a president, vice-presidents, chief judges, associate chief judges, and judges. The president is elected or removed by the NPC. He has a term of office of five years and may serve for no more than two consecutive terms. In addition, the Standing Committee of the NPC exercises the power to appoint or dismiss the vice-presidents, chief judges, associate chief judges, and judges of the Supreme Court.

The Supreme Court is designed to try three types of case: (a) cases of first instance which are assigned by laws and decrees to its jurisdiction or which it considers should be tried by itself. Specifically, the Supreme Court has first-hearing right to try criminal and civil cases of major national importance, and it also has first-hearing jurisdiction over administrative cases that are substantially important and complicated; (b) appeals and protests lodged against judgments and orders of higher people's courts and special people's courts; and (c) protests lodged by the Supreme People's Procuratorate in accordance with the procedures of judicial supervision.[12]

In addition to trying cases, the Supreme Court also exercises the following powers: supervision of lower courts and special courts; approval of death penalty cases; issuing of judicial interpretations on how to apply laws and writs; and leading and managing the judicial administration of courts at all levels across the country. In particular, the practice of the Supreme Court interpreting laws and decrees has developed as a form of "judicial legislation" in recent years. This form of legislation is not included in the Chinese Constitution, but many people argue that judicial legislation can perform the function of filling gaps in and resolving conflicts and vagueness among the laws, so that effective enforcement can be carried out by the judicial branch.[13]

Special problem: cyberspace

Among the major features of cyberspace is its international, border-defying scope. This has raised significant questions about whether a court can claim jurisdiction over the parties in cyberspace-related legal disputes. To claim jurisdiction, a court must meet two requirements: (a) it must have the ability to hear the type of problem brought before it, known as subject matter jurisdiction. This essentially involves the division of jurisdiction over cases of first instance between the courts at different levels, which has been explained above; and (b) it must also have the ability to enforce its ruling over the involved parties, known as personal jurisdiction. This mainly involves the division of jurisdiction over cases of first instance between courts at the same level. Due to the borderless nature of the Internet, the issue of personal jurisdiction becomes particularly evident in Internet-related cases, and is thus the focus of the following discussion.

According to China's civil procedure law, a civil lawsuit comes under the jurisdiction of the court in the place where the defendant has his domicile. However, it is often problematic to apply this provision to cyberspace-related civil disputes because the anonymous nature of online communication often makes it difficult to discover real information about the defendant, including his domicile. Therefore, China's courts are increasingly relying on special jurisdiction provisions to deal with Internet-related civil cases. In November 2000, the Supreme Court promulgated a judicial interpretation concerning the laws applicable to the trial of copyright disputes involving the Internet. It stipulates that copyright infringement cases involving the Internet should fall within the jurisdiction of the court of the place where the infringement occurred or where the defendant has his domicile. The place where the infringement occurred mainly refers to the place where such equipment as network servers and computer terminals involved in the alleged infringement are located. If it is difficult to determine the place where the infringement occurred or where the defendant has his domicile, the place where such equipment as computer terminals are located on which the plaintiff found the infringing content may be deemed the place where the infringement occurred. Indeed, this interpretation has become a legal source for resolving the problem of personal jurisdiction over a variety of Internet-related civil disputes.[14]

In a civil lawsuit involving foreign interests, if the infringing act or the infringing results take place within the territory of China, the lawsuit should be under the jurisdiction of Chinese courts. For a case over which both Chinese and foreign courts have jurisdiction, if one involved party appealed to a foreign court and the other involved party appealed to a Chinese court, the Chinese court has the right to accept the case.[15] In judicial practice, the major problem raised in cyberspace is so-called forum shopping, that is, the plaintiff files a lawsuit with the court that is thought most likely to provide a favorable judgment. The court may be in China or in another country. Commentators argue that, in order to avoid the undesirable consequences of forum shopping in civil cases involving foreign interests, the defendant should be given legal measures to dispute the plaintiff's unreasonable choice of court, and the involved court should also have the right not to hear the case.

According to China's criminal procedure law, a criminal case is under the jurisdiction of the court in the place where the crime takes place. This principle applies to Internet-related criminal cases. Furthermore, the places whether cybercrimes occur can be divided into three categories: (a) the place where the crime is committed, which mainly refers to the place where such equipment as network servers and computer terminals involved in the alleged crime are located; (b) the intended place of occurrence of the crime results, that is, the place whether the offender hopes the crime results will take place; and (c) the factual place where the crime results occur, that is, the place where such equipment as network servers and computer terminals are located on which the victim discovered the crime.[16] In judicial practice, different cybercrime cases follow different standards on territorial jurisdiction. For instance, for criminal cases involving the violation of copyright and reputation, the place where the network server or the computer terminal on which the infringing content is found can be deemed the place where the crime takes place; for criminal cases involving the online sale of fake or shoddy goods, however, the place where the computer terminal is located on which the crime is committed may be deemed the place where the crime occurs.[17]

With regard to criminal cases involving foreign interests, China currently adopts territorial jurisdiction as the fundamental principle, while taking nationality jurisdiction, protective jurisdiction, and universal jurisdiction as the complementary principles. In judicial practice, however, it is often difficult to apply these principles to cybercrime cases. According to the principle of territorial jurisdiction, all crimes which occur in China should be subject to the rule of Chinese criminal law. However, many cybercrimes are international and there is often controversy about which country can claim jurisdiction over crime. Under the principle of nationality jurisdiction, all crimes which are committed by Chinese citizens in foreign countries should be subject to Chinese law. The problem is that most online communication is anonymous, and it is futile to attempt to obtain information about the offender. The principle of protective jurisdiction provides that all crimes which involve the violation of China's national interests or Chinese citizens' interests by foreigners should be subject to Chinese law. This principle also is not applicable to cybercrimes, which by nature are borderless and complex. In addition, the principle of universal jurisdiction provides that all crimes which are stipulated in international treaties should be subject to Chinese law. So far, China has not joined any international treaties related to cybercrimes. This means that universal jurisdiction cannot be applied to cyberspace-related criminal cases in China.

The legal procedure

Law is either substantive or procedural. Most of what this book describes is the substance of Chinese Internet law—the actual rules of conduct people must live by. Procedural law, on the other hand, deals with the rules for how substantive law is created and applied. Indeed, the rights and duties prescribed by the substantive law can only be exercised through the application of proper procedure. So the procedural aspect of law is equally important in the Chinese legal system.

There are several fundamental principles that apply to Chinese judicial procedure. These include: (a) open trial. All cases in the courts must be open to the public, except for those involving state secrets and individual privacy, or crimes committed by minors. For cases that are not openly tried, the verdict must be publicized when passed; (b) the defense system. The accused has the right to a proper defense. He may defend himself, or he may be defended by lawyers, his custodians or relatives, or persons recommended by his employer or other legal organizations. When necessary, the court may appoint a counsel to defend him; (c) the challenge system. Judicial officers are required to withdraw from a case if they have special relationships with the case or litigants; (d) the collegial system. Cases of first instance in a court must be tried by a collegial panel of judges or of judges and people's assessors, although simple civil cases can be tried by a single judge. Appealed or protested cases must also be handled in court by a collegial panel of judges. In addition, all courts are required to set up a judicial committee; (e) second instance being final. If the case is brought to a higher court by the involved parties or the procuratorate, the court (i.e., the court of second instance) will review the case and then pass a judgment or ruling finalizing the case; and (f) the judicial supervision system. This is in fact a remedy to the principle of second instance being final. The prerequisite for initiating a judicial supervision is that the judgment and rulings that have already taken effect have been found to include errors in the establishment of facts or in the application of laws. Judicial supervision can be initiated by the presidents of people's courts or people's procuratorates.

In practice, the procedure for a legal action varies according to many factors, the most important of which is whether the action is criminal, civil, or administrative. A criminal action is brought by a prosecutor against an individual for committing a crime. The immediate purpose of the prosecution is to impose punishment, which includes fines, imprisonment, execution, education, labor, and skills training. A civil action normally involves two private individuals or organizations that cannot resolve a dispute. The purpose of a civil suit is to right a wrong, honor an agreement, or settle a dispute. Usually the remedy sought is compensation in the form of money. An administrative action may be brought by the subject of a regulation against the administrative agency. The application of a regulation to a party can be appealed by the party; and the decisions by the agency on fines and orders can be upheld, adjusted, or dismissed.

Criminal procedure

In China, the criminal justice system is uniform throughout the country, featuring just one criminal code and one criminal procedure law. The *Criminal Procedure Law* was adopted in 1979 and amended in 1996.[18] This law stipulates five principal stages for handling a criminal case: initiation, investigation, prosecution, adjudication, and execution of the sentence.

The filing or initiation of criminal cases is often carried out by the police or procuratorates. The standard for filing a case is relatively vague. Article 83 of the *Criminal Procedure Law* provides that a case should be filed for investigation "upon discovering facts of crimes or criminal suspects." Article 86 provides that if, after examining the materials provided by a complainant or informant, the responsible official "believes that there are facts of a crime and criminal liability should be investigated," then he shall file a case; if not, or if "the facts are obviously incidental and do not require investigation of criminal liability," then he shall not file a case.[19] Therefore, when establishing the standards for initiating a case, Chinese procedural law assumes that it is possible, even at this early stage, to ascertain whether there are some facts of a crime. This contrasts with the criminal system in many other countries. The American system, for instance, acknowledges that uncertainty about the facts of a crime is inevitable, and so provides a "probable cause" threshold for bringing a criminal case.[20]

Once a case is filed, the police may carry out an investigation, collecting and obtaining evidence to prove the criminal suspect guilty or innocent or to prove the crime to be minor or grave. During the investigation, active criminals or major suspects may be detained first. Within three to seven days of the initial detention, the police must seek the procuratorate's approval for formal arrest. In most cases, however, this time limit may be extended to 30 days. If the approval is denied, the police may seek a review, but they must release the detainee. If the approval is obtained, the police may lawfully continue to detain the criminal suspect. To approve a formal arrest, the procuratorate must find that: (a) "there is evidence to support the facts of a crime"; (b) the "criminal suspect or defendant could be sentenced to a punishment of not less than imprisonment"; and (c) "such measures as allowing him to obtain a guarantor pending trial or placing him under residential surveillance would be insufficient to prevent the occurrence of danger to society."[21] If the case is transferred from the police to the procuratorate for prosecution, the time limit for holding a person in custody under formal arrest may be extended to seven and a half months.

A criminal suspect must be interrogated within 24 hours of detention or arrest. A suspect who need not be detained or arrested may be summoned to a designated place for interrogation. The time for interrogation through summons or forced appearance is limited to 12 hours. During an interrogation, there must be no fewer than two investigators participating. When interrogating a suspect, investigators must "first ask the suspect whether or not he has committed any criminal act, and let him state the circumstances of his guilt or explain his innocence; then they may ask him questions."[22] The suspect is required to respond truthfully to the investigators' questions, but he has the right to refuse to answer any questions irrelevant to the case. In addition to interrogation, investigators may also use other investigative techniques, such as the questioning of witnesses, inquest and examination, search, seizure of material and documentary evidence, and expert evaluation. However, Chinese law prohibits the use of torture, threats, enticements, or deceit to obtain evidence.

After collecting evidence, investigators may submit the case, along with relevant evidence, to the procuratorate for prosecution. The procuratorate must make a decision within one month of receiving the case; an extension of half a month may be allowed for major or complex cases. When reviewing the case, the procuratorate must interrogate the criminal suspect and his representative, and consult the victim and his representative. If the procuratorate considers that "the facts of a criminal suspect's crime have been ascertained, the evidence is reliable and sufficient, and criminal liability should be investigated," it will then initiate a public prosecution in a court.[23] If the case is minor, causing no serious harm, the procuratorate may decide not to initiate a prosecution. The procuratorate may also excuse the suspect from prosecution or send the case back to the public security organ for further investigation.

Once the procuratorate has decided to initiate prosecution, the case then advances to the court of first instance. In most cases, the court tries the case within one and a half months after accepting it. Trials begin with the public procurator reading the indictment. Then the adjudicator questions the defendant about his identity, status, and the basic process of the case to that point. The other parties, such as the procuratorate, defense, and victim, may also interrogate the defendant. During this stage, the witnesses are examined by the adjudicator and the procuratorate, and the defendant and his defender may be given permission to question the witnesses. The next step is "court debate," in which the procuratorate, the defendant, and the victim (if any) all have an opportunity to orally argue the case. The defendant is given the right to make a final statement. Finally, the judicial panel has a brief adjournment and then returns to announce the verdict and sentence. Once sentenced, a convict is turned over to the penal authorities for execution of the sentence.

If the defendant, private prosecutors, or their legal representatives refuse to accept the decision rendered by the court of first instance, they are allowed to appeal in writing or orally to the next higher level of court, within a specified period of time. Similarly, if the procuratorate is displeased with the first instance court's disposition of the case, it can present a protest to the higher court. The higher, second instance court then conducts a complete review of the facts as well as the application of law in the case of first instance.[24] After the court of second instance has made a decision, the case is legally closed. This principle is called "second instance being final," as discussed earlier. The decision of second instance may still not be final, however; it may be subject to challenge via the adjudicatory supervision system, which may risk damaging the authority of the court.

Civil procedure

China's first codification of civil procedure, the *Provisional Civil Procedure Law*, was passed by the NPC in 1982. This provisional code was replaced in 1991 through the enactment of the *Civil Procedure Law*, which was subsequently amended in 2007.[25] This law provides that in a court of first instance, a civil case will proceed under one of two forms of procedure, either summary procedure or ordinary procedure.

When trying a simple civil case in which the facts are evident, the rights and obligations clear, and the disputes trivial in nature, the court of first instance (usually the primary court) may apply the summary procedure, deciding the case in a less formalistic manner. The plaintiff's claims may be presented orally, or the disputing parties may go to court together for an immediate resolution. Only one judge tries the case.

Under the ordinary procedure, a case is initiated by filing a writ with a court, which will examine the writ to determine if the requirements for bringing a lawsuit have been met. The requirements include: (a) the plaintiff must be a citizen, a legal person, or an organization that has a direct interest in the case; (b) there must be a definite defendant; (c) there must be specific claims, facts, and causes for the case; and (d) the case must be within the scope of acceptance for civil actions by the court.[26] If all these requirements are met, then the court may file the case. If the court decides not to file the case, this decision can be appealed by the plaintiff.

Prior to the commencement of trial, it is the court's duty to examine and verify the case and carry out investigations and the collection of necessary evidence. Also, before the trial, the court may conduct conciliation, with the hope that the parties can settle their dispute on a voluntary basis. If the conciliation is unsuccessful, the court must notify the parties that the case is going to proceed to trial.

The ordinary trial procedure includes three stages: court investigation, court debate, and judgment of the case. During the investigation, the court questions the parties and witnesses, and there are also presentations of material and documentary evidence. With the permission of the court, the parties may question the witnesses, expert witnesses, and inspectors. Court debate is comprised of the parties and their legal agents offering their arguments. At the end of the debate, the court makes a judgment, assuming that the conciliation proves once again to be a failure.

Appeals can be taken to a court of second instance by any of the parties concerned. A collegial panel from the court will review the facts of the case, make investigations, and question the parties. An opening trial may be conducted, but it is not required; the court may make a judgment or a written order. Also, the court of second instance can still try conciliation between the parties. The decision by the court of second instance is assumed to be final and legally valid. As in criminal procedure, however, it can still be challenged by a court, a party, or a procuratorate via the adjudicative supervision system.

Administrative procedure

The *Administrative Procedure Law of the PRC* was passed in 1989 by the NPC.[27] It allows citizens, legal persons, and organizations to bring legal challenges against certain concrete administrative actions. The review of administrative actions is often carried out by a local court. The types of administrative action that can be challenged include: administrative punishments such as detentions, fines, and rescission of a license; coercive administrative measures such as restricting personal freedom and seizing and freezing property; interference with the operations of enterprises; refusal to take actions or perform a statutory duty; illegal demands for performance of duties; and violations of one's personal or property rights.[28] However, a court is not allowed to review administration actions involving national defense and foreign affairs. Nor is it permitted to accept suits against administrative legislation.

Citizens, legal persons, and organizations may ask an administrative organ at the next higher level or as prescribed by the law to review the case. If displeased with the review decision, they may bring the case to a court of first instance; or they may bring the case directly to the court without such a review. The court must not mediate between the parties. If the plaintiff applies for withdrawal of the case, the court needs to decide whether or not to grant approval. After hearing a case, the court of first instance may uphold the administrative action or amend the administrative sanction. If it finds that the action involves an inadequacy of major evidence, erroneous application of the law, violation of the legal procedure, or abuse of power, the court may annul or partially annul the action and also require the defendant to undertake a new specific action. If the court considers that the government officials in the case have violated administrative disciplines or committed a crime, it must transfer the relevant materials to the administrative organ or to the public security and procuratorial organs respectively. Finally, the decision by the court of first instance can be appealed by any of the parties within a specified period of time, and the parties are required to perform the legally effective judgment or order of the court.

Finding the law

This book attempts to provide an introduction to and overview of key areas of Chinese Internet law, but you may wish to supplement it with research in primary and secondary sources, in English and even in the

Chinese language. To help you navigate through China's complex and diverse legal materials, the book tries to identify some of the most useful sources of legal information. These sources can be divided into two broad categories: print and online. While both printed and online legal information systems are in the early stages of construction, the rapid development of the online system has significantly contributed to the process of building up a modern legal information system in China.[29]

Printed sources

Printed sources are traditionally identified in terms of primary sources and secondary sources. Primary sources refers to the actual documents that constitute the law, such as statutory laws, administrative regulations, and case decisions. Secondary sources refers to the literature that analyzes, interprets, and discusses primary documents, such as legal periodicals. The primary and secondary sources of Chinese laws and regulations identified below may be English, Chinese, or bilingual. When using English versions of Chinese laws, we should bear in mind that the English version, even when issued by the government, may be not quite authentic with the Chinese version. When there is a conflict between the English and the original Chinese versions, the latter should be treated as authentic.

Let us first examine primary sources. It should be noted that Chinese laws and regulations are often arranged in the form of compilation rather than of codification. The leading compilations include: (1) *China Law Reference Service*, Hong Kong: Asia Law and Practice, 1996–, quarterly. This bilingual, loose-leaf service classifies Chinese laws and regulations into five subjects: government, administration, and the legal system; economic law; tax and finance; real estate, infrastructure, and transport; and trade, commerce, and industry. It includes most of the national and provincial laws issued in mainland China since 1979. They are available in both print and web versions, and presented in the form of digests or in full English translation. Full translation is often accompanied by an editor's note offering expert commentary on what the law means and how it is implemented in practice; (2) *China Laws for Foreign Business*, North Ryde, N.S.W.: CCH Australia Ltd., 1985–. This bilingual, loose-leaf service is a comprehensive collection of key business laws and regulations of the PRC. It consists of seven volumes and three parts, namely, business regulation, taxation and customs, and special zones and cities. Presented with Chinese and English text side-by-side, it allows for easy cross-referencing between the original legislation and the translation; and (3) *Laws and Regulations of the People's Republic of China*, Beijing: China Legal Publishing House, 1995–, annual. Edited by the Legislation Affairs Committee of the NPC Standing Committee, this publication has two separate editions: Chinese and English. The Chinese, loose-leaf legal compilation consists of six volumes which contain 1,435 laws and regulations currently in force; it is supplemented bimonthly by adding new laws and regulations or removing invalid items. The English edition publishes the translations of selected Chinese laws and regulations.

The leading secondary sources include: (1) *China Law and Practice*, Hong Kong: China Law and Practice Ltd., 1987–, 10 issues per year. This English magazine publishes translations of Chinese legal documents as well as analysis of legal and business developments in China. The main contents of each issue include features and analysis, full text translation, legislation digest, latest news, and business law bulletins. All legislation digests in this magazine are later recompiled and published in the *Encyclopedia of Chinese Law*. In addition, this magazine offers a new range of online services, including a full archive of articles and legislation translation dating backing to 1999 and a free weekly e-mail newsletter on the latest legal developments in China; (2) *China Law*, Hong Kong: China Law Magazine Ltd., 1996–, quarterly. This bilingual magazine provides Chinese legal information in the fields of foreign trade and economy, democracy and rule of law, human rights, judicial reform, four jurisdictions within one country, and international legal issues. Its main content includes authoritative views, complete laws and regulations, landmark cases, and extensive and up-to-date legal information; and (3) *Chinese Law and Government*, White Plains, NY: M.E. Sharpe Inc., 1968–, quarterly. This English publication translates materials relating to Chinese law and government from Chinese publications. The materials translated for publication are carefully selected, including laws, regulations, court records, policy directives, and official or scholarly reports and analyses of critical issues.

Online sources

Online sources of Chinese legal information can be divided into commercial services and official services, both of which may contain primary sources and secondary sources. Among numerous commercial services, the major ones include: (1) *Chinalawinfo*, which is provided by

Chinalawinfo Co., a legal information and education company established by Peking University Law School. Chinalawinfo Co. operates the Chinese language website Chinalawinfo.com and its English language sister site lawinfochina.com. The Chinese language website contains almost all the laws, regulations, cases, and other legal information promulgated by the Chinese central government and most of the local governments since 1949. The English language website selectively provides English translations for those Chinese laws, regulations, cases, and legal information since 1949. To supplement these services, Chinalawinfo also offers online database services on Sino-foreign tax treaties, official gazettes, the WTO and China, and law journals in both Chinese and English. (2) *Isinolaw*. Founded by a group of Chinese legal professionals and entrepreneurs, this bilingual commercial database has extensive coverage of Chinese law, regulations, cases, pronouncements, and other legal information. It is argued to be the best place for the time being to find English versions of newly enacted Chinese laws or regulations; (3) *Sinolaw*. Developed by Chinese legal experts and professional legal translators, Sinolaw Legal Online is the first English language legal database in China. It provides up-to-date English translations of all the major business laws and regulations. Though the website emphasizes commercial and business laws, it also consists of constitutional and basic laws, major statutes and administrative regulations of China; and (4) *China Academic Journals*. This online database offers the most comprehensive range of periodical articles. It has an English index as well as Chinese full texts of Chinese legal literature. The database is updated on a daily basis.

Some of the most useful official services include: (1) the website of the NPC. This website, operated by the General Office of the NPC, reports all major legislative activities of the Chinese congress and its standing committee and contains all major Chinese laws and regulations enacted since 1949. The Chinese version of this website was established in 2005, and its English version came into operation one year later;[30] (2) the website of the Supreme People's Court. The Chinese version of this website contains a wide variety of legal information, including laws and regulations, important cases, legal news, and information from the courts throughout the country. The English version mainly provides English translations of some important laws, regulations, and cases. It also contains judicial news as well as information on Chinese grand justices and the judicial system;[31] and (3) other official websites. Most of the central government agencies have also established their own websites, which usually contain laws and regulations related to their authorities.

Regarding the Internet, we can get relevant regulation information from the websites of the following agencies: the Ministry of Industry and Information Technology, the Ministry of Public Security, the Information Office, the State Administration of Radio Film and Television, the General Administration of Press and Publication, the State Intellectual Property Office, and so on.

Notes

1. See John W. Head and Yanping Wang (2005) *Law Codes in Dynastic China: A Synopsis of Chinese Legal History in the Thirty Centuries from Zhou to Qing*, Durham, NC: Carolina Academic Press; Derk Bodde (1981) "Basic Concepts of Chinese Law: The Genesis and Evolution of Legal Thought in Traditional China," in *Essays on Chinese Civilization*, ed. Charles Le Blanc and Dorothy Borei, Princeton: Princeton University Press.
2. The names of these laws are abbreviated for the sake of simplicity. Their full names usually include "of the People's Republic of China," such as "The Patent Law of the People's Republic of China."
3. This law was enacted in 2000 for the purpose of standardizing law-making activities, improving state legislative institutions, and strengthening the rule of law in the country.
4. State Council Information Office (2008) "China's Efforts and Achievements in Promoting the Rule of Law," *Chinese Journal of International Law* 7.
5. This law was promulgated in 1981 by the NPC Standing Committee. The full text (Chinese language) can be accessed at http://www.law-lib.com/law/law_view.asp?id=2249.
6. Thomas A. Schwartz (2003) "The Law in Modern Society," in *Communication and the Law*, ed. W. Wat Hopkins, Northport, AL: Vision Press.
7. For simplicity, the names of these regulations are abbreviated. Their full names usually include "of the People's Republic of China," as in "The Telecommunications Regulation of the People's Republic of China."
8. Peter Howard Corne (1997) *Foreign Investment in China: The Administrative Legal System*, Hong Kong: Hong Kong University Press.
9. WIPO (the World Intellectual Property Organization) is a specialized agency of the United Nations that is dedicated to developing a balanced and accessible international intellectual property system.
10. Article 15(1) of the treaty stipulates that "performers and producers of phonograms shall enjoy the right to a single equitable remuneration for the direct or indirect use of phonograms published for commercial purposes for broadcasting or for any communication to the public."
11. In practice, a tribunal of this nature is often set up in big towns or townships where there is a concentrated population.
12. The Supreme People's Procuratorate is the highest state organ for legal supervision in China. Under Chinese Constitutional Law, the Supreme Procuratorate has the power to perform legal supervision of the judicial

process of courts and investigation of criminal cases, and also can lodge protests against valid but wrong decisions and rulings made by various courts with the Supreme People's Court.

13. See Chenguang Wang (2004) "Law-making Functions of the Chinese Courts: Judicial Activism in a Country of Rapid Social Changes," *Frontiers of Law in China* 4:1, pp. 524–549.

14. It should be noted that defamation cases are an exception. According to a judicial interpretation issued by the Supreme People's Court, the domicile of the plaintiff can be deemed the place where the results of infringement occur, so that the plaintiff can file a lawsuit in the place where he has a domicile.

15. Refer to Article 306 of the Opinion on Several Issues Concerning the Applicability of the Civil Procedure Law of the PRC issued by the Supreme People's Court in 1992.

16. See the article "On the Determination of Jurisdiction over Cybercrime Cases," which can be retrieved at http://china.findlaw.cn/jingjifa/dianzishangwufa/swjf/qqgx/61160.html.

17. See the article "On the Determination of Jurisdiction over Cybercrime Cases," which can be retrieved at http://china.findlaw.cn/jingjifa/dianzishangwufa/swjf/qqgx/61160.html.

18. The full text of the Criminal Procedure Law of the PRC can be accessed at http://www.npc.gov.cn/englishnpc/Law/2007-12/13/content_1384067.htm.

19. See Article 86 of the Criminal Procedure Law of the PRC.

20. See Ira Belkin (2000) "China's Criminal System: A Work in Progress," *Washington Journal of Modern China* 6.

21. See Article 60 of the *Criminal Procedure Law* of the PRC.

22. Article 93 of the *Criminal Procedure Law* of the PRC.

23. Article 141 of the *Criminal Procedure Law* of the PRC.

24. China's second instance courts can be compared to American appellate courts, which, however, only review the first instance courts' application of the law, rather than seeking new evidence.

25. The full text of the *Civil Procedure Law* of the PRC can be accessed at http://www.npc.gov.cn/englishnpc/Law/2007-12/12/content_1383880.htm.

26. Article 108 of the *Civil Procedure Law* of the PRC.

27. The full text of the *Administrative Procedure Law* of the PRC can be accessed at http://www.npc.gov.cn/englishnpc/Law/2007-12/12/content_1383912.htm.

28. See Article 11 of the Administrative Procedure Law of the PRC.

29. Luo Wei and Joan Liu (2003) *Complete Research Guide to the Laws of the People's Republic of China* (LLRX).

30. The English legal database of the NPC can be accessed at http://www.npc.gov.cn/englishnpc/Law/Integrated_index.html.

31. The English legal database of the Supreme People's Court can be accessed at http://en.chinacourt.org/news/?location=0400000000.

2

Regulating the Internet

Abstract: This chapter first provides basic information about the Internet, including its history, structure, and functions. It then examines why and how the Internet is regulated in China. The regulatory mechanisms examined include laws and regulations, administrative licensing, architectural control, technical protection, administrative enforcement, industry self-regulation, and public supervision. In addition, the chapter briefly discusses the problems with China's Internet regulation.

Key words: the Internet, legal regulation, administrative licensing

The Internet is one of the most important inventions of recent decades. It has fundamentally changed people's lives, and it is still evolving rapidly. With the explosive growth of the Internet, Internet regulation has become an imperative and challenging issue around the world. The first part of this chapter provides basic information on the Internet, its history, structure, and functions. The rationales for Internet regulation in China and the various regulatory mechanisms – laws and regulations, administrative licensing, architectural control, technical protection, administrative enforcement, industry self-regulation, and pubic supervision – are then examined. The chapter concludes with a brief discussion of problems with China's current system of Internet regulation.

Internet basics

Brief history of the Internet

The term "Internet" refers to a global system of interconnected computer networks in which users/computers are able to communicate with each other. The origin of the Internet dates back to the 1960s when the U.S. Department of Defense funded its research division to build a distributed communications network. Known as the ARPANet, the network connected computers in four universities that were heavily involved in government and military research—Stanford; University of California, Los Angeles; University of California, Santa Barbara; and the University of Utah. The unique advantage of this network was that communications "traffic" would be less likely to become congested at a single point or to be destroyed in the event of military attacks or natural disasters, because multiple paths linked one computer site to another.[1] In the 1980s, ARPANet was superseded by NSFNet, a high-speed communications network created by the National Science Foundation. This new network linked computers together across the country. Research in the United States has since generated worldwide participation in the development of networking technologies. Researchers first linked small computer networks to form a large network, and then connected the large networks around the world; thus was born the Internet. Over the past decade, the Internet has experienced explosive global growth: as of June 2010, an estimated one quarter of the global population used Internet services.[2]

In China, the first computer network—CANET (China Academic Network)—was established in 1986 by the Beijing Institute of Computing Applications, with help from the Universität Karlsruhe in Germany. A year later, the IHEP (Institute of High Energy Physics) in Beijing began connecting to CERN, the European Organization for Nuclear Research in Geneva, representing China's first international connection. In 1994, the IHEP achieved China's fully functional connection to the Internet by opening a 64 kbps international dedicated line to the Internet, making China a country with fully functional Internet accessibility. In 1995, the Internet became available to the public through the services provided by China Telecom and ChinaNet, both of which were operated by the government.

The Chinese government plays a dominant, vital role in the development of the Internet.[3] From 1997 to 2009, it invested a total of 4.3 trillion RMB, and built up a nationwide optical communications network with a total length of 8.267 million kilometers.[4] By the end of 2009, China had established 7 land–submarine cables and 20 land cables, with a combined capacity of more than 1,600 Gb, China's international outlet bandwidth reached 866,367 Gbps, and China's major telecommunications companies possessed 136 million broadband Internet access ports.[5] The large-scale development of Internet infrastructures has greatly enhanced the diffusion and application of the Internet around the country. By the end of 2009, the number of Chinese Internet users reached 384 million, which was 618 times the number in 1997 and represented an average annual increase of 31.95 million users. In 2009, the Internet penetration rate in China reached 28.9%, higher than the world average; the total number of IPv4 addresses reached 232 million, making China the second-largest owner of IPv4 addresses in the world; and the total number of domain names reached 16.82 million, a historic high point.[6]

The structure of the Internet

Physically, the Internet resembles and is part of existing public telecommunications networks. Large telecommunications companies, called network service providers (NSPs), offer long-distance data transport services through national and international fiber optic cables. These transport services are accessed by individuals and organizations via Internet service providers (ISPs), which are physically linked to NSPs. People connect to ISPs through such channels as dial-up connection, Wi-Fi, and landline broadband. Once connected, they have access to various services provided by the ISPs, including access to the Internet, access to ISP resources, and user resource hosting.[7]

What technically distinguishes the Internet from traditional telecommunications services is its use of a set of communication protocols that is commonly referred to as Internet Protocol Suite. A protocol is a set of rules or standards that enable computers to connect and transmit data to one another. The Internet Protocol Suite is constructed as a set of layers which includes the application layer, transport layer, Internet layer, and link layer. Each layer solves a set of problems related to data transmission and corresponds to the environment or scope in which its service operates. At the top of the Suite, the application layer "defines the type of information contained in the collection of packets and what is to be done with it."[8] Important protocols in the application layer include HTTP, SMT, POP, IMAP, and FTP. The transport layer provides end-to-end communications services for applications. TCP, the most notable transport protocol, controls how data are sent out on the Internet. At the Internet layer, all transport protocols use the Internet protocol (IP) to carry data from the original host across network boundaries, if necessary, to the destination host. The link layer is the lowest layer in the hierarchy of the Suite. It is used to interconnect hosts between adjacent network nodes in a local area network segment or a wide area network connection. The Internet Protocol Suite is also commonly known as TCP/IP, named from two of the most critical protocols within it. The TCP/IP model breaks down information from one network into packets, allows packets to be repackaged for transmission, and then reassembles them at the receiving computer in another network.

The functions of the Internet

First of all, the Internet provides an infinite amount of information for users to access and retrieve. The World Wide Web plays a particularly important role in this regard: it enables users to access any type of information located on the Web anywhere in the world. The Web has three major components: the Uniform Resource Locator (URL)—the address of content placed on the Web; the hypertext transfer protocol (HTTP)—the primary protocol used by Web servers and browsers for sending and receiving documents on a website; and the hypertext markup language (HTML)—the programming language used to create Web pages and links.[9] Although the Web has grown immensely in complexity in the past decade, these three basic elements remain central to its operation. Also, Web browser software such as Firefox and Internet Explorer enables users to navigate from one Web page to another. Additionally, through the use of keywords, Internet search engines like Google and Baidu[10] allow users to locate their desired, specific content in the sea of online information nearly instantly.

Second, the Internet provides an effective tool for users to communicate with each other. Among the various communication tools, e-mail is arguably the most important. E-mail refers to a message sent from one computer user to another across a network. Major portal sites like Yahoo! and Microsoft have offered free e-mail accounts to attract users to their sites, and e-mail communication is in fact the first Internet activity for many users. Communication on the Internet has grown beyond e-mail, however. Users now can chat with one another in real time through instant messaging (IM) services. Major global IM services include Skype, Microsoft's MSN, and Yahoo!'s Messenger. In China, the most popular instant messaging program is provided by Tencent QQ, whose simultaneous online users exceeded 100 million in 2009.[11] Most of these services are free, but they do not adhere to a common standard. Users therefore have to be using the same program in order to communicate with each other via instant messaging. Another communication service enabled by the Internet is Internet telephony, also known as Voice-over-Internet Protocol (VoIP). As the Internet carries the voice traffic, VoIP can be free or cost much less than traditional telephone services, though its voice quality still varies from call to call. In addition, due to the development of webcam technologies, the new communication tools video chat room and video conferencing are becoming increasingly popular among users.

Third, large amounts of data can be transferred over the Internet. A major practice in this regard is file sharing, which refers to the distribution or the provision of access to digitally stored information, such as music, film, video, photography, electronic books, and computer programs. There are two types of file sharing: peer-to-peer networks and file hosting services. In the peer-to-peer networks, users can use software like Gnutella and Napster to search for and directly download shared files from other users' computers that have been connected to the network. File hosting services are a simple alternative to peer-to-peer software. They are specifically designed to host static content, which can be accessed through file transfer protocol (FTP). File hosting services typically include video sharing, visual storage, and remote backup. In all these applications, access to the file may be controlled via user verification, and the transfer of the data may be obscured by encryption.[12]

Last, the Internet has been evolving rapidly as a mass medium, though the path it follows remains unclear. This process involves a number of players, most of which are referred to as Internet content providers (ICPs). The major players include traditional newspapers such as the *New York Times*, *Wall Street Journal* and the *People's Daily*[13] that publish news online; existing radio/television broadcasters and movie studios that develop streaming media to promote Internet "feeds" of their live audio and video programs; and new media publications like *Slate* and *Salon* that have no traditional print components. There are also aggregate sites such as Yahoo!, Google, and Sina[14] that put together an enormous amount of Internet content and then help people to find specialized information. More important is the emergence of user-generated sites, such as weblogs, video-sharing sites, picture-sharing sites, wiki websites, and social networking sites. These new types of site can be operated by anyone who has a computer, an Internet account, and something to say; they open up the world of publication and broadcasting to the general public.

Legal regulation

Since the popularization of the Internet in 1995, China has actively pursued the regulation of the Internet. For the Chinese government, the objectives of regulating the Internet are "to promote general and hassle-free Internet accessibility, and sustainable and healthy development, guarantee citizens' freedom of speech online, regulate the order of Internet information transmission, promote the positive and effective application of the Internet, create a market environment for fair competition, guarantee the citizens' rights and interests as vested in the Constitution and other laws, and guarantee safety for Internet information and state security."[15] In practice, China has built up a highly complicated system for regulating the Internet, which mainly involves legal regulations, administrative licensing, architectural control, technical protection, administrative enforcement, industry self-regulation, and public supervision. Legal regulation is reviewed in this section, while other mechanisms are addressed in the following two sections.

In 1996, the State Council promulgated *Provisional Regulations for the Administration of International Connection of Computer Information Network*, which is considered China's first attempt to regulate the Internet. This regulation aimed at strengthening the control of computer information networks connecting to the international network, and safeguarding the healthy development of international computer information exchange. In September 2000, the executive meeting of the State Council passed the *PRC Telecommunications Regulations*, in which the Internet was included as an integral part of telecommunications business and thereby subjected to telecommunications regulations. During the same meeting, the State Council also passed the *Administrative Measures for Internet Information Services*, which in fact functions as China's "fundamental law" on the administration of Internet services. This "fundamental law" provides the legislative basis for the subsequent introduction of various Internet regulations, including *Administrative Provisions on Electronic Bulletin Service, Interim Provisions on the Administration of Internet Publishing, Administrative Provisions on Internet Audio-Visual Programs, Interim Provisions on the Administration of Internet Culture, Administrative Provisions on Internet News Service*, and *Interim Administrative Measures on the Registration of Internet Domains in China*.

The above-mentioned administrative regulations are not only purported to solve specific problems in cyberspace but also establish Internet jurisdiction for administrative agencies. In accordance with the *PRC*

Telecommunications Regulations, the Internet is part of the telecommunications business, and its major regulator is the Ministry of Industry and Information Technology (MIIT), which sets up subordinate telecommunications regulatory agencies in all Chinese provinces, autonomous regions, and municipalities.[16] In addition, the Internet is subject to regulation by many other administrative organs for the provision of specific Internet services. For example, websites engaging in Internet publishing are regulated by the General Administration of Press and Publication (GAPP) and its local subordinates; websites providing audio-visual programs are regulated by the State Administration of Radio Film and Television (SARFT) and its local subordinates. To date, at least 14 regulatory agencies have been involved in Internet regulation, and these agencies have promulgated more than 50 administrative rules and regulations on the Internet. It is thus said that China has built up the most comprehensive system of Internet regulation.[17]

In 2000, the NPC Standing Committee passed the *Decision on Safeguarding Internet Security*, which is the highest legislation concerning the Internet and the communications industry in general. The *Decision* argues that the Internet has played an important role in facilitating the development of the national economy, science and technology, and the informationalization of social services; meanwhile, it has also aroused general concerns about how to ensure the operational and information security of the computer network. The purpose of enacting the *Decision* was to enhance the healthy development of the Internet, safeguard national security and the public interest, maintain social order and the socialist market economic order, and protect the lawful rights and interests of individuals, legal corporations, and other organizations. This is essentially the focus of the whole legal system concerning the Internet. The main contents of the *Decision* are as follows:

1. For the purpose of ensuring the operational security of the computer network, anyone who commits any of the following acts, which constitutes a crime, shall be investigated for criminal responsibility in accordance with the relevant provisions in the Criminal Law:

   (1) invading the computer data system of state affairs, national defense buildup or the sophisticated realms of science and technology;

   (2) intentionally inventing and spreading destructive programs such as computer viruses to attack the computer system and the communications network, thus damaging the computer system and the communications network; or

(3) in violation of state regulations, discontinuing the computer network or the communications service without authorization, thus making it impossible for the computer network or the communications system to operate normally.

2. For the purpose of preserving the security of the State and maintaining social stability, anyone who commits any of the following acts, which constitutes a crime, shall be investigated for criminal responsibility in accordance with the relevant provisions in the Criminal Law:

(1) making use of the computer network to spread rumors, libels or publicize or disseminate other harmful information for the purpose of whipping up attempts to subvert state power and overthrowing the socialist system, or to split the country and undermine unification of the State;

(2) stealing or divulging state secrets, intelligence or military secrets via the computer network;

(3) making use of the computer network to stir up ethnic hostility or discrimination, and thus undermining national unity; or

(4) making use of the computer network to form cult organizations or contact members of cult organizations, thus obstructing the implementation of State laws and administrative regulations.

3. For the purpose of maintaining order of the socialist market economy and ensuring the administration of public order, anyone who commits any of the following acts, which constitutes a crime, shall be investigated for criminal responsibility in accordance with the relevant provisions in the Criminal Law:

(1) making use of the computer network to sell shoddy products or give false publicity to commodities or services;

(2) making use of the computer network to jeopardize another person's business credibility and commodity reputation;

(3) making use of the computer network to infringe on another person's intellectual property right;

(4) making use of the computer network to fabricate and spread false information which affects the exchange of securities and futures or other information which disrupts financial order; or

(5) establishing on the computer network pornographic websites or web pages, providing services for connecting pornographic websites, or spreading pornographic books and periodicals, movies, audiovisuals or pictures.

4. For the purpose of protecting the lawful rights of the person and property of individuals, legal corporations and other organizations, anyone who commits any of the following acts, which constitutes a crime, shall be investigated for criminal responsibility in accordance with the relevant provisions in the Criminal Law:

(1) making use of the computer network to humiliate another person or to libel another person with fabrications;

(2) in violation of the law, intercepting, tampering with or deleting other persons' e-mails or other data, thus infringing on citizens' freedom and privacy of correspondence; or

(3) making use of the computer network to commit theft, fraud or blackmail.

In addition, the *Decision* stipulates that anyone who makes use of the Internet to commit any of the above-mentioned illegal acts that is in violation of the administration of public security but does not constitute a crime, shall be punished by the public security organ; anyone whose illegal acts violate administrative regulations or other laws and do not constitute a crime, shall be given administrative punishment by the relevant regulatory agency; and anyone who makes use of the Internet to infringe on another person's lawful rights and interests and whose illegal acts constitute a tort, shall be bear civil liability in accordance with the law.

It should be noted that China's Internet laws and regulations are basically developed from existing laws, combined with the characteristics of the Internet. The major goal of China's legislation on the Internet is to illustrate the application of existing laws to the Internet. For example, the *Decision on Safeguarding Internet Security* confirms that many crimes stipulated in the existing *Criminal Law* apply to the Internet. In order to safeguard national security and social stability, the *Decision* reiterates the crime of inciting secession stipulated in Article 103, the crime of inciting the subversion of state power in Article 105, the crime of illegally obtaining state secrets in Article 282, the crime of disclosing state secrets in Article 398, the crime of inciting ethnic hatred or ethnic discrimination in Article 249, and the crime of organizing and using cults to undermine law enforcement in Article 300 of the PRC *Criminal Law*; and in order to protect the lawful rights and interests of individuals, legal corporations, and other organizations, the *Decision* reiterates the crime of insult or libel provided in Article 246, the crime of infringing upon the right to freedom of correspondence in Article 252, the crime of fraud in Article 266, the crime of theft in Article 264, and the crime of extortion in Article 274 of the *Criminal Law*. On the other hand, since the Internet has many new features, it is sometime necessary to make certain adjustments to existing laws in order to resolve legal disputes arising from cyberspace. For example, the provisions on "intercepting, tampering with or deleting other persons' e-mails or other data, thus infringing on citizens' freedom and privacy of correspondence" included in the *Decision* are obviously an extension of the *Criminal Law* provisions on "illegally opening others' mail." To conclude, Internet activities need to comply with China's current Constitution, criminal law, civil law and other Internet-related basic laws; they should also follow new legislation that focuses on the Internet. This will be discussed in detail in the following chapters.

Administrative licensing

China's other important means of controlling the Internet is by implementing the administrative licensing system. The term "administrative licensing" refers to the permission granted by the administrative organs to citizens, legal corporations or other organizations to engage in special activities as detailed in their applications. In 2003, the NPC Standing Committee passed the *Administrative Licensing Law*. It provides for administrative licensing to be established by laws; if such kinds of laws have not been enacted, it can be enabled through administrative regulations; and, when necessary, the State Council may issue a decision to establish administrative licensing. However, the *Administrative Licensing Law* does not give powers to establish administrative licensing to departments of the State Council, in order to prevent self-authorization and subsequent abuse of power by the departments. In addition, the administrative licenses that have already been released by the departments may be confirmed by the State Council by the enacting of administrative regulations.

China's Internet-related regulations have set up numerous administrative licenses. This allows the government to exercise direct or indirect control over Internet users, as well as over Internet service providers, for the purpose of protecting civil rights, public interest, and national security. At present, China's licensing tool is primarily used for value-added telecommunications services, news and information services, online audio and video programs, Internet publishing, and Internet-related cultural enterprises.

Licensing telecommunications services

China has a licensing system for the operation of telecommunications business, which is divided into basic telecommunications services and value-added telecommunications services. Basic telecommunications services refers to the provision of the public network infrastructure, public data transmission, and basic voice communications services, such as fixed telephone services, mobile phone services, network and data communication services, and information services. Value-added telecommunications services refers to the telecommunications and information services provided through the public network infrastructure, such as Internet access services and Internet content services.

Under the *PRC Telecommunications Regulations* and the *Administrative Measures for the Licensing of Telecommunications Business Operation*, the following conditions must be met in order to operate basic telecommunications services: the operator should be a legally established company that specializes in basic telecommunications services and the state-owned shares of the company should be not less than 51%; there should be a feasible business development plan and a relevant technical plan for formation of the network; there should be suitable funds, facilities, and specialized personnel to carry out business activities; the operator should have the capability and/or reputation to provide a long-term service to its customers; if the operator provides services only within a province, the minimum registered capital should be 100 million yuan; if the operator provides services nationwide or across provinces, the minimum registered capital should be 10 billion yuan; and the major shareholders and executives of the company should not have a record of violating telecommunications regulations over the past three years.

In a similar vein, the *PRC Telecommunications Regulations* and the *Administrative Measures for the Licensing of Telecommunications Business Operation* also mandate that the following conditions shall be met in order to operate value-added telecommunications services: the operator should be a legally established company; there should be funds and specialized personnel commensurate with the business activities to be developed; the operator should have the capability and/or reputation to provide a long-term service to its customers; the minimum registered capital for operating business within a province should be 1 million yuan; the minimum registered capital for operating business nationwide or across provinces should be 10 million yuan; the operator should have the necessary facilities, physical space, and technology plans; and the company's key shareholders and management personnel should have no record of violating telecommunications regulations over the past three years.

The MIIT is charged with the licensing of basic telecommunications business as well as value-added telecommunications services that are provided across provinces. The subordinates of the MIIT in a province are responsible for the licensing of value-added telecommunications services that are mainly operated within that province. Foreigners may invest in China's telecommunications business, including both basic telecommunications services and value-added telecommunications services. The licensing of foreign-funded telecommunications business[18] shall be under the *Administrative Provisions on Foreign-Funded Telecommunications Enterprises.*[19]

Licensing Internet information services

In the *Administrative Measures for Internet Information Services*, Internet information services are defined as the service activities of providing information services through the Internet to online users. There are two types of Internet information service: commercial and non-commercial services. Commercial Internet information services refers to the paid-for provision of information services to online users via the Internet, website production, and etc. Non-commercial Internet information services refers to the unpaid provision of public information to online users via the Internet. The government registers commercial Internet information services in a licensing system and non-commercial Internet information services in a record-filing system. No one may engage in the provision of Internet information services without first obtaining a license or carrying out record-filing procedures.

Under the *Administrative Measures for Internet Information Services* the following conditions must be met in order to engage in the provision of commercial Internet information services: having a business development plan and a relevant technical plan; having in place sound procedures to ensure network and information security, including procedures to ensure network security, a system to preserve state secrets, and a system to protect user privacy; and if the services to be provided fall under the services covered in Article 5 thereof,[20] having obtained the written consent of the relevant competent authority.

The above-mentioned "procedures to ensure network security" mainly refer to the requirements proposed in the *Administrative Measures for Safeguarding the Safety of International Connecting of Computer*

Information Networks, which was promulgated in 1997 by the Ministry of Public Security. These requirements include: implementing technical measures to protect the operational and information security of the network; educating its users on the issue of network security; registering individuals and organizations that publish information on the website; establishing user registration and an information management system for its electronic bulletin services; and deleting harmful or illegal information from the website or even closing down the website when necessary.

As for "the system to preserve state secrets," this means that the operator of Internet information services shall follow a set of requirements stipulated by the State Secrecy Bureau in the *Administrative Provisions on the Preservation of State Secrets in the International Networking of Computer Information System*. These requirements mainly include: computer information systems involving state secrets may not be directly or indirectly connected to the Internet or other public information networks; information involving state secrets may not be stored in, processed on, or transmitted through computer information systems which are internationally networked; any information to be provided to, or published on, an internationally networked website must be subjected to secrecy maintenance review and approved by the relevant government agency; except for information which has been published through other news media, individuals or organizations shall obtain the permission of the information provider before publishing any information which has been collected for public use; and no individuals or organizations may disseminate state secrets via e-mail, in chat rooms, or on electronic bulletin boards.

Current prevailing practices to establish "the system to protect user privacy" include: setting full access permission for users; ensuring effective management and protecting the confidentiality of user information; designating personnel to keep web access records; establishing the liability system for information editing, auditing, and publishing; setting the bounds of Internet service providers' authority over user information management; and in the event of privacy disclosure, taking effective measures to stop it and also reporting it to the relevant government organ.

Anyone who plans to engage in the provision of commercial Internet information services shall apply to the MIIT or its province-level subordinates for a value-added telecommunications service operating permit. Anyone who plans to engage in the provision of non-commercial Internet information services shall go through record-filing procedures with the MIIT's province-level subordinates, including submitting the application materials such as the basic information about the Internet service provider, and the website's URL and the services to be provided.

One important part of Internet information services is electronic messaging services. This refers to the services that enable users to publish information on the Internet in an interactive form, such as bulletin boards, whiteboards, discussion forums, chat rooms, and message boards. According to the *Administrative Measures for Electronic Mail Services*, if an Internet service provider plans to launch electronic messaging services, it should meet the following conditions: having determined the categories of electronic messaging services; having formulated the rules and procedures for such services; having adopted measures to ensure the operational security of such services; and having found appropriate professional administrative personnel and technical personnel to effectively monitor such services.

Licensing Internet news services

Under the *Administrative Provisions on Internet News Services*, "news" includes reports and commentaries on social and public affairs; "Internet news services" includes online publication of news and commentaries, distribution of news and commentaries to users through e-mail or news groups, and provision of electronic bulletin boards on which users can discuss current and political affairs. There are three types of website that are allowed to provide Internet news services, each of which needs to meet certain but different requirements in order to obtain an operating license.

The first type of website is established by traditional news media, and it is allowed to publish news and commentaries beyond the scope of what has been published by the media outlet in original format, provide electronic bulletin board services on current and political affairs, and send news and commentaries to Internet subscribers through e-mail or news groups. To establish an Internet news service website, the traditional news organization needs to meet the following requirements: have sound rules and mechanisms for administration of Internet news services; have five or more full-time news editors who have engaged in journalism for three or more years in news organizations; and have the necessary equipment, funds, and facilities to operate the website. In fact, only news organizations directly under the central or provincial government are allowed to operate this type of website; and they should apply for operating permits to the Information Office of the State Council.

The second type of website is established by non-news media organizations, and it is not allowed to publish news collected by itself, but needs to disseminate news and commentaries published by the news organizations directly administered by the central or provincial government. To establish this type of website, the applicant should meet the following three requirements, i.e., have sound rules and mechanisms for administration of Internet news services; have ten or more full-time news editors, of whom at least five have engaged in journalism for three or more years in news organizations; and have the necessary equipment, funds, and facilities to operate the website. The applicant must be a legal person who has engaged in Internet business for over two years, and also has no record of violating relevant laws and regulations during the past two years. If the applicant is a legal corporation, its registered capital should not be less than 10 million yuan. Similarly, the applicant should apply to the Information Office of the State Council for operating permits.

The third type of website is also established by traditional news media, but it is only allowed to publish news and commentaries which have already been published in original format by those media. To establish this type of website, the applicant needs to carry out the record-filing procedure with, instead of obtaining permit from, the Information Office of the State Council or its local subordinates in provinces.

Traditional news media include newspapers, magazines, radio stations, television stations, and news agencies established in accordance with the law. It is obvious that the purpose of implementing the above-mentioned licensing or record-filing mechanisms is to ensure that all news and commentaries on the Internet are provided only by traditional news media, and eventually to help the government control the dissemination of harmful or illegal information on the Internet.

News media organizations are allowed to cooperate with non-news media organizations in providing Internet news services. If 51% or more of equity interest in the news website is owned by the news organization, the website will be regarded as established by a news media organization; otherwise, it will be regarded as established by a non-news media organization. It should be noted that such cooperation is open only to domestic enterprises. At present, no organization is allowed to provide Internet news services in the form of a Sino-foreign equity joint venture, Sino-foreign cooperative joint venture, or wholly foreign-owned enterprise.

Licensing Internet audio-visual programs

Under the *Administrative Provisions on Internet Audio-Visual Programs*, Internet audio-visual program services refers to the activities of producing or editing audio-visual programs, and providing the programs to the general public via the Internet; they also include providing services for the public to upload and disseminate audio-visual programs. To launch Internet audio-visual program services, the service provider must meet the following requirements: be a state-owned or state-controlled enterprise and have no record of law violation within the three years before the date of application; have sound institutional arrangements and technical measures to protect information security; have the necessary facilities, equipment, technology, and funding to launch the services; have technical solutions in line with national standards, industry standards, and technical formats, etc. The SARFT is in charge of the regulation of Internet audio-visual programs. The service provider should apply to the SARFT for an operating permit.

It should be pointed out that under the *Administrative Provisions on Internet Audio-Visual Programs*, only state-owned or state-controlled enterprises are eligible to apply for a permit to provide Internet audio-visual program services; private and foreign enterprises are not allowed to enter this field of business. The introduction of this provision generated much concern within the Internet industry, since the majority audio-visual websites were in fact established by private enterprises, which were often funded by foreign venture capital. Responding to pressure from the industry, the SARFT later provided a written explanation, allowing such websites to continue to operate as long as they had no record of violating the law.

Licensing Internet publishing

In the *Interim Provisions on the Administration of Internet Publishing*, Internet publishing refers to the situation whereby Internet service providers select, edit, and process works created by themselves or others and subsequently publish such works on the Internet or send such works to users via the Internet. The works mainly include: (i) the content of publications such as books, newspapers, periodicals, audio and video products, electronic publications or works that have been made public in other media; and (ii) edited works of literature, art, natural science, social science, engineering technology, etc. Internet publishers refers to

Internet content providers that engage in Internet publishing business with the approval of the GAPP and the MIIT. There are currently four types of Internet publisher, i.e., websites established by existing publishing houses as a supplement to their traditional format of publication; websites specializing in Internet publishing, including the publication of online literature, online games, and online music; Internet journals or e-book sections launched by portal websites as part of their Internet business; and online publishing generated by digital libraries. To engage in Internet publishing, the website operator must meet the following requirements, i.e., have a definite scope of publication; have articles of association that comply with laws and regulations; and have the necessary funds, equipment, facilities, and personnel. In addition, the website operator needs to submit an application to the GAPP for review and approval.

Licensing Internet cultural services

In the *Interim Provisions on the Administration of Internet Culture*, Internet cultural products are cultural products produced for and disseminated through the Internet, which mainly include audio/video products, game products, live shows, art, and cartoons on the Internet. Internet cultural activities refers to the activity of providing Internet cultural products and services, which mainly include: (i) the activities of producing, reproducing, importing, wholesaling, retailing, leasing or broadcasting Internet cultural products; (ii) the activities of publishing cultural products online, or sending cultural products through the Internet to such user devices as computers, fixed telephones, mobile phones, radios, TV sets, games consoles, etc. for individual use; and (iii) the activities of displaying Internet cultural products or holding contests on Internet cultural products. In addition, Internet cultural activities are also divided into commercial and non-commercial ones. Commercial Internet cultural activities refers to the provision of Internet cultural products and services for profit by charging Internet users or by advertisement, sponsorship, or electronic commerce. Non-commercial Internet cultural activities refers to providing Internet users with Internet cultural products and services not for the purpose of making profits.

Under the *Interim Provisions on the Administration of Internet Culture*, to engage in Internet cultural service, the enterprise must meet the following conditions: have a definite scope for Internet cultural activities; have a legal name, physical site, organizational structure, and articles of association; and have the necessary funds, equipment, facilities, and personnel. Furthermore, to launch commercial Internet cultural activities, the enterprise must have at least 1 million yuan of registered capital and at least eight professional editors and technicians. Enterprises that intend to provide Internet cultural products and services should apply to the Ministry of Culture for review and approval. Foreign enterprises are currently excluded from investing in Internet cultural business in China.

Other regulatory issues

Along with legal regulation and administrative licensing, China has also adopted several other mechanisms to regulate the Internet. First, China advocates the use of architectural means for effective administration of the Internet. Specifically, China divides Internet networks into two categories: backbone networks and access networks. Backbone networks directly connect to international websites through international leasing circuits. Access networks, commonly referred to as ISPs, are those networks that link indirectly to the international Internet; they are required to obtain such a link through the backbone networks. There are four backbone networks in China, all of which are controlled and administered by government agencies. They include the MIIT's CHINANET and CHINAGBN, the Ministry of Education's CERNET, and the Chinese Academy of Science's CSTNET. All connections to international websites are required to go through MIIT's international gateway, and only backbone operators are permitted to link directly to the international Internet via that gateway. Through the use of backbone networks and the gateway, China is able to increase its capability to monitor Internet content and Internet users, while maintaining MIIT's monopoly of the international gateway. On the other hand, diversity and competition are recognized and established, since there are at least four backbone networks that compete with one another. In addition, there is no specific attempt to centralize the ownership of access networks, which are encouraged to coexist and compete.

Second, China advocates the use of technical means to control the Internet. Indeed, almost all major telecommunications operators and Internet content providers are required to take technical measures to prevent the dissemination of illegal and harmful information in cyberspace. The most frequently used techniques include keyword filtering and selective website blocking, both of which are primarily conducted at the router level. Routers are devices that forward packets of data along computer networks. In China, routers are programmed to channel URLs through proxy servers, which act as intermediaries for requests from clients seeking resources from other real servers. Proxy servers may look for, say, politically sensitive words and then send back error messages to the client who requested the information. Websites are blocked in a similar manner. As in other countries, there are many ways to get around such blocking. But the Chinese government has been constantly updating its technical monitoring system, in which the Golden Shield Project is gaining much attention. Beginning operation around the country in 2003, this project aims to establish an all-encompassing surveillance network that integrates such data and applications as credit records, closed-circuit television, face and speech recognition, and Internet monitoring technologies. The major monitoring techniques in the project include IP blocking, DNS filtering and redirection, URL filtering, packet filtering, and connection resetting. Despite these kinds of effort, the effectiveness and consequences of China's technical control of the Internet remain unclear.[21]

Third, administrative enforcement actions are also employed, especially when the government regards such actions as necessary for resolving certain urgent problems. In 2002, for example, following a fire in an Internet café in Beijing that killed 24 people, the authorities shut down more than 3,000 Internet cafés in Beijing.[22] The implication for Internet cafés is that, in order to stay in business, it is necessary to adhere to the relevant regulations. In 2009, in order to stop the spread of online pornography, violence, and indecency, the authorities reviewed 1.8 million websites across the country, among which 16,000 pornography sites as well as 136,000 unregistered sites were shut down.[23] Rigorous administrative enforcements like these may help the authorities to quickly achieve their regulatory objectives, but they may also have a suppressing effect on the development of the whole industry. It is argued that, in the long run, abnormal measures cannot be a real solution to increasingly complicated problems that occur in relation to the Internet.[24]

Fourth, China actively encourages self-regulation within the Internet industry. The most notable example is the establishment of the Internet Society of China (ISC). This is a national organization that was co-established in 2001 by more than 70 Internet-related entities, including Internet technology providers, Internet service providers, Internet content providers, and research and education organizations. This organization has issued a series of self-disciplinary regulations, such as the Public

Pledge of Self-Discipline for China's Internet Industry, the Public Pledge of Self-Discipline on Anti-Internet Virus, and the Declaration of Self-Discipline on Copyright Protection of China's Internet Industry. These disciplines are expected to be obeyed by all of its members. The ISC has arguably contributed to the healthy development of the Internet. It is reported that the organization has helped to reduce the global percentage of Chinese spam e-mail from 23% in 2002 to 4.1% in 2009.[25]

Finally, the Chinese government asks each individual and company to be responsible for what is published online, thus making everyone his own self-censor.[26] The government also solicits help from its citizens in order to effectively monitor Internet content. This practice is sometimes referred to as public supervision. Since 2004, the government has established a network of online reporting centers, which include the China Internet Illegal Information Reporting Center, Network Crimes Reporting Websites, 12321 Harmful and Spam Internet Information Reporting and Reception Center, 12390 Pornography Crack-Down and Press and Publication Copyright Joint Reporting Center. These reporting systems include a component of reward that encourages citizens to report illegal or harmful information. It is reported that by October 2004, 50 citizens had been rewarded 500 to 2,000 RMB for reporting pornography and 18 citizens had been rewarded 3,000 to 10,000 RMB for reporting illegal online gambling.[27]

China may be successful in achieving some of its regulatory objectives, but there are several problems that are deserving of discussion. One of the major problems is that the system arguably puts much more emphasis on government intervention than on other mechanisms such as self-regulation or market regulation. It is widely recognized that government intervention should be adopted mainly as a response to market failure, rather than play a central, dominant role in the market-oriented economy. Indeed, the Chinese government clearly acknowledges this supplemental approach. For example, Article 13 of the *Administrative Licensing Law* prescribes that if a target problem can be solved by individuals and organizations themselves, or can be effectively regulated by the mechanism of market competition, administrative licensing should not be pursued. In practice, however, China's Internet regulators can hardly meet this kind of requirement. They have not clearly identified what aspects of the Internet should be regulated and what aspects should not be managed. Neither have they found a way to help the Internet market to correct its own problems. Although self-regulation mechanisms like the ISC have been established, they are still a result of governmental coordination, to a large extent.

In the area of government intervention, the current system of regulation arguably stresses the imposition of restrictions on Internet activities rather than protecting the rights of participants. So far the most important legislation regarding the Internet is the *Decision on Safeguarding Internet Security* enacted by the NPC Standing Committee in 2000. The main part of the resolution is specification of the criminal or administrative punishment for behaviors that may endanger the safety of Internet operation or for individuals who conduct illegal activities through the Internet. Most of the subsequent Internet regulations also focus on preserving order in cyberspace and stipulating the liabilities for Internet users and business operators who violate the law. It is argued that the emphasis of China's Internet legislation is currently on restricting the rights of Internet users, while the objective of legislating for the protection of their rights remains unfulfilled.[28]

In addition, many Internet regulations are not operable in practice. Take as an example the *Interim Provisions on the Administration of Internet Websites Engaged in News Posting Operations* promulgated by the State Council Information Office (SCIO) in 2000. Article 14 of the *Interim Provisions* provides that "the linking of an Internet site to a news website outside China and the publication of news released by news media and Internet sites outside China must be specifically reported for approval to the SCIO." This provision attempts to impose some restrictions on the publication of foreign news. But it does not indicate how to handle foreign news that has been published by domestic newspapers and magazines. Do Internet publishers still need to apply for approval from the SCIO in this case? Operational problems like these also exist in many other regulations on the Internet.

It can be concluded that China's regulatory regime for the Internet is highly complicated. Although different agencies promulgate laws and regulations to respond to different aspects of the Internet, there are often overlaps or even conflicts among their jurisdictions. For example, Article 15 of the *Interim Provision on the Administration of Internet Websites Engaged in News Posting Operations* stipulates that if anyone publishes news without permission, the SCIO or its subordinate provincial offices will issue a warning or order rectification within a given time frame; or, if the offender has already obtained permission but violated relevant laws regarding online news publishing, the information offices have the right to revoke such permission. This *Interim Provision* was promulgated by the SCIO, but the *Administration of Internet Information Service Procedure*, which is promulgated by the State Council and has a higher authority than the *Interim Provision*, does not give the SCIO the aforementioned power. Another example of conflicting jurisdictions involves the nationwide movement on curbing Internet indecency that was discussed earlier. A total of seven agencies joined this movement. Some ISP owners complained that they did not know which agency they should report to because all of the agencies claimed to have ruling power over their websites.[29] In the following chapters, we will find that China's regulations on the Internet are becoming increasingly complicated, and are in need of clarification in order to be better understood.

Notes

1. Richard Campbell, Christopher R. Martin, and Bettina Fabos (2008) *Media and Culture: An Introduction to Mass Communication*, 6th edition, Boston, MA: Bedford/St. Martin, p. 45.

2. See Internet World Stats (2010) "World Internet Users and Population Stats," retrieved June 18, 2009 from http://www.internetworldstats.com/stats.htm.

3. Since the advent of the Internet, the Chinese government has worked out a series of policies, identifying phased priorities to boost Internet development across the country. As early as 1997, the government formulated the 9th Five-Year Plan for State Informationization and the Long Range Objective for the Year 2010, which included the Internet as part of the national information infrastructure and set the goal of facilitating national economic informationization through rigorous development of the Internet. In 2002, the government promulgated the Specialized Plan for Informationization in the 10th Five-Year Plan for National Economic and Social Development, setting up electronic government, electronic commerce, and the software industry as the development priorities. In 2006, the NPC passed the 11th Five-Year Plan for National Economic and Social Development, advocating the integration of the networks of telecommunications, radio, television, and the Internet. In 2007, the 17th National Congress of the Communist Party of China (CPC) developed the strategy of "developing modern industrial systems, integrating informationization with industrialization, and transforming scale-oriented industries into strength-oriented industries." These strategic policies contributed directly to the rapid development of the Internet in China.

4. See State Council Information Office (2010) *The White Paper on the Internet in China*. The original, Chinese version of the document can be retrieved from http://www.scio.gov.cn/zfbps/ndhf/2010/201006/t662572.htm; its English translation can be retrieved from http://www.chinadaily.com.cn/china/2010-06/08/content_9950198.htm.

5. See State Council Information Office (2010) *The White Paper on the Internet in China*.

6. China Internet Network Information Center (2010) "The 25th Statistical Survey Report on Internet Development in China," retrieved May 15, 2010 from http://www.cnnic.net.cn/en/index/0O/02/index.htm.

7. Chris Reed (2004) *Internet Law: Text and Materials*, 2nd edition, Cambridge, UK: Cambridge University Press.

8. Chris Reed (2004) *Internet Law: Text and Materials*, 2nd edition, Cambridge, UK: Cambridge University Press, p. 13.

9. Ralph E. Hanson (2008) *Mass Communication: Living in a Media World*, 2nd edition, Washington, DC: CQ Press.

10. Currently the No. 1 search engine in China, Baidu.com, provides Chinese and Japanese language Internet search and community services. Its search service allows users to find such online data as web pages, news, images, maps, blogs, and multimedia files. It also offers Baidu Baike, an online collaboratively built encyclopedia, and a searchable keyword-based discussion forum.

11. See "Tencent QQ 24-Hour Update Statistics of Online Users" (2010) retrieved June 19, 2010 from http://im.qq.com/online.shtml#qq.

12. See Wikipedia (2010) "Internet," retrieved June 15, 2010 from http://en.wikipedia.org/wiki/Internet.

13. The *People's Daily* is an organ of the Central Committee of the Communist Party of China (CPC), providing direct information on the policies and viewpoints of the Party. It is published worldwide with a circulation of 3 to 4 million; it also maintains an online presence at peopledaily.com.cn.

14. Sina.com is the largest Chinese language commercial news portal in China, claiming approximately 95 million registered users and 3 billion page views every day.

15. See State Council Information Office (2010) *The White Paper on the Internet in China.*

16. Before 1994, there was a power struggle between the former Ministry of Posts and Telecommunications (MPT) and the former Ministry of Electronics Industry (MEI) over the control of the Internet. These agencies held different interests and could not work together, consequently stifling the development of the Internet. The State Council thus created the National Joint Conference on State Economic Informationization in 1994, which was reorganized into the Steering Committee of National Information Infrastructure (NII) in 1996. However, the Steering Committee was seriously handicapped in its decision-making power since it lacked legislative power, financial means, and political support. In order to solve the problem of constant power struggle, China combined the MPT with the MEI and created the Ministry of Information Industry (MII) in 1998. This super ministry was responsible for the regulation and development of software, information, and telecommunications industries. In March 2008, the Ministry of Industry and Information Technology (MIIT) was established, superseding the MII as the major regulator of the information industry. Regarding the Internet, the MIIT is specifically in charge of the planning and administration of Internet infrastructure, the licensing or filing of Internet-related businesses, and the allocation and coordination of electronic bandwidth, domain names, and Internet addresses.

17. Yongzheng Wei (2006) *Lectures on Journalism and Communication Law*, 2nd edition, Beijing, China: Renmin University of China Press.

18. Foreign-funded telecommunications enterprises refer to Sino-foreign equity joint ventures that are jointly invested in and established in China by foreign investors and Chinese investors in accordance with the law and that are engaged in the provision of telecommunications services.

19. The *Administrative Provisions on Foreign-Funded Telecommunications Enterprises* can be retrieved from the following website: http://www.gov.cn/zwgk/2008-09/12/content_1094487.htm.

20. According to Article 5, the provision of Internet information services concerning news, publishing, education, medical treatment, health, and pharmaceuticals or medical apparatus must be reviewed and approved by the relevant authority.

21. See Ronald J. Deibert (2002) "Dark Guests and Great Firewalls: The Internet and Chinese Security Policy," *Journal of Social Issues* 58, pp. 143–159; Jason Lacharite (2002) "Electronic Decentralization in China: A Critical Analysis of Internet Filtering Policies in the People's Republic of China," *Australian Journal of Political Science* 37, pp. 333–346; Bin Liang and Hong Lu (2010) "Internet Development, Censorship, and Cyber Crimes in China," *Journal of Contemporary Criminal Justice* 26:1, pp. 103–120.

22. Guosong Shao (2010) "China's Regulations on Internet Cafes," *China Media Research* 6:3, pp. 26–30.

23. Tianai Wu and Xiaoyu Wu (2010) "The Internet Is Being Strictly Regulated in China," *IT Times*, March 25.

24. Tianai Wu and Xiaoyu Wu (2010) "The Internet Is Being Strictly Regulated in China," *IT Times*, March 25.

25. See State Council Information Office (2010) *The White Paper on the Internet in China*.

26. Lokman Tsui (2003) "The Panopticon as the Antithesis of a Space of Freedom: Control and Regulation of the Internet in China," *China Information* 17, pp. 65–82.

27. Michelle W. Lau (2005) "Internet Development and Information Control in the People's Republic of China," *CRS Report*, November 22, retrieved July 15, 2010 from http://www.cfr.org/publication/9844/crs_report.html,

28. See Xudong Qin, "On Internet Regulation and Legislation," retrieved July 1, 2011 from http://www.shoubu.com/second/content.asp?no=1125.

29. See Tianai Wu and Xiaoyu Wu (2010) "The Internet Is Being Strictly Regulated in China," *IT Times*, March 25.

Internet speech

Abstract: This chapter first examines the concept of freedom of speech, including its meaning and scope, major restrictions, and special problems caused by the Internet. It then discusses in detail how China regulates Internet speech that may harm national security, the social order, and one's reputation. The discussion also involves evaluation of how China strikes a balance between protecting free speech and preserving national security, the social order, or people's reputation.

Key words: Internet speech, freedom of speech, seditious speech, disclosure of state secrets, pornography, cults, superstition, fabricated terrorist information, fabricated stock market information, commercial speech, defamation

While freedom of speech is protected by China's Constitution, unfettered speech always stirs fear and anger both in government and among citizens. Under the label of freedom of speech, a political activist may advocate secession, an artist may illustrate sexual activities in his works, an advertiser may release deceptive ads, and a journalist may defame celebrities in his writing. These kinds of speech arguably may endanger the public interest or the rights of individuals. The problem is how to strike a balance between protecting free speech and preserving public interests or individuals' rights. Such a problem is becoming particularly urgent in the context of the Internet, which has fundamentally facilitated people's capability to exercise their right to freedom of speech. Focusing on the issue of Internet speech in China, this chapter first introduces the concept of freedom of speech and then investigates how China imposes legal restrictions on Internet speech that may cause damage to national security, the social order, and one's reputation.

Freedom of speech

In order to understand how speech in cyberspace is regulated, it is necessary to become familiar with how speech is regulated in general. This section thus examines the meaning of freedom of speech in China. It also investigates such fundamental questions as what speech may be restricted and how speech may be restricted. The section concludes with a discussion of how existing freedom of speech constructs may apply to speech in cyberspace.

The meaning of freedom of speech

Freedom of speech refers to the right to disseminate, seek, and receive information and ideas either orally, in writing, or in print, in the form of art, or through any other media. It is regarded as a fundamental right of Chinese citizens. Since the founding of the PRC in 1949, the NPC of China has adopted four constitutions,[1] all of which have provided for the protection of freedom of speech. In China, freedom of speech mainly covers three aspects, i.e., the right to express, the right to make criticisms and suggestions, and the right to know.

The right to express is explicitly protected by the current Chinese Constitution (1982). Article 35 of the Constitution provides that Chinese citizens enjoy "freedom of speech, of the press, of assembly, of association, of procession, and of demonstration." These six types of freedom, considered crucial for Chinese citizens to participate in public affairs, are summarized as the right to expression. In addition, the Constitution stipulates the freedom of correspondence under the law in Article 40 and the freedom to engage in scientific research, and literary and artistic creation and other cultural pursuits, in Article 47. These two types of freedom are considered an integral part of the right to express.

In accordance with the constitutional provisions, the right to expression can be defined as the right of Chinese citizens to publicly or privately express or disseminate thoughts, feelings, information, and opinions in a variety of ways without infringement by others. The right to expression involves both the content and the form of expression. Regarding the content of expression, it includes not only issues of concern to special interest groups but also such general issues as national politics and the economy. In terms of the form of expression, it includes not only private conversation or correspondence but also the use of newspapers, radio, television, film, the Internet, and other mass media. Expression is not limited merely to being verbal; it also can be symbolic, such as through images, painting, sculpture, music, and gesture. In addition, social rituals like mourning and floral tributes can also be a form of expression. Among various forms of expression, voting is considered the most important, the most formal, and the ultimate form of expression. When it is difficult to reach agreement over significant issues, people should have the right to express their opinion through voting.

The right to make criticisms and suggestions is also protected by the Chinese Constitution. Under Article 41 of the Constitution, Chinese citizens have the right to criticize and make suggestions to any state organ or functionary. The right to make criticisms means that citizens have the right to criticize the shortcomings and wrongdoings of state organs and their staff; and the right to make suggestions means that citizens have the right to suggest how state organs and their staff can improve their work. Simply stated, suggestions are positive comments while criticisms are negative comments. Suggestions mainly concern certain policies, while criticisms mainly concern specific persons and events.[2] Criticisms and suggestions are not necessarily made to specific persons or organizations; they can be publicized through the mass media. When citizens exercise their right to make criticisms and suggestions through the mass media, the supervision of public opinion may be put in place. By definition, the supervision of public opinion refers to a situation in which citizens make use of mass media like newspapers, radio, television, and the Internet to express their views and opinions, and then public opinion may be formed, functioning as a curb on illegal or unethical behaviors by state organs, political parties, social organizations, and civil servants and public officials. It has become the most important and the commonest way for citizens to exercise their right to make criticisms and suggestions in China.

The right to know means that citizens have the right to seek and receive information. In contemporary society, it is also seen as an integral part of freedom of speech. Such international conventions as the *European Convention on Human Rights* and the *International Convention on Human Rights* provide that freedom of speech includes the right to seek and receive information and ideas. The Chinese Constitution does not explicitly propose the concept of the right to know, but its stipulation on the right to make criticisms and suggestions implicitly includes the right to information. That is because the right to criticize and make suggestions cannot be exercised without the necessary information. In other words, the right to know is a prerequisite for the right to make criticisms and suggestions. In addition, under Article 2 of the Chinese Constitution, all power belongs to the people, who "administer state affairs and manage economic, cultural and social affairs through various channels and in various ways in accordance with the law." This provision also indirectly confirms the existence of the right to know. There are two types of right to know: negative and positive. The term "negative rights" means that anyone is obligated not to infringe on others' rights to seek and receive information that has already been publicized; and "positive rights" means that certain individuals and state organs have the obligation to publicize information for citizens to seek and obtain.[3] Both types of right to information have been mandated in the *Regulation on the Disclosure of Government Information*, which was promulgated in 2007 by the State Council.

The scope of freedom of speech

Freedom of speech is constitutionally protected as a fundamental right in many countries. The major arguments for free speech include enhancing democracy, preserving social stability, discovering truth, and advancing autonomy.[4] However, there is also little disagreement that freedom of speech is not absolute, and that protection of free speech does not extend to situations in which one's speech impinges upon the legal interests and rights of other citizens and of society. This leaves room for the government to establish the scope of freedom of speech. In the United States, for example, an important solution to the scope of free speech is the categorical approach. The Supreme Court has indicated that there are three levels of protection for speech, which were summarized by Justice John Paul Stevens in *R.A.V.* v. *City of St. Paul.* He wrote in a concurring opinion: "our First Amendment decisions have created a rough hierarchy in the constitutional protection of speech. Core political speech occupies the highest, most protected position; commercial speech and non-obscene, sexually explicit speech are regarded as a sort of second-class expression; obscenity and fighting words receive the least protection of all."[5] Theoretically, defining categories of most protected, less protected, and unprotected speech provides greater guidance than a system in which almost all speech cases have to be reviewed on a case-by-case basis. But there is a great deal of debate about why some categories of speech are protected while others are not. There is also a recurring problem of whether the Court's definitions of the categories are sufficiently specific and applicable.

In China, while the Constitution provides protection for freedom of speech, it also stipulates that the exercise by citizens of their freedoms and rights may not infringe upon the interests of the state, society, and other citizens. This is a basic principle which citizens are required to comply with in their exercise of the right to free speech. Explicating this provision, China has set up a wide range of restrictions on the freedom of speech for the purposes of protecting individual, social, and national interests. These restrictions are contained in such regulations as the *Regulations for the Administration of Audio-Visual Products* (enacted in 1994), the *Regulations for the Administration of Broadcasting and Television* (1997), the *Regulations for the Administration of the Printing Industry* (1997), the *Regulations on Publication Administration* (enacted in 1997, revised in 2002), and the *Decision of the NPC Standing Committee on Safeguarding Internet Security* (2000). Under these regulations, the following content is prohibited from being published or disseminated:

1. Anything that goes against the basic principles determined by the Constitution;
2. Anything that endangers the unification, sovereignty, and territorial integrity of the country;
3. Anything that endangers state security, reputation and interests;
4. Anything that instigates national separatism, infringes on the customs and habits of minority nationalities and disrupts solidarity of nationalities;
5. Anything that discloses state secrets;
6. Anything that publicizes pornography and superstition or plays up violence, endangers social ethics and the fine traditions of national culture; and
7. Anything that insults or slanders others.

The "basic principles determined by the Constitution" listed above in item 1 refer generally to the four cardinal principles that China must adhere to, namely, the socialist road, the people's democratic dictatorship, the leadership of the Communist Party, and Marxism-Leninism and Mao Zedong Thought. These principles were proposed in 1979 by Deng Xiaoping, the general architect of China's reform and opening up, and adopted in the Chinese Constitution in 1982. Thus, any speech that attempts to challenge such core principles will be found to be in violation of Chinese law. Items 2, 3, 4, and 5 above all concern national security.

In Chinese political culture, national security, honor, and interests are traditionally considered more important than individual rights and freedom; so speech that may endanger national interests or incite the overthrow of the government is strictly restricted by Chinese law. In essence, the prohibited content in item 1 also concerns national security, since opposing the four core principles is essentially about opposing the existing political system. Item 6 concerns social order. Any act of disseminating pornography, cults, superstition, gambling, and violence is prohibited by Chinese law. The last item concerns personal rights and reputation. This right is relatively new, but has been increasingly acknowledged by Chinese law.

Moreover, China's *Criminal Law*, *General Principles of the Civil Law* and other basic laws all include provisions on the scope of free speech. In order to safeguard national security, for example, the *Criminal Law* makes it a crime to incite secession, ethnic hatred and discrimination, the overthrow of the government, and violent resistance to the enforcement of laws and regulations. In order to maintain social order, the *Criminal Law* also makes it a crime to disseminate pornography, organize and make use of cults, superstition, and secret societies to undermine the implementation of state laws and administrative regulations. In addition, the tort provisions in the *General Principles of the Civil Law* are often used to protect the reputation of individuals and organizations.

Major restrictions on speech

We have examined what speech the Chinese government may restrict. The next question is how. The Chinese Constitution clearly stipulates that citizens, in exercising their freedoms and rights, may not infringe upon the interests of the state, of society or of the collective, or upon the lawful freedoms and rights of other citizens. This provides constitutional support for the government to impose restraints on speech. In practice, the state mainly employs the following measures to restrict speech: prior restraint, subsequent punishment, and vagueness and overbreadth.

Prior restraint

By definition, prior restraint involves "submitting all proposed publications to government censors who exercised considerable discretion regarding the content to be proved for publication, and it was imposed specifically on publication in advance of the publication."[6] Prior restraint may appear in different forms, but is often controversial. One form of prior restraint is to stipulate what kind of information is prohibited from dissemination. It may be stipulated by laws and regulation, as shown in the above-mentioned scope of free speech. It may also be stipulated by the central or local propaganda departments, which send out notices to editors informing them which news topics are completely forbidden. In some cases, the government may even suggest what stories newspapers should print and even how the stories should be portrayed.

Prior restraint may also come out as "prior review," whereby some proposed publications are required to be reviewed and approved by relevant authorities. For example, a directive jointly promulgated by the GAPP and the Central Propaganda Department mandates that manuscripts on major Party and national leaders must be subject to review by the administrative organ in advance of publication.[7] Another directive enacted by the GAPP stipulates that all proposed publications on important topics are to be filed with the GAPP.[8] These include topics that concern documents or literature of the Party or the nation, former or current leaders of the Party or the nation, Party secrets or state secrets, nationality problems or religious problems, national defense, the Cultural Revolution, the former Soviet Union and Eastern European countries, and so on. The scope of the selected topics is not fixed, however; it is subject to adjustment by the regulatory authority. If a topic that has been prohibited by the GAPP is published, the publisher will be subject to administrative or even criminal punishment.

In addition, prior restraint is reflected in the licensing scheme, by which the government requires individuals or organizations to obtain a permit in order to lawfully engage in media business. In China, the government directly or indirectly controls the amount, structure, distribution, and coordination of publishing and broadcasting within the country. A series of regulations on publication clearly state that individuals or organizations may not legally engage in any form of publishing unless they obtain permission from the relevant authorities. According to the *Administrative Measures for Internet Information Service*, for instance, all commercial Internet information services are required to receive a license from, and all non-commercial Internet information services are required to file with, their local telecommunications regulatory authority. Similarly, the *Administrative Provisions for Internet Audio-Visual Programs* stipulates that no one may operate an Internet broadcast business for news-related audio/visual programs without permission from the State Council Information Office.[9]

Subsequent punishment

Subsequent punishment refers to the situation whereby the news media are punished for and after publishing irresponsible or unlawful articles. In China, subsequent punishment is employed against irresponsible speech just as much as is prior restraint. It may come in the form of fines, closure, defamation lawsuit, and dismissals, demotions, or imprisonment of the editors or journalists involved. Compared to prior restraint, punishment after publication is generally considered a more acceptable way to deter irresponsible speech. That is because, firstly, subsequent punishment is imposed on individual publications, but prior restraint may affect all publications.[10] Secondly, the system of subsequent punishment allows the communicator rather than the government to decide what to publish, and only thereafter to be punished if the decision was inappropriate.[11] Thirdly, in many countries subsequent punishment is usually a criminal procedure, while prior restraint is administrative. The criminal procedure involves the presumption of innocence, burden of proof, and strict rules of evidence, all of which make the courts fairer and more deliberate forums than administrative agencies.[12] But it should be pointed out that punishment after the fact may also be an administrative proceeding, since the regulatory authorities have the right and ability to directly penalize alleged abuses. Finally, subsequent punishment provides an opportunity for public appraisal, which is often lacking in prior restraints that feature internal administrative procedures. Despite the above arguments, there may be little practical difference between subsequent punishment and prior restraint. It is argued that when the laws are very vague, or the punishment is overly harsh, "the prospect of subsequent sanctions may serve to chill expression as much as prior orders not to publish."[13] Therefore, in the United States and some other countries, punishment after the fact may be allowed for certain categories of irresponsible speech, but is required to follow carefully tailored lines set by the courts.[14]

Vagueness and overbreadth

Regulatory schemes are regarded as vague if "a reasonable person cannot tell what speech is prohibited and what is permitted."[15] China's legislation on speech arguably features vague language. For example, the *Regulation on Publication Administration* enacted by the GAPP stipulates that "no publication" may contain content "harming the honor or the interests of the nation" and "disturbing social order, disrupting social stability." In this regulation, what constitutes national honor, national interests, social order, and social stability remains undefined. This may cause some freedom of speech problems. One of the problems is about fairness—it is unfair to punish the innocent by not providing clear notice as to what was prohibited.[16] Vagueness also risks selective enforcement. Without providing some "minimum" guidelines, a law may permit government officials to choose whom to punish for their views or politics.[17] But the most disturbing aspect of vague regulations is that they may chill constitutionally protected speech. Vague laws tend to obscure the boundaries of free expression, and people whose expression is constitutionally protected may well refrain from exercising their rights for fear of stepping into the unlawful zone. An undesirable consequence is that people censor themselves to varying degrees, and protected speech is greatly inhibited.

China's laws on speech are also characterized by overbreadth, i.e., "they regulated substantially more speech than the constitution allows to be regulated."[18] For instance, the *Administrative Measures for Safeguarding the Safety of International Connecting of Computer Information Networks* prescribes that no unit or individual may utilize the Internet to produce, copy, look up, or transmit information "harming the credibility of a government agency," which is obviously overbroad in terms of regulating Internet speech. Like vagueness, overbreadth may cause such problems as unfairness, selective enforcement, and the chilling effect on free speech. Thus, in countries like the United States, legal provisions with overbreadth are made constitutionally invalid. It should be noted that vagueness and overbreadth are often overlapping. Particularly in China, many vague regulations on speech are potentially overbroad, and many clearly overbroad regulations are in fact potentially vague. It is argued that regulations on speech would not necessarily be vague and overbroad if the legislative authorities provided more specific guidelines regarding the scope of freedom of speech. So far, China has not established such guidelines.

Special problem: Internet speech

The emergence of the Internet brings a brand new channel for Chinese citizens to express their opinions. E-mail, blogs, Twitter, web pages, instant messaging, public bulletin boards, video sharing sites, social networking websites, and many other forms of communication are fundamentally changing the way people communicate with one another.

According to official statistics, over 80% of Internet users rely mainly on the Internet for getting information. About 80% of Chinese websites provide electronic bulletin board services to Internet users. Every day Chinese Internet users publish a total of over 3 million pieces of information through a variety of Internet channels. More than 66% of Chinese Internet users frequently take part in online discussions on various issues. In addition, most government websites provide the e-mail address and phone number of the government so that the public can report problems and make criticisms and suggestions to the government in a timely way.

The constitutional protection of free speech basically applies to the Internet in China. Meanwhile, speech in cyberspace is subject to almost the same restrictions as are traditional communication activities. Under the *Administrative Measures for Internet Information Services*, Internet information service providers may not produce, reproduce, disseminate, or broadcast information with content that opposes the fundamental principles established in the Constitution; endangers national security or subverts state power; harms national honor and national interests; incites ethnic hatred or ethnic discrimination; sabotages state religious policy or propagates cults or superstitions; disseminates rumors, disturbs social order, or disrupts social stability; propagates obscenity, pornography, gambling, violence, or fear, or incites the commission of crimes; and insults or slanders others or infringes upon others' rights and interests. These kinds of restriction on Internet service providers also appear in the *Interim Provisions on the Administration of Internet Publishing*, *Administrative Provisions on Internet Audio-Visual Programs*, *Administrative Provisions on Internet News Services*, and so on.

However, the Internet is not traditional media. It in fact presents a unique set of problems for regulating speech, such as anonymity and accountability. Genuine anonymity in cyberspace means that "no one could trace the source of electronic message."[19] The positive value of anonymous communication is that it induces individuals to be more active in expressing their ideas or criticizing government officials. But there is also an inherent danger, that is, anonymity allows individuals to escape responsibility for their abusive or negligent postings. In China, genuine anonymity is not allowed in general. All ISPs are required to keep records of the real identity of pseudonymous traffic so that abusers can be identified and reprimanded. In spite of these requirements, Chinese Internet users can still find ways technically to avoid the disclosure of their true identities. Another related issue concerning

Internet speech is accountability, which refers to "the acceptance of responsibility for one's actions."[20] When a harmful or abusive message occurs, it may involve several parties, such as the individual who initiates the message, the individuals who help to disseminate the message, the ISP where the message is initially posted, and the websites where the message also appears. Without accountability, there is no basis upon which a prosecutor or an injured party can initiate a criminal or civil procedure. The question is, if the initiator of an abusive message is anonymous and cannot be identified, who would be liable for that message? If the ISP containing the message is held liable, it will be transformed into a censor, a role that none of them wishes to play.

To conclude, free speech constructs can basically apply to the regulation of Internet speech, but the unique features of the Internet have created some problems that challenge the traditional legal system to some extent. This may be seen in the following discussion of the tension between protecting free speech and preserving national security, social order, or one's reputation.

Risks to national security

In China, speech in cyberspace, like that in physical space, is literally protected by the Constitution. If Internet speech is severely restrained, perhaps the most likely situation is when it is deemed to endanger national security. The fundamental question is how to strike a balance between protecting free expression and preserving national security in cyberspace. This section first examines crimes in which speech may endanger national security, including seditious speech and disclosure of state secrets. Then it investigates when and how Internet speech may be censored or punished because of national security concerns. Two cases are presented for the purposes of illustration.

Seditious speech

Seditious speech refers to "the advocating, or urging, of an attempt to overthrow the government by force, or to disrupt its lawful activities with violence." In the *Criminal Law* enacted in 1979, seditious speech was treated as a counter-revolutionary crime, which refers to the act of overthrowing the political power of the dictatorship of the proletariat and the socialist system. In 1997, the NPC Standing Committee made revisions to the *Criminal Law*, replacing crimes of counter-revolution with crimes of endangering national security, which refers to acts aimed at "endangering the sovereignty, territorial integrity and security of the state, splitting the state, subverting the state power of the people's democratic dictatorship and overthrowing the socialist system."[21] The revised *Criminal Law* specified 12 types of crimes of endangering national security, among which 4 concern seditious speech, namely, inciting the overthrow of state power, inciting secession, inciting ethnic hatred and ethnic discrimination, and inciting violent resistance to law enforcement.[22] The following paragraphs will discuss the basic principles of these four crimes, which have been largely applied to Internet speech.

The crime of inciting the overthrow of state power

The crime of inciting the overthrow of state power involves acts of instigating others to overthrow the state power and the socialist system by spreading rumors, libel, or by any other means. China's Constitution stipulates clearly that the PRC is a socialist country under the people's democracy dictatorship, which is led by the working class and based on the alliance of workers and peasants; the socialist system is the basic state system, so any attempt to overthrow the state power and the socialist system is considered to be a serious harm to national security, and will be severely punished by Chinese law.

The crime of inciting the overthrow of the government can be analyzed from four perspectives, i.e., the subject of the crime, the object of the crime, the subjective aspect of the crime, and the objective aspect. The subject of this crime is a natural person who has reached the official age of criminal liability; it can be divided into ringleaders, active participants, and other participants, each of whom bear differentiated criminal liability for their acts. The object of this crime is the people's democratic dictatorship and the socialist system. In terms of the subjective aspect of the crime, the offender must be proved to have deliberately instigated others to overthrow the state power and the socialist system. In terms of the objective aspect, this crime refers to the act of instigating others to overthrow the state power and socialist system by means of rumor, defamation, or other ways. Rumor and defamation refers to facts that are fabricated or distorted for the purpose of damaging and defaming the state power and the socialist system. Anyone who produces, copies, distributes, and disseminates publications with the knowledge that such publications contain content inciting the overthrow of state power, or who makes use of the Internet to incite the overthrow of the government, may be convicted of a crime. Anyone who organizes and uses cult organizations to subvert state power may be also convicted of a crime. As long as the offender incites the overthrow of state power through the means of rumor, libel and other ways, no matter whether or not his audience believes what he says, no matter whether or not he/she in fact carries out the activities of overthrowing the government, he/she may still be convicted of the crime of inciting the overthrow of the government.

Under Article 105 of the *Criminal Law*, a person who is convicted of the crime shall be sentenced to a fixed term of imprisonment of not more than five years, criminal detention, public surveillance, or deprivation of political rights; the ringleaders or others who commit major crimes shall be sentenced to fixed terms of imprisonment of not less than five years. Further, a person who commits this crime shall be deprived of political rights, and could also be sentenced to confiscation of property.

The crime of inciting secession

The crime of inciting secession involves acts of inciting others to split the state or undermine the unity of the country. The subject of this crime is a natural person who has reached the official age of criminal responsibility. Chinese citizens, foreign citizens, and stateless persons all can be the subject of this crime. The object of this crime is the unity of the state. The subjective aspect of this crime is that the offender has direct intent to split the country and undermine its national unity. The objective aspect of this crime is that the offender commits an act of inciting secession. Incitement refers to a situation whereby the offender urges or persuades others to commit secession through the use of language, text, images, or other communication tools, but does not to commit secession himself. This is the fundamental difference between the crime of inciting secession and the crime of committing secession.

Simply stated, to be convicted of the crime of inciting secession, the offender must have direct intent and also commit an act of inciting secession. If someone has only a narrow-minded nationalistic sentiment or complains only about local or national policies towards ethnic minorities, but does not intend to split the country or incite others to split the country, he should not be viewed as committing the crime of inciting secession. Further, if someone gains access to information that advocates secession only for personal use in advocating secession, his act does not constitute a crime; but if he disseminates such information to others and to society at large, his act may constitute a criminal offense. The crime of inciting secession is determined by the existence of an action. As long as a person commits the act of inciting others to split the country, no matter whether his audience is incited as a result, and no matter whether he acts in accordance with his seditious speech, his behavior still constitutes a criminal offense.[23]

In Chinese judicial practice, anyone who commits one of the following acts for the purpose of splitting the country or undermining national unity will be investigated for criminal responsibility: distorting and fabricating history, or through discussion of hot topics, promoting ethnic separatism, disseminating offensive attacks on the Communist Party leadership and the socialist system; promoting "Pan-Islamism," "Pan-Turkism," or advocating the establishing of a country ruled by theocracy or the Qur'an; advocating the establishment of separatist organizations, "governments in exile," or "Islamic militants"; advocating "jihad" or "jihad history"; propagating "colonial rule," "foreign invasion, anti-Han," or hatred against non-Islamic believers; promoting "self-determination", or "liberation of the oppressed Muslims;" making use of folk culture activities to advocate secession; producing, suspending, posting, or distributing the "flags" and "national emblems" of separatist organizations; producing, publishing, suspending, posting, or distributing slogans, flyers, and other forms of material that advocate secession; making use of international conferences, cultural seminars, or academic research to engage in the propaganda of secession; making use of radio, television, and the Internet to promote secession or ethnic separatism; inciting the masses to refuse using the RMB, the various documents issued by the government, and the mosques built by the government; and committing other acts that incite secession.[24] According to Article 103 of the *Criminal Law*, persons who incite secession shall be sentenced to a fixed term of imprisonment of not more than five years, criminal detention, public surveillance, or deprivation of political rights; the ringleaders and those who commit major crimes shall be sentenced to fixed terms of imprisonment of not less than five years.

The crime of inciting ethnic hatred or discrimination

China is a unitary multinational state built up jointly by the people of all its nationalities. Under the Chinese Constitution, all nationalities in China are equal. The state protects the lawful rights and interests of the minority nationalities and upholds the principles of equality, unity, and mutual assistance among all of China's nationalities. Discrimination against and oppression of any nationality are prohibited; any acts that undermine the unity of the nationalities or instigate their secession are prohibited. Also, under the *International Covenant on Civil and Political Rights* that China has signed, "any advocacy of national, racial or religious hatred that constitutes incitement to discrimination, hostility or violence shall be prohibited by law." Thus, an act of inciting ethnic hatred or discrimination constitutes a crime in China. The subject of this crime is a natural person who has reached the official age of criminal liability. The object of this crime is ethnic equality, which means that all of China's nationalities enjoy equal political and legal rights. The incitement of ethnic hatred or discrimination may lead to separatist sentiment and even secession, so that this crime indirectly endangers national security. The subjective aspect of this crime is that the offender has the subjective intention to incite ethnic hatred or ethnic discrimination. The objective aspect of this crime is that the offender commits an act of inciting ethnic hatred or discrimination. It should be noted that incitement to ethnic hatred or discrimination will constitute a crime only in serious cases. "In serious cases" generally refers to one of the following situations: the offender's motive is despicable, such as to cover up their illegal or criminal acts; the offender plays dirty tricks, such as making use of insult, libel, and rumor; the offender repeatedly agitates; a relatively large number of people are agitated; or the consequences of such agitation are serious. In accordance with Article 249 of the *Criminal Law*, whoever incites ethnic hatred or discrimination, if the circumstances are serious, shall be sentenced to a fixed term of imprisonment of not more than three years, criminal detention, public surveillance, or deprivation of political rights; if the circumstances are especially serious, he shall be sentenced to a fixed term of imprisonment of not less than three years but not more than ten years.

Another related crime is the crime of publishing materials purported to discriminate against or humiliate an ethnic group. The subject of this crime is the person who is directly responsible for the publication. The object of this crime is also ethnic equality. The subjective aspect of this crime is that the offender has the subjective intent to publish such materials. The objective aspect is that the offender publishes materials that discriminate against or humiliate an ethnic group. In other words, the establishment of this crime requires two elements: first, the discriminating or insulting content must be published, such as in books, video tapes, audio tapes, pictures, posters, calendars, and more; second, the published content must be discriminating or insulting. Discrimination here refers to treatment or consideration of, or making a distinction in favor of or against, an ethnic group based on that group's origins, history, customs, or culture. Insult here refers to treatment of or making a statement about an ethnic group with contemptuous rudeness based on that group's origins, history, customs, or culture. Under Article 250 of the *Criminal Law*, only when the circumstances are flagrant and the consequences are serious, will the publication of materials purported to discriminate against or insult an ethnic group constitute a crime; and the persons who are directly responsible for the offense shall be sentenced to a fixed term of imprisonment of not more than three years, criminal detention, or public surveillance.

The crime of inciting violent resistance to law enforcement

The crime of inciting violent resistance to law enforcement involves acts of deliberately inciting the masses to resist law enforcement. Any natural person who has reached the age of criminal responsibility can be the subject of this crime. The object of this crime is public order, which is often established through legislation and required to be complied with by the public. The subjective aspect of this crime is that the offender has the subjective intent to incite the masses to resist law enforcement, although he knows such law should be abided by. The objective aspect of this crime is that the offender incites the masses to resist law enforcement and disturb public order in a violent way. It should be noted that "the masses" here refers to three or more persons, who can be either criminals or law-abiding citizens, and "law" includes the constitutional law, basic laws, local laws, and administrative regulations. This crime is established by the existence of the act. As long as the offender commits the act of inciting, regardless of the consequence, he will be convicted of this crime. Under Article 278 of the *Criminal Law*, anyone who incites the masses to violently resist law enforcement shall be sentenced to a fixed term of imprisonment of not more than three years, criminal detention, public surveillance, or deprivation of political rights; if the consequences are serious, he shall be sentenced to a fixed term of imprisonment of not less than three years but not more than seven years.

Judicial practice concerning sedition law

Sedition law is not unique to China. In England, a statement was seditious if it intended to "bring into hatred or contempt, or excite hostility towards, the Crown, government, Parliament, and administration of justice, or with the aim of inducing reform by unlawful means or of promoting class warfare".[25] In the United States, the Congress passed the Sedition Act of 1798, which made it a crime to publish "any false, scandalous, and malicious writing with intent to stir up contempt for the federal government officials, or their official acts."[26] This traditional view of sedition would in fact cover much of political speech, and thus have the effect of stifling any serious criticism of government officials and public policies. Over time, the law on sedition has been liberalized in a number of approaches. In England, the courts tried to differentiate between incitement to revolutionary change and advocacy of lawful reform and the removal of grievances. In *R. v. Burns*, for example, the defendant was acquitted after making a passionate public speech calling attention to the plight of unemployed workers in London. A number of subsequent English cases also emphasize that for the offense to be committed, the speaker must intend to cause violence, and for such intention to be established, the jury must consider the character of the audience and the current state of public feeling, i.e., the circumstantial nature of the offense.[27] In the United States, the Supreme Court has attempted to distinguish the expression of political opinion from the incitement of violent political action. In *Gitlow* v. *New York*, the Court made a distinction between the expression of philosophical abstraction and the language of direct incitement; only the latter could be punished because of its tendency to endanger public security. Similarly, in *Yates* v. *U.S.*, the Court made a distinction between advocacy of abstract political doctrine and advocacy designed to promote specific action; only the latter could be made a crime by the government. Later, the United States has seemingly become more protective of speech than many other democratic countries. This is particularly reflected in the case of *Brandenburg* v. *Ohio*, in which the Supreme Court ruled that a conviction for incitement is constitutional only if several requirements are met: imminent harm, a likelihood of producing illegal action, and an intent to cause imminent illegality.[28]

Compared with Western countries, China's judgment of seditious speech remains ambiguous. This ambiguity allows some government agencies and officials to make use of the law to suppress criticism of their poor governance. Moreover, unlike American courts, Chinese courts do not have the right to constitutional review or constitutional interpretation. This results in a lack of protection of free speech in the trial of criminal cases, although free speech is a fundamental right guaranteed by the Chinese Constitution. When handling secession cases, Chinese courts have not intentionally adhered to certain judicial principles. However, it is argued that they have to some extent adopted the test of "the tendency to endanger national security," as proposed in *Gillow v. New York*. This means that the court will punish any speech that has a tendency to harm national security, no matter whether or not that speech can cause substantial, imminent harm. This principle has been criticized on the grounds that it may place excessive restrictions on freedom of speech. Since there is no clarified standard for how to establish secession in Chinese law, more and more Chinese lawyers are citing the *Johannesburg Principles on National Security, Freedom of Expression and Access to Information* as a defense for their clients' problematic speech. Under this international convention, no one may be subjected to any sort of restraint, disadvantage, or sanction because of his or her opinions or beliefs; expression may be punished as a threat to national security only if a government can demonstrate that: (a) the expression is intended to incite imminent violence; (b) it is likely to incite such violence; and (c) there is a direct and immediate connection between the expression and the likelihood or occurrence of such violence. These provisions are very close to the "imminent lawless action" test established in *Brandenburg v. Ohio*. Chinese courts so far tend not to accept this kind of test, however; they still tend to extinguish "reactionary political speech" at the very beginning.

Disclosure of state secrets

Simply stated, disclosure of state secrets refers to acts of making state secrets known to persons who should not know them. Chinese law has provided a systematic approach to the protection of state secrets. The Chinese Constitution (enacted 1982) stipulates that all citizens have the obligation to safeguard state secrets. The *Criminal Law* (1979) makes it a crime to disclose state secrets. Both the *Law on Guarding State Secrets* (1988) and the *State Security Law* (1993) provide further clarification on the crime of disclosing state secrets. The revised *Criminal Law* (1997) divides the crime of divulging state secrets into three categories: the crime of intentionally or negligently leaking state secrets; the crime of stealing, spying into, buying, or unlawfully supplying state secrets or intelligence for individuals or organizations outside the territory of China; and the crime of unlawfully holding documents, materials, or other objects classified "top secret" or "highly secret" state secrets.[29]

The crime of leaking state secrets

In Chinese judicial practice, this crime is often divided into two categories: the crime of intentionally leaking state secrets, and the crime of negligently leaking state secrets. Both crimes have the same subject, object, and objective aspects, but they have different subjective aspects. The subject of both crimes is the functionaries of state organs. This is because only the functionaries of state organs are able and qualified to hold and be aware of state secrets. The object of both crimes is state secrets, which is often required to be clarified in the trial of criminal cases. In terms of the subjective aspect, the crime of intentionally leaking state secrets obviously focuses on the intentionality of the offender, while the crime of negligently leaking state secrets focuses on the negligence of the offender. The objective aspect of both crimes is that the offender must commit acts of leaking state secrets in violation of the provisions of the *Law on Guarding State Secrets*. Leakage refers to disclosure without the authorization of official sanction. Leakage can be conducted orally, in writing, or through steganography, photocopying, recording, and other methods. If others obtain state secrets through stealing, detecting, decoding, or telemetry, and the functionaries of state organs have not violated the law of guarding state secrets, such a situation does not constitute the crime of leaking state secrets. Under the relevant Chinese law, the People's Procuratorate courts should file for investigation of cases if the functionaries of state organs commit one of the following acts: leaking "top secret" or "highly secret" state secrets; leaking more than three pieces of "confidential" state secrets; disseminating state secrets to the public; leaking state secrets with serious consequence; making use of authority to mandate or force others to unlawfully leak state secrets; leaking state secrets for the seeking of personal gain; and other serious circumstances. For the action to constitute a crime, the offender must commit acts of disclosing state secrets and the consequence of his action must also be serious. If the consequence is not serious, the offender should not be prosecuted as a criminal, although he may be punished administratively. Under Article 398 of the *Criminal Law*, any functionary of a state organ who intentionally or negligently leaks state secrets, if the circumstances are serious, will be sentenced to a fixed term of imprisonment of not more than three years, or criminal detention; if the circumstances are especially serious, he will be sentenced to a fixed term of imprisonment of not less than three years but not more than seven years.

The crime of illegally providing state secrets to foreign entities

The subject of this crime is Chinese citizens who have reached the age of criminal responsibility. Foreign citizens and stateless people cannot be the subject of the crime. The object of the crime is national security. The subjective aspect of the crime is that the offender has the subjective intention to commit these acts. The objective aspect of the crime is that the offender commits acts of stealing, spying into, buying, or unlawfully supplying state secrets or intelligence for individuals or organizations outside the territory of China. It should be noted that the organizations outside the territory of mainland China mentioned here include organizations in Hong Kong, Macao, Taiwan, and all foreign countries as well as the agencies or branches of those organizations established in mainland China. If the offender commits any one of these acts, i.e., stealing, spying into, buying, or unlawfully supplying state secrets, he will be charged with this crime. If the offender was apprehended or failed to obtain state secrets when committing the above acts, he will be charged with attempted crime. Under Article 111 of the *Criminal Law*, anyone who steals, spies into, buys, or unlawfully supplies state secrets for individuals or organizations outside the territory of China shall be sentenced to a fixed term of imprisonment of not less than five years but not more than ten years; if the circumstances are especially serious, he shall be sentenced to a fixed term of imprisonment of not less than ten years or life imprisonment.

The crime of illegally obtaining or holding state secrets

Under Article 282 of the *Criminal Law*, whoever unlawfully obtains state secrets by stealing, spying, or buying shall be sentenced to a fixed term of imprisonment of not more than three years, criminal detention, public surveillance, or deprivation of political rights; if the circumstances are serious, he shall be sentenced to a fixed term of imprisonment of not less than three years but not more than seven years; whoever unlawfully holds documents, material, or other objects classified as "top secret" or "highly secret" state secrets and refuses to explain their sources and purposes shall be sentenced to a fixed term of imprisonment of not more than three years, criminal detention, or public surveillance. The subject of these two crimes is a natural person who has reached the age of criminal responsibility, including Chinese citizens, foreign citizens, and stateless persons. The object of the crimes is state secrets. The subjective aspect of the crimes is that the offender has the subjective intent to commit such acts. The objective aspect of the crimes is that the offender obtains state secrets through such unlawful means as stealing, spying, and buying; or the offender unlawfully holds state secrets and refuses to explain his sources and purposes. If the offender can explain his sources and purposes, and demonstrate that he really has no knowledge of the nature of state secrets, he may not be charged with this crime. Overall, these two crimes focus on the unlawful obtaining or holding of state secrets, no matter whether the offender discloses the secrets or not.

What are state secrets?

With regard to the case of disclosing state secrets, one of the most important issues is how to define state secrets. If the definition of "state secrets" remains ambiguous, the right of citizens to obtain government information may be restricted to a large extent. In the United Kingdom, United States, and some other Western countries, there are mainly two solutions to this issue. First, to establish the principle of a "presumption of openness," i.e., open information is the rule, while closed information is the exception. Second, based on that principle, to specify what kind of information should not be publicized, for the purpose of limiting the discretionary power of public officials. In the United States, for example, the term "state secrets" is defined as any information that, if disclosed, would be reasonably likely to cause significant harm to the national defense or foreign relations of the United States.[30] Specifically, American laws classify only the following information as state secrets: military plans, weapons systems, or operations; foreign government information; intelligence activities, sources, or methods, or cryptology; foreign relations or foreign activities of the United States, including confidential sources; scientific, technological, or economic matters relating to national security, which includes defense against transnational terrorism; United States government programs for safeguarding nuclear materials or facilities; vulnerabilities or capabilities of systems, installations, infrastructures, projects, or plans, or protection services relating to national security, which includes defense against transnational terrorism; and weapons of mass destruction.[31] In addition to stipulating the scope of classified information, the American legal system also provides a series of mechanisms to curb the unlawful expansion of the scope of classified information and to facilitate the declassification of some classified information.

In the United Kingdom, Parliament passed the Freedom of Information Act in 2000, which also provides for the exemption from disclosure of certain types of information. Under this Act, there are two forms of exemption: absolute exemption and qualified exemption. If information falls within an absolute exemption, it is not subject to any public interest test. Examples of such exemption include information relating to or dealing with security matters, information contained in court records, and information provided in confidence. If information falls within a qualified exemption, it must be subject to a public interest test, i.e., "balancing the public interest in maintaining the exemption against the public interest in disclosing the information." Examples of qualified exemption include prejudice to international relations, information intended for future publication, information held for purposes of investigations and proceedings conducted by public authorities, and information relating to the formation of government policy, ministerial communications, advice from government legal officers, and the operation of any ministerial private office. However, this Act has been criticized on the grounds that the range of exemptions is so wide that it may significantly undermine the right of citizens to government information.

In 2010, China revised the *Law on Guarding State Secrets*, which was originally enacted in 1988. This law defines state secrets as matters concerning national security and interests, determined in accordance with statutory procedures, and known to a limited number of people for a given period of time. Furthermore, the law on state secrets divides state secrets into three categories: top secret, highly secret, and secret. "Top secret" refers to the most vital state secrets, the disclosure of which will cause extremely serious harm to state security and national interests; "highly secret" materials refers to important state secrets, the disclosure of which will cause serious harm to state security and national interests; and "secrets" refers to ordinary state secrets, the disclosure of which will cause harm to state security and national interests.

Under the revised law, materials classified as state secrets should meet three conditions. First, they concern state security and national interests. The law provides that any information that, if disclosed, would be likely to cause harm to national security and interests in the areas of political, economic, defense, and foreign affairs, should be identified as state secrets. It includes secrets concerning major policy decisions on state affairs; secrets in the building of national defense and in the activities of the armed forces; secrets in diplomatic activities and in activities related to foreign countries, as well as secrets to be maintained as commitments to foreign countries; secrets in national economic and social development; secrets concerning science and technology; secrets concerning activities for the safeguarding of state security and the investigation of criminal offenses; and other matters that are classified as state secrets by the department for guarding state secrets.

Second, they are determined in accordance with statutory procedures. Under the revised law on state secrets the specific scope and categories of state secrets must be stipulated by the department for guarding state secrets together with the Ministries of Foreign Affairs, Public Security, and State Security, and other central organs concerned. The specific scope and categories of state secrets related to national defense must be stipulated by the Central Military Commission.[32] Matters may only be classified as "top secret" by central or provincial government authorities or their authorized organs; and matters may only be classified as "highly secret" or "secret" by government authorities at the municipal level or above or their authorized organs. If it is unclear whether or not a certain matter is a state secret or into which category of state secrets it should be classified, the question shall be determined by the department for guarding state secrets or its local subordinates in provinces or large cities, or an organ approved by the department for guarding state secrets.

Third, they are known to a limited number of people for a given period of time. In the past, only the classification level of the state secret would be marked, and the length of time for which the secret should be protected would not be marked. As a result, information classified as state secret might be protected permanently. This has been changed in the revised law on state secrets, which adds provisions on the length of time that state secrets should be protected. Unless otherwise specified by law, the duration of "top secret," "highly secret," and "secret" state secrets is up to 30 years, 20 years, and 10 years respectively. All state secrets should be automatically declassified when the time period for guarding them has expired, unless it is extended by the relevant authorities prior to their expiry. In addition, state organs should conduct periodic audits of all classified state secrets; and they should promptly declassify a secret during the period of classification if it no longer needs to be guarded. The revised law on state secrets also stipulates that the range of those with knowledge of state secrets should be restricted to the smallest number possible, as required by work. If the number of those with knowledge of state secrets can be limited to specific people, it should be so limited; it cannot be limited to specific people, it should be limited to a state organ, which, in turn, shall limit it to specific people. The personnel outside the range of those with knowledge of state secrets, and whose work requires knowledge of state secrets, should be approved by the person in charge of the state organs that originally classified the secrets.

Compared with Western countries, China seems to have a relatively wider and more ambiguous definition of state secrets. This is particularly evident when the law provides that state secrets also include "other matters that are classified as state secrets by the state secret-guarding department." This provision arguably gives state organs vast discretionary power to establish state secrets. On the other hand, the revised law on state secrets has also established such mechanisms as automatic declassification and periodic audits of classified information, which may help to alleviate the possible negative effect of the discretionary power of the secret-guarding organs.

The Regulation on the Disclosure of Government Information

In revising the law on state secrets, the Chinese government has unveiled the importance of striking a balance between protecting state secrets and disclosing government information. That is because "when the government information is appropriately disclosed, the state secrets can be better protected."[33] In 2007, the State Council enacted the *Regulation on the Disclosure of Government Information* in order to ensure that citizens and organizations can obtain government information and to enhance the transparency of the work of government. Under the *Regulation*, administrative agencies should on their own initiative disclose government information that satisfies any one of the following basic criteria: information that involves the vital interests of citizens, legal persons, or other organizations; information that needs to be extensively known or participated in by the general public; information that shows the structure, function, and working procedures of, and other matters relating, to the administrative agency; and other information that should be disclosed on the administrative agency's own initiative according to laws, regulations, and relevant state provisions. Meanwhile, the regulation stipulates that when facilitating the process of disclosing government information, administrative agencies should also establish and improve mechanisms to examine for secrecy the government information to be released. Administrative agencies should not disclose government information that involves state secrets, commercial secrets, or individual privacy, unless they have the consent of the rights holder or believe that non-disclosure might give rise to a major impact on the public interest. When administrative agencies are unclear whether certain government information should be disclosed, they should submit the matter for determination to the relevant department in charge or to the department for safeguarding secrecy at the same level as the administrative agency. If the information of which a citizen requests the disclosure involves state secrets, the relevant state organs must first examine it for the possibility of declassification, and then determine whether or not it can be disclosed.

The provisions discussed above show that the disclosure of government information is heavily influenced by the concept of state secrets. In other words, if the concept of state secrets cannot be clearly delineated, the impact on society of the open government information regulation may be considerably weakened. Furthermore, since the law on state secrets was enacted by the NPC Standing Committee, while the open government information regulation was made by the State Council, the former has higher legal authority than the latter. As a result, some administrative agencies may refuse to disclose certain government information under the higher-level law on state secrets, which does not include mandates on the disclosure of government information. In this case, who should be responsible for supervision of the disclosure of government information? This issue so far has not been addressed by Chinese law.

National security and Internet speech

In Chinese judicial practice, the above-mentioned laws on protecting national security have been applied to dangerous speech in cyberspace. In 2000, the NPC Standing Committee passed the *Decision on Safeguarding Internet Security*, which further reinforced such application. Under *the Decision*, nobody should be allowed to make use of the Internet to incite secession, to divulge state secrets, to advocate the overthrow of state power and the socialist system, to provoke ethnic hatred or discrimination, or to propagate violent resistance of law enforcement. Anyone who commits any of these acts, which constitutes a crime, shall be investigated for criminal responsibility. To many people, compared to traditional mass media, the Internet is a much more powerful tool for the dissemination of unlawful information that endangers national security, and thus more attention should be paid to it by the government. An example is the riot in Urumqi on July 5, 2009. This deadly riot left 197 people dead and about 1,600 injured. It is argued that this riot was incited directly through the Internet.[34]

The subject of the crime stipulated in the *Decision on Guarding Internet Security* is mainly a natural person who has reached the age of criminal responsibility. However, the *Administrative Measures for Internet Information Service enacted in 2000* also clearly stipulates the liability of Internet service providers. This regulation mandates Internet service providers not to produce, copy, promulgate, or disseminate information that may endanger national security, such as inciting secession, disclosing state secrets, advocating the subversion of state power, etc. If Internet service providers discover such unlawful information transmitted through their websites, they must immediately stop the transmission thereof, save the relevant records, and make a report thereon to the relevant authority; otherwise, their operating licenses may be suspended or revoked, or they may be required to stop operation, or even to shut down their websites. Similar provisions also appear in several other Internet regulations, such as the *Interim Provisions on the Administration of Internet Publishing* and the *Administrative Provisions on Internet Audio-Visual Programs*. Here, the real issue is how to identify the transmitted content that endangers national security. In order to avoid any legal trouble, websites may prevent the transmission of normal criticisms of state organs and their functionaries as dangerous speech, eventually infringing on people's right to free speech.

In 2010, China revised the *Law on Guarding State Secrets*, particularly strengthening control over the disclosure of state secrets in cyberspace. Under Article 24 of the revised law, no individual or organization shall engage in the following actions: connecting computers or storage devices dealing with secrets to the Internet or other public information networks; exchanging information between a secrets information system and the Internet or other public information networks without adopting protective measures; using computers or storage devices that do not deal with state secrets to save or process state secret information; uninstalling security technology programs or administrative programs from a secrets information system without authorization; and giving away, selling, or discarding decommissioned computers and storage devices that have dealt with state secrets but have not gone through technology security procedures. This Article essentially aims at controlling the source of state secrets that may be transmitted on the Internet. Article 26 of the revised law on state secrets focuses on control over the dissemination of state secrets in cyberspace. Under this Article, all of the following actions are prohibited: duplicating, recording, or storing state secrets in violation of the law; the transmission of state secrets through wired or wireless communication, the Internet, or other public information networks without taking secret-guarding measures; and dealing with state secrets in private contact and correspondence, such as through electronic mail. Whoever violates the above two articles may be investigated for criminal responsibility. The revised law on state secrets also stipulates the responsibility of Internet service providers. In Article 28 of the law, Internet service providers and other public network operators are required to: cooperate with the competent government authorities in investigating leakages of state secrets; upon discovering a leak of a state secret, cease making such information available on the Internet, keep records, and report to the relevant authorities; and delete state secret information upon the request of the relevant authorities. Any website which violates this Article will be administratively penalized by the relevant regulatory authorities. Again, the key issue for implementing these provisions involves the definition of state secrets, about which individuals, organizations, and Internet service providers often call for further clarification.

Another important regulation on the online disclosure of state secrets is the *Administrative Provisions on the Preservation of State Secrets in the International Networking of Computer Information System*, which was promulgated in 2000 by the State Secrets Bureau. This provision also emphasizes the principle of physically isolating secret secrets from the Internet, requiring computer information systems involving state secrets not to directly or indirectly connect to the Internet. It also stipulates that information involving state secrets, including state secrets which, after examination and approval, have been legally exchanged with a specific party abroad, may not be stored in, processed on, or transmitted through computer information systems which are internationally networked. In addition, this provision establishes a set of norms on specific Internet activities for the protection of state secrets. For example, except for information which has been made public through other news media, the organizer shall obtain the consent of the information provider before placing it on a website. The establishment of electronic bulletin boards, chat rooms or network news groups by any individual or organization must be subject to examination and approval by the relevant secrecy maintenance authority, which shall clarify the secrecy requirements and responsibilities. No individual or organization may publish, discuss, or disseminate state secret information on electronic bulletin board systems or in chat rooms or network news groups. If the operator of an electronic bulletin board system, chat room or network news group discovers the presence of information relating to secrets, it shall promptly adopt measures and report to the local department for the maintenance of secrets. In addition, individuals who exchange information via e-mail shall also comply with the relevant state secrets law and regulations. They are prohibited from using electronic mail to disseminate state secrets. Overall, both Internet users and Internet service providers need to perform their specialized duties of guarding state secrets in cyberspace; otherwise, they may be subject to administrative or criminal penalties, in accordance with law.

Case 3.1   Huang Qi case: using the Internet to incite subversion and secession[35]

A typical case concerning seditious speech in cyberspace is the Huang Qi case. On January 11, 2001, the People's Procuratorate of Chengdu, Sichuan filed a public prosecution of Huang Qi at the Immediate People's Court of Chengdu, Sichuan. It charged that from March through June 2000, defendant Huang Qi set up such sections as "Trends Forum," "Recovered from the Web," and "Viewing China from Far Away" on his website "Tianwang Disappeared Persons." In "Trends Forum," he posted seditious articles such as "Guiding Principles of Chinese Democratic Party" and "The Independent Consciousness of Xingjiang Uighur: Because Historically We Have Always Been an Independent Country." In "Recovered from the Web," he posted seditious articles like "An Unpredictable Future for China" and "June Fourth Was neither an Incident nor a Disturbance; It Was a Massacre". In the section "Viewing China from Far Away" he posted links to information from abroad that was published by the Information Center for China Human Rights and Democracy such as "Two Citizens Arrested for Demanding Vindication of June Fourth" and "Amnesty International: 213 June Fourth Political Criminals Imprisoned."

The Chengdu People's Procuratorate cited the following evidence in court in order to prove the crime: a list of the evidence obtained by public security authorities from the "Tianwang Disappeared Persons" website, using Huang Qi's computer; an electronic physical evidence verification certificate from the Sichuan Public Security Office; testimony obtained from witnesses Zeng Li, Zeng Hong, Zeng Quanfu, Liu Honghai, and Li Yu; an enterprise Internet access contract signed by the Chengdu Tianwang Disappeared Persons Service Center and the Chengdu Huamei Computer Network Limited Company; and a statement made by Huang Qi to the public security authority. The public prosecution authority believed that Huang Qi's acts constituted the crimes of inciting secession and inciting the overthrow of state power, and that he should be sentenced in accordance with articles 103, 105, and 69 of the *PRC Criminal Law*.

Defendant Huang Qi denied charges, and argued that the articles in the "Trends Forum" section had been posted by other people, and had stayed online because he did not know how to delete them. He took responsibility only for articles on the "Recovered from the Web," and "Viewing China from Far Away" sections before March 30, 2000, because after March 30, 2000 the website had been closed down within China and transferred to a Chinese person in North America to manage the finding of missing relatives. Further, Huang Qi's defense attorneys claimed that the public security authorities had no evidence of when Huang Qi had disseminated the aforementioned articles of which he was charged, or with what computer, and they pointed out that Huang Qi had freedom of speech and could disseminate his views regarding a given incident.

The Immediate People's Court of Chengdu, Sichuan found that defendant Huang Qi had used the Internet to disseminate and spread articles regarding issues such as "democracy movements," "June Fourth," and "Falun Gong," and that his use of rumor mongering and defamation to incite the overthrow of state power and the socialist system amounted to the crime of inciting the overthrow of the government and should be punished in accordance with the law. The facts charged in the indictment by the public prosecution authority, that Huang Qi had committed the crime of inciting subversion of the state power, had been established, the application of the law was correct, and the charges should be upheld.

Regarding the charge by the public prosecution authority that Huang Qi had committed the crime of inciting secession, the court found that the electronic forum on Huang Qi's website contained articles with content that promoted ethnic separatism that had been posted by him, and that Huang Qi, as the person responsible for the website, had a responsibility to delete these articles, but had failed to do so. However, these articles had not initially been written, edited, or disseminated by him, and there was no evidence that Huang Qi's intention was to incite secession. The court therefore did not uphold this charge.

Regarding defendant Huang Qi's claim that he was responsible only for articles appearing on "Viewing China from Far Away" and "Recovered from the Web" prior to March 30, 2000, after an investigation, based on the Xi'an evidence, it was confirmed that from March 30, 2000 until the crimes were exposed, the articles posted on the "Tianwang Disappeared Persons" website's "Viewing China from Far Away," and "Recovered from the Web" were compiled, edited, and disseminated by Huang Qi. Regarding the claim of defendant Huang Qi and his defense attorneys, that the public security authorities had no evidence to prove when, where, or from which computer Huang Qi disseminated the articles, the court found that the prosecution had collected a large quantity of corroborating evidence in the case, which formed a complete chain of evidence confirming that the articles relating to the incitement of subversion of state power posted on the "Tianwang Disappeared Persons" website were Huang Qi's. The court did not accept the claims of the defense.

The defense attorneys also argued that defendant Huang Qi had freedom of speech and was free to disseminate his views with respect to given incidents. The court found that freedom of speech is a political right of Chinese citizens but, in exercising this right, they may not jeopardize national interests and security, and may not use rumor or defamation to incite subversion of the government. The court therefore did not accept the case of the defense, which emphasized the rights of the defendant and ignored his responsibilities.

Based on the facts of the crime that defendant Huang Qi had committed, the nature of the crime, the circumstances and the degree of harm caused to society, pursuant to the provisions of articles 105(2), 55(1), and 56(1) of the *PRC Criminal Law*, the court determined on February 22, 2003 as follows: Defendant Huang Qi committed the crime of inciting subversion of state power, and is sentenced to five years' imprisonment with one year's deprivation of political rights.

Case 3.2   Shi Tao case: using the Internet to disclose state secrets[36]

An influential case involving disclosure of state secrets through the Internet is the Shi Tao case. On January 31, 2005, the People's Procuratorate of Changsha, Hunan filed a public prosecution of Shi Tao at the Immediate People's Court of Changshang, Hunan for prosecution. The public prosecution authority charged that from February 11 to April 22, 2004, defendant Shi Tao was employed by Hunan's *Contemporary Business News*, where he held the position of head of the Editorial Department. At around 5:00 on the afternoon of April 20, after a routine newspaper review meeting and a pre-editorial meeting, assistant editors-in-chief of *Contemporary Business News* Wang XX and Yang XX convened a special meeting of the heads of the newspaper's Front Page News Department, the Mobile Hotline Department, and the Editorial Department. During this special meeting, Wang XX verbally communicated a summary of the main contents of a top-secret document issued by the General Office of the Central Committee of the Communist Party of China (CPC) and the General Office of the State Council entitled "A Notice Regarding Current Stabilizing Work" (CPC General Office Document No. 11 [2004]). He also emphasized that this was a top secret document and that notes must not be taken on it and that it should not be disseminated. However, defendant Shi Tao secretly did take notes on the summary of the document's main content. Between approximately 7:00 pm on that day and approximately 2:00 am the following morning, defendant Shi Tao used his personal e-mail account in his office to send the notes he had secretly taken on the above-mentioned summary of the main contents of CPC General Office Document No. 11 (2004) to the e-mail account of Hong Zhesheng, one of the founders of the "Asia Democracy Foundation" located in New York, USA and editor-in-chief of the foreign website "Democracy Forum" and the electronic publication "Democracy News." He gave "198964" as the alias of the person who provided the document and asked Hong Zhesheng to find a way to distribute it as quickly as possible without using Shi Tao's name. That day, the above-mentioned summary of the main contents of CPC General Office Document No. 11 (2004) was posted for publication on the "Democracy Forum" under the name of "198964." It was later reposted for publication on other foreign websites such as "Boxun News" and the "China Democracy & Justice Party."

Regarding the above-mentioned facts as charged, the prosecution authority provided such corroborating evidence as the oral testimony of witnesses, a secrecy-degree verification certificate, related material and written evidence, materials on the process of taking Shi Tao into custody, photos of the crime scene and photos of material evidence, information proving the defendant's identity, and the defendant's confession. The prosecuting organ claimed that defendant Shi Tao's actions violated Article 110 of the *PRC Criminal Law* and that his actions constituted the crime of illegally providing state secrets outside of the country.

Neither defendant Shi Tao nor his defense attorney raised any objections to the criminal facts as charged in the indictment or to the characterization of this case. Defendant Shi Tao argued in his defense: "My criminal act of providing state secrets to foreign entities did not involve especially serious circumstances." His defense attorney stated: "Considering that defendant Shi Tao's actions did not cause extremely serious damage to state security or interests and that his attitude in admitting his crimes was good, please punish him leniently."

The Changsha Immediate People's Court found that in order to leak information to hostile elements outside of the country, defendant Shi Tao intentionally and illegally provided information that he knew to be top secret state secrets to an entity outside of the country. Endangering state security and involving especially serious circumstances, his actions constituted the crime of illegally providing state secrets to foreign entities.

Therefore, the court accepted the prosecution's charge that Shi Tao's actions constituted the crime of illegally providing state secrets to foreign entities. Defendant Shi Tao argued in his defense: "My criminal act of providing state secrets to foreign entities did not involve especially serious circumstances." This was investigated and it was found that, according to Item 1 of Article 2 of the Supreme People's Court's "Explanation on Certain Questions Regarding the Specific Application of the Law when Trying Cases of Stealing, Gathering, Procuring, or Illegally Providing State Secrets or Intelligence Outside of the Country," stealing, gathering, procuring, or illegally providing state secrets are crimes with "especially serious circumstances." The state secrets that defendant Shi Tao illegally provided outside of the country were verified by the State Secrecy Bureau as being top secret state secrets, and his actions should be considered to involve especially serious circumstances. Therefore, the defense argument could not be accepted by the court. Shi Tao's defense attorney stated: "Considering that defendant Shi Tao's actions did not result in

> causing extremely serious harm to state security or interests and that his attitude in admitting his crimes was good, please punish him leniently." This was investigated and found to conform with the facts; therefore, the opinion of the defense could be accepted by the court.
>
> On April 27, 2005, the court determined that in accordance with Article 111, 5(1), and 56(1) of the *Criminal Law*, defendant Shi Tao was sentenced to ten years' imprisonment with two years' subsequent deprivation of political rights for committing the crime of illegally providing state secrets to foreign entities.[37]

Threats to social order

Besides controlling Internet speech that endangers national security, China also imposes restrictions on Internet speech that may break the social order. This mainly involves making use of the Internet to disseminate pornographic information, advocate cults and superstition, spread fabricated terrorism information, spread fabricated capital market information, and release deceptive or illegal ads. These behaviors are deemed as threatening the public order or the order of the market economy, and are thus subject to legal restrictions.

Pornography

In China, it is widely accepted that the spreading of pornographic materials will harm children's growth, corrupt social morals, and bring out criminal behaviors. Therefore, the production and dissemination of pornographic materials have for a long time been prohibited in China. China's legal control of pornography can be traced back to the 1979 *Criminal Law*, which established the crime of producing and selling pornographic books and pictures. The law has since been amended several times, and its provisions on pornography have developed into the crime of producing, selling, and disseminating obscene materials. Given that the channels and methods for disseminating pornography have become increasingly diversified and complicated, the Chinese government has enacted a series of regulations in response. For example, the *Customs*

Law enacted in 1987 prohibits transporting, carrying, and mailing obscene materials across national boundaries. The *Regulations on the Administration of Publishing* (1997), the *Regulations on the Administration of Broadcasting and Television* (1997), and the *Decision of the NPC Standing Committee on Safeguarding Internet Security* (2000) prohibit the dissemination of pornographic materials through print media, electronic media, and Internet publication or release, respectively. In addition, the *Regulations on Administrative Penalties for Public Security* enacted in 2005 stipulate that a person who produces, transports, duplicates, sells, lends, or disseminates pornographic materials shall be subject to administrative penalty if his act is insufficient to constitute a crime.

Defining pornography

Regarding the regulation of pornography, the key issue is to determine what constitutes pornography. In China, the most frequently cited definition of pornography is given in the *Criminal Law*, which provides that pornographic materials refers to obscene books, periodicals, movies, video- and audio-tapes, pictures, etc. that explicitly describe sexual conduct or blatantly appeal to the prurient interest. It can be seen that pornography consists of two important elements. The first is "explicitly describe sexual conduct," which refers to explicit representations or depictions of the genitals, masturbation, excretory functions, and ultimate sexual acts (normal or perverted, actual or simulated). The second is "blatantly appeal to the prurient interest," which means that the material patently purports to excite lewd, lascivious, or shameful thoughts about sex. In addition, the *Criminal Law* also stipulates that materials that have serious scientific, literary, or artistic value do not fall into the category of pornography. First, scientific works on human physiology or medical knowledge are not considered pornographic materials. These include science and social science works on human anatomy, human reproduction, sexually transmitted diseases, sexual psychology, sexual physiology, sexual pathology, sexual sociology, sexual morality, etc. These works are allowed to be published because they can contribute to the advancement of medical science and social science. Second, literary and artistic works that contain erotic content are not regarded as pornographic materials either. *The Plum in the Golden Vase* is a great example in this regard. This naturalistic Chinese novel depicts sexuality in a graphically explicit manner, but has been highly praised as mature literature that deals with such important social issues as sexual politics and the role of women in ancient Chinese society. Therefore, it is not treated as pornography.

Compared with the *Criminal Law*, the GAPP provides a more specific definition of pornography in the *Interim Provision Concerning the Determination of Pornographic Publications*, which it enacted in 1998. This regulation divides pornographic publications into three categories: obscene publications, erotic publications, and literary and artistic works partly containing obscene or erotic content. "Obscene publications" refers to publications that propagate obscene behavior throughout, that intend to incite people's sexual desire and lead ordinary people to be morally degenerate, that lack artistic or scientific value, and that contain one of the following: (1) explicit depictions of sexual behaviors, sexual intercourse, or its psychological effects in an indecent way; (2) open propagation of pornographic or lewd images; (3) description or impartation of sexual skills in an indecent way; (4) explicit depictions of the means, procedures, or details of incest, rape, or other sexual crimes, sufficient to induce the commission of crime; (5) explicit depictions of sexual behavior by juveniles and children; (6) explicit depictions of sexual behavior by homosexuals or other deviant sexual behavior, or explicit depictions of violence, cruelty, and humiliation related to deviant sexual behavior; or (7) other indecent depictions of sexual behavior that ordinary people would not be able to tolerate. Publications include books, newspapers, magazines, prints, picture albums, wall calendars, audio and video products, and printed publicity materials. "Ordinary people" refers to physically and mentally normal adults. Publications that are considered obscene will be strictly banned; individuals or organizations which publish, print, store, sell, rent, and store obscene publications will be subject to administrative or criminal penalty.

"Erotic publications" refers to publications that are not obscene throughout but that partially contain content falling within the above-mentioned seven categories that intends to poison the mental and physical health of ordinary people, especially juveniles, and that lacks artistic and scientific value. The difference between obscene publications and erotic publications is that the former, taken as a whole, propagate pornography while the latter propagate pornography only partly. In other words, the whole purpose of obscene publications is to propagate pornography; without pornographic material, the works simply cannot be established. In comparison, erotic publications partly include pornographic content; and taken as whole, propagating pornography is not their ultimate purpose. In spite of this, erotic publications are also considered as having a negative impact on people, especially on minors. So, like obscene publications, erotic materials are also legally prohibited from being published, stored, sold, and disseminated in China.

Artistic and scientific works with obscene or erotic content include literary works that have artistic value, artistic works that express the beauty of the human body, and scientific works that concern human anatomy and reproduction, disease prevention, and other knowledge relating to sex, sexual morality, and the sociology of sex. These types of publication are not deemed to be pornography and can be lawfully published and disseminated, as stipulated in both the *Criminal Law* and the GAPP provisions. It should be noted, however, that the manuscript is subject to the review and approval of the GAPP prior to publication.

As for such visual communication media as television and film, the relevant authorities have established a stricter set of standards for determining what is considered pornographic in terms of content. Under the *Provisions for Film Examination* promulgated in 1997 by the SARFT, content that is considered pornography or illegal sexual speech and thus shall be edited or deleted from films includes obscene and vulgar images or language; the inappropriate representation or description of sex and sex-oriented plots; the illustration of full frontal nudity of the male or female body; the positive representation or description of extramarital affairs and pre-marital cohabitation; images of lengthy kissing and caressing that cause strong sensory stimulation; the detailed description of promiscuity, rape, prostitution, and homosexuality; and dialogue or visual/audio messages featuring vulgar content and poor taste. Similarly, the *Interim Provisions for Television Drama Examination* enacted in 1999 by the SARFT stipulate that the language, images, or plot of a television drama, if containing any of the following pornographic content, shall be modified or cut out: explicit representation of sexual behavior; images of male and female sex organs and female breasts; kissing, caressing, and other sex-related images that cause strong sensory stimulation; the specific representation or description of promiscuity, rape, adultery, and prostitution; speech that is vulgar, obscene, or in poor taste; and vulgar actions, music, and sound effects. In 2006, the SARFT made some revisions to the provisions concerning pornography in the *Interim Provisions for Television Drama Examination*, and the *Interim Provision for the Archival Filing of Film Scripts (Outlines) and the Administration of Films*, which treat the following content as pornography: that mixed up with indecent and sexy, vulgar, and meaningless content; the representation or description of plots of promiscuity, rape, prostitution, wenching, sexual behavior, parasexuality, and the sex organs and other concealed parts of a man or woman; that mixed up with dirty and vulgar dialogue, song, background music, and sound effects, etc. If these types of content are included in a film, they shall be cut or revised. From what has been presented above, we can see that in China the definition of pornography is becoming more complicated, but not necessarily better clarified.

Regulating pornography in cyberspace

In 2000, the NPC Standing Committee passed the *Decision on Safeguarding Internet Security*, which prescribes that anyone who establishes pornographic websites or web pages, provides services for connecting pornographic websites, or spreads pornographic books and periodicals, movies, and audio or visual materials in cyberspace may be investigated for criminal responsibility. Based on this provision, the Supreme People's Court and the Supreme People's Procuratorate successively published two judicial interpretations under the same title, the *Interpretations of Several Issues on the Specific Application of Law in the Handling of Criminal Cases about Producing, Reproducing, Publishing, Selling, and Disseminating Pornographic Electronic Information via the Internet, Mobile Communication Terminals and Sound Message Stations* in 2004 and 2010 (hereinafter referred to as the *2004 Interpretation* and the *2010 Interpretation*). These interpretations provide a set of specific implementation guidelines for regulating online pornography.

Under these judicial interpretations, "pornographic materials" refers to materials that explicitly describe sexual conduct or blatantly appeal to the prurient interest in the digital forms of video, audio, pictures, articles, or publications; however, neither electronic information related to the physiology and medical knowledge of the human body nor digitalized literary and artistic works that contain pornographic content but have artistic value shall be considered pornography. This definition is obviously similar to that given by the *Criminal Law*, as mentioned above. What is more, the *2010 Interpretation* also provides a definition of pornographic websites: this refers to websites that were established for the purposes of producing, copying, publishing, selling, and spreading electronic pornographic information; or that, after being established, mainly engaged in such activities. A website usually consists of multiple web pages, columns, or channels. The *2010 Interpretation* suggests that a court should not treat a website as pornographic merely because part of a web page, column, or channel on the website contains pornographic content; rather, the court should take into account the purpose of establishing the website or the main business of the website after its establishment. If a web page, column, or channel was established for producing, copying, publishing, selling, or spreading pornography or mainly engaged in such activities after its establishment, then it should be identified as a "pornographic website." These provisions are designed to ensure that a web page, column, or channel that does not include pornographic content will not be treated as pornographic; they are also designed to make sure that a comprehensive website will not be identified as a pornographic one.[38]

The *2004 Interpretation* stipulates that anyone who commits any of the following actions for commercial purposes via the Internet or any mobile communication tool shall be punished for criminal liability: (1) producing, reproducing, publishing, selling, or disseminating 20 or more pornographic cinematic, performance, motion picture, or other video files; (2) producing, reproducing, publishing, selling, or disseminating 100 or more pornographic audio files; (3) producing, reproducing, publishing, selling, or disseminating 200 or more pornographic electronic publications, pictures, articles, etc.; (4) producing, reproducing, publishing, selling, or disseminating pornographic electronic information with the click number reaching 10,000 or more; (5) publishing, selling, or disseminating pornographic electronic information by subscription, with the number of registered subscribers being 200 or more; (6) charging advertising fees, membership registration fees, or other fees by making use of pornographic electronic information, with the illegal gains being 10,000 yuan or more; or (7) the quantities or amounts failing to reach the respective standards as prescribed in items 1 to 6 above, but reaching 50% of the standards as prescribed in two or more of the items. In other words, Internet users or websites will be subject to criminal punishment once the pornographic information which they process or disseminate reaches a certain level. Even if the purpose of processing or disseminating pornography is not for profit, the offender may still be subject to criminal liability, although the minimum amount required for criminal liability is relatively less.

To combat online pornography, the *2004 Interpretation* puts emphasis on the regulation of Internet users and pornographic websites. However, this has proved insufficient to curb the spread of online pornography. It is well observed that online pornography has developed into an industry that involves multiple parties such as pornographic websites, telecommunications operators, advertisers, and third-party payment platforms. It is argued that, in order to effectively crack down on pornographic websites, the judicial organs should impose restrictions on all major participants. This argument has been accepted by and reflected in the *2010 Interpretation*, which clearly prescribes the legal responsibility of each major participant. Specifically, the *2010 Interpretation* stipulates that: (1) where a telecommunications operator or an ISP knows that a website is a pornographic one, but provides it with such services as Internet access, server hosting, network storage, data transmission channels, and fee collection for profits, it may be punished with criminal liability; (2) where an individual or an organization knows that a website is a pornographic one, but provides it with direct or indirect financial support or service through advertising or other means, he/it may be punished with criminal liability; and (3) where the founder of or the administrator directly responsible for a website knows that an Internet user is producing, reproducing, publishing, selling, and disseminating electronic pornographic information, but allows or connives in the publication of such information on the website or a web page of the website, he may be punished with criminal liability.[39] By specifying the legal liability of each participant, the judicial organs aim to cut off the interest chains behind pornographic websites.[40]

Many of the above-mentioned provisions involve the concept of "knowing." In judicial practice, offenders often attempt to evade punishment by claiming that they have no knowledge that they are involved in the production or dissemination of pornographic content. To ensure the applicability of the principle of "knowing", the *2010 Interpretation* thus prescribes several specific situations in which the offender shall be viewed as subjectively "knowing" that he is dealing with pornographic information. These situations include that: (1) after being informed by the relevant authority that certain content is pornography, the offender continues to produce or disseminate it; (2) after being informed by the relevant individual that certain content is pornography, the offender fails to take necessary measures to handle it; (3) where the offender provides a website with such services as Internet access, server hosting, network storage, data transmission channels, and fee collection, the service charge is obviously higher than the market price; and (4) where the offender advertises on a website, the hit rate of the advertising is abnormally high. In judicial practice, however, the circumstance is often complicated: the "knowing" case may not be limited to these four situations; or even in these four situations, the offender may be found not to subjectively "know." In response, the *2010 Interpretation* prescribes some inclusive as well as exceptional principles, respectively.

In addition, both of the judicial interpretations protect children from pornography in cyberspace. Article 6 of the *2004 Interpretation* stipulates that anyone who produces, reproduces, publishes, sells, or disseminates electronic pornographic information that depicts the sexual behavior of minors under the age of 18, or sells or disseminates electronic pornographic information to minors under the age of 18, shall be subject to heavy punishment. Compared to the first interpretation, the second one reduces by half the minimum amount or quantity of pornographic publications involving any minors under the age 14, for the conviction of an offender who produces or disseminates such information in cyberspace. This reflects the trend in China of strengthening the protection of children against online pornography.

Case 3.3   Wei Dawei and Qi Benhou case: disseminating pornographic materials for profit[41]

A typical case concerning online pornography is the Wei Dawei and Qi Benhou case. Since August 2008, defendant Wei Dawei had successively established such websites as "Porno Girl", "Mature Girl with Fornication", "Go to Porn," and "Lu Cheng Entertainment" for commercial purposes. And defendant Qi Benhou paid Wei Dawei 3,000 yuan for releasing ads on those sites. The court held that the first three sites were all porn sites, while the last site, "Lu Cheng Entertainment," contained 26 obscene videos as well as 792 obscene pictures/articles. In 2009, defendant Qi Benhou founded a website named "Aizhilin Sex Toys" to sell sex products online. To make more profit, he decided to advertise his website on porn sites. The court held that Qi Benhou put his ads on 32 different porn sites, along with Wei Dawei's website "Lu Cheng Entertainment." The court determined that where defendant Wei Dawei made use of the Internet to spread 26 obscene videos and 792 obscene pictures/articles in order to make a profit, his act constituted the crime of disseminating pornographic materials for profit; where defendant Qi Benhou knew that those sites were porn sites but still put ads there for commercial purposes, his act also constituted the crime of disseminating pornographic materials for profit. The court sentenced Wei Dawei to 2 years and 6 months in prison and a fine of 10,000 yuan. It also sentenced Qi Benhou to 1 year and 8 months in prison and a fine of 10,000 yuan.

Cults and superstition

Article 300 of the *Criminal Law* provides that a person who uses cult organizations or superstition to undermine law enforcement shall be subject to criminal liability. This means that in China it is illegal to propagate cults or superstition via the Internet or other communication tools. The key issue involves how to determine what is a cult and what is superstition.

Propagating cults

According to a judicial interpretation by the Supreme Court, cult refers to illegal organizations that are set up using religions, Qigong or other things as a camouflage, deify their leading members, and confuse, poison, and deceive people, recruit and control their members, and endanger society by fabricating and spreading superstitious heresies.[42] Based on this definition, Chinese scholar Wei Yongzheng has summarized the characteristics of a cult as follows: a cult is not a religion. It is often positioned as a religion or Qigong, but lacks doctrines and beliefs inherent to a religion; a cult avidly engages in deifying activity, especially fabrication of the leading member as a savior or the representative of a god; a cult fabricates and spreads rumors, fallacies, and heresies, such as "Judgment Day and the End of the World"; a cult is passionate about developing and controlling its members, and often forms associations/societies in secret; and a cult often endangers public security and social stability, including deceiving people out of their money, seducing people to commit suicide, engaging in terrorist activities, violently resisting law enforcement, and inciting and creating social turmoil. For the Chinese government, to propagate a cult is not only a blasphemy against religion, but also an act that seriously jeopardizes public order and social stability. Therefore, China insists that any cult organizations and activities should be vigorously suppressed.[43]

As mentioned earlier, the *Criminal Law* established a crime of organizing and using cult organizations to undermine law enforcement. In 2001, the Supreme Court and the Supreme Procuratorate jointly released the *Interpretation on the Concrete Application of Law on Handling the Cases of Committing Crimes by Organizing and Using Cult Organizations*, providing specific restrictions on the propagation of cults. Under this interpretation, those who produce and disseminate cult materials, propagate cults, violate the enforcement of laws and regulations, and conduct one of the following activities shall be penalized in accordance with the criminal law: (1) producing and disseminating more than 300 copies of cult flyers, pictures, slogans, or newspapers, more than 100 cult books, more than 100 cult CD-ROMs, or more than 100 cult audio or video tapes; (2) producing and disseminating the original version of a CD, VCD, DVD that advocates a cult; (3) making use of the Internet to disseminate information on cult organizations; (4) propagating a cult through hanging banners, writing or painting slogans in public places with serious consequences; (5) producing and disseminating cult propaganda materials after having been criminally or administratively punished for producing and disseminating cult materials; and (6) other serious situations related to the production and dissemination of cult propaganda materials. These provisions cover almost all kinds of actions of propagating cults. It is worth noting that an offender may have a direct intention to propagate a cult, i.e., only for the purpose of propagating and organizing a cult; an offender may also have an indirect intention to propagate, say, only for the purpose of making a profit from the production and dissemination of cult materials. No matter whether the intention is direct or indirect, both situations are viewed as criminal offenses.

The emergence of the Internet enables an offender to disseminate cult materials in a much faster way to a much wider audience. Take Falun Gong as an example. Since the Chinese government banned it as a cult in 1999, Falun Gong has mainly used the Internet to propagate its doctrines, develop members, and organize activities. According to the analysis of Chinese scholar Fang Hanqi, Falun Gong has established websites in 25 countries and regions, using a total of 13 languages; and in the United States, it has established 80 websites in 46 states. All of these sites are based overseas, but could technically be accessed by

Internet users in mainland China. Accordingly, the Chinese government has strengthened its control over the dissemination of cults via the Internet. All major Internet regulations, including the *Decision of the NPC Standing Committee on Safeguarding Internet Security* and the *Administrative Measures for Internet Information Services*, mandate that no one is permitted to take advantage of the Internet to propagate cults, and a violator will be investigated for criminal liability. Furthermore, the Supreme Court stipulates in the above-mentioned interpretation that, regardless of the scale of dissemination, whoever uses the Internet to disseminate cult information shall be subject to criminal punishment.

Case 3.4   Zheng Ruihan and Liu Yinglan case: dissemination of Falun Gong materials[44]

From 2003 to 2005, defendants Zheng Ruihan and Liu Yinglan downloaded various Falun Gong materials from the Internet, converted part of the materials into publications, flyers, and slogans, and then distributed them to several workers in the Shengli Oil Field.[45] As a result, each defendant was charged with committing the crime of using cult materials to violate law enforcement and sentenced to a fixed term of imprisonment of five years.

Propagating superstition

Superstition generally refers to "a belief or practice resulting from ignorance, fear of the unknown, trust in magic or chance, or a false conception of causation."[46] In China, it specifically refers to an irrational faith or a blind trust in such superstitious methods and phenomena as Feng Shui, fortune-telling, divination, astrology, and ghosts and gods. The nature of superstition lies in its followers' irrationally abject attitude of mind towards such methods and phenomena. For the Chinese government, superstition may hinder the advancement of science and technology, incite its followers to break the law and disturb public order, and even cause damage to a person's life and property. Any act of spreading superstition is thus prohibited by the government.

Back in 1979, China enacted its first *Criminal Law*, which established a crime of spreading "feudal superstition." The law was amended in

1997. The revised law retained the crime, but removed the word "feudal" from the term. This was mainly because the legislators recognized that something feudal was not necessarily a superstition; it might be a traditional custom or culture. In 1999, the GAPP and the Central Propaganda Department jointly released the *Notice Regarding Prohibition on Publishing Publications with Contents which Propagate Ignorant Superstitions and Pseudo-Sciences*, which reaffirmed that all publication units shall not publish publications that propagate such superstitions and pseudo-sciences as fortune-telling, divination, astrology, and Feng Shui under the name of studying traditional customs and culture. The problem is that there is lack of clarification on the difference between superstitions and traditional customs/culture, so that administrative or judicial organs are given discretionary power to determine what is superstition and what should be banned. With the development of information technology, more and more people are gaining access to information on superstitions via the Internet.[47] Accordingly, China's Internet-related regulations such as the *Administrative Measures for Internet Information Services* and the *Interim Provisions on the Administration of Internet Culture* have imposed restrictions on the dissemination of superstition in cyberspace.

Fabricated terrorist information

In past decades, China has witnessed a rapid increase in the number of criminal cases involving the spread of fabricated terrorist information via the Internet and other communication tools. Such false terrorist information often focuses on public organizations, large companies, and public places such as shopping malls and hotels, and is likely to create and incite large-scale public panic and social turmoil. Therefore, when Chinese legislators amended the *Criminal Law* in 2001, they added a crime of fabricating and intentionally disseminating false terrorist information. Specifically, Article 8 of the Amendment provides that whoever fabricates such terrorist information as explosive, biochemical, radioactive, or other threats, or intentionally disseminates terrorist information while clearly knowing that it is fabricated, thereby seriously disturbing the public order, shall be subject to criminal punishment such as criminal detention, public surveillance, or imprisonment.

According to the Amendment, the crime of fabricating and intentionally disseminating false terrorist information is made up of two elements. First, the offender has committed the act of fabricating or intentionally disseminating false terrorist information (e.g., explosive, biochemical, radioactive, or other threats). As long as the offender has committed one of these two acts, he will meet this element required to prove a crime. The term "fabricating or intentionally disseminating" implies that the act must be a deliberate offense. Therefore, where a person has disseminated false terrorist information without knowing of its falsity, he should not be investigated for criminal liability. Second, the offender's act has seriously disrupted public order, that is, the act has caused public panic and seriously disturbed the normal life of the public. To constitute a crime, the offender's fabrication or dissemination of false terrorist information must have seriously disturbed the public order. Therefore, where a person has fabricated or disseminated false terrorist information but did not disrupt social order, he shall not bear criminal liability; or where a person has fabricated terrorist information but did not spread it, this might disturb the social order but lack serious consequences, so that he shall not bear criminal liability.

Case 3.5 Chen Zhifeng case: fabricating terrorist information[48]

A case involving the dissemination of fabricated terrorist information via the Internet is that of Chen Zhifeng. During end of May and early June of 2008, defendant Chen Zhifeng published on 163.com[49] fabricated terrorist information, asserting that a disastrous level-9 earthquake was going to take place in Guangxi province. In fewer than five days, this post was viewed 13,242 times by Internet users. Furthermore, the defendant took technical measures to unlawfully delete all content and application procedures of the Guangxi Network for Earthquake Prevention and Disaster Reduction, the official website of Guangxi Earthquake Bureau, thus causing panic among the public, who were unable to acquire information from the official website. Based on these facts, the court held that the defendant had committed both the crime of fabricating and intentionally disseminating false terrorist information and the crime of destroying a computer information system. The court thus sentenced the defendant to a fixed term of imprisonment of four years.

Fabricated stock market information

Over the past few decades, China's rapid economic growth has resulted in the prosperity of Chinese securities and futures markets. In order to protect the interests of investors and maintain the market economic order, the Chinese government has gradually strengthened its regulation of the dissemination of securities and futures market information. Article 181 of the *Criminal Law* revised in 1997 clearly stipulates that whoever fabricates and spreads false information affecting stock exchange or futures trading, and disrupts the stock exchange market and futures exchange market, shall bear criminal liability if the consequences are serious. This paved the way for subsequent legislation on the dissemination of capital market information. In 1998, the NPC Standing Committee adopted the *Securities Law*, which specified the liability of all major parties involved in the stock exchange. Under Article 78 of the *Securities Law*, it is prohibited for government employees and news media practitioners to fabricate and disseminate false information that seriously disturbs the securities market; it is prohibited for stock exchanges, securities companies, securities registration and clearing institutions, securities trading service institutions, securities industry associations, securities regulators, and these institutions' functionaries to make any false statement or give any misleading information about the activities of securities trading; and the securities market information as disseminated by any media shall be true and objective. Given that the Internet is becoming an important channel for publishing securities information, Article 2 of the *Decision of the NPC Standing Committee on Safeguarding Internet Security* prescribes that whoever uses the Internet to fabricate and spread false information that influences the exchange of securities and futures or other information that disrupts the financial order will be investigated for criminal liability in accordance with the relevant provisions of the *Criminal Law*.

In accordance with the above laws, the crime of fabricating and spreading false stock market information is composed of two elements. The first element is that the offender committed both acts of fabricating and disseminating false stock information. Where either a person fabricated the information but did not spread it or the information a person disseminated was not fabricated by him, he shall not be punished for this crime. In addition, this crime is a deliberate one, that is, the offender knew that the acts of fabricating and spreading information would affect the stock market, but still took such actions. Otherwise, he shall not be punished for this crime. The second element is that the acts of fabricating and spreading false stock market information seriously disturbed the securities and futures market. If such acts did not disrupt the stock market, or the disruption did not produce serious consequences, they shall not constitute a crime. By "serious consequences" is meant that the false stock market information fabricated and disseminated by the offender resulted in strong price fluctuations in securities and futures markets, caused panic among investors and induced them to sell or purchase a large amount of stocks or futures contracts, invoked significant economic loss to investors, had a serious adverse impact on society, and so on.

So far only a few criminal cases have involved the fabrication and dissemination of false stock market information.

Case 3.6   Li Dingxing case: fabrication and dissemination of false acquisition information[50]

In October 1993, defendant Li Dingxing lost a lot of money in the purchase of shares of Jiangsu Sanshan Industry & Co. To recoup the loss, he fabricated and disseminated false acquisition information about the company through a regional newspaper, resulting in the improvement of the stock price in his favor. After a public hearing, the court held that the defendant had committed the crime of fabricating and disseminating false stock information and sentenced him to a fixed term of imprisonment of two and a half years as well as a 10,000 yuan fine.

Case 3.7   Shanghai Pudong Development Bank: fabricated stock information[51]

A recent case of fabricated stock information concerns the Internet. On February 19, 2008, news of Shanghai Pudong Development Bank's 40 billion refinancing quickly spread on the Internet. The next day, the share price of the bank dropped from 50.5 to 45.98; on subsequent days, it continued to drop, eventually causing a sharp drop in both the Shanghai and Shenzhen stock exchanges. This piece of fabricated stock information proved to have originated from the Internet, but regulators found it hard to trace the initiator of the message and were thus unable to punish the perpetrator.

Commercial speech

Commercial speech, commonly referred to as advertising, is directly associated with the development of the market economy. Since adopting the policy of reform and opening up in 1978, China has experienced rapid economic growth, which is accompanied by the prevalence of advertising in people's daily lives. According to statistics from the State Administration of Industry and Commerce (SAIC), advertising sales in 2009 reached more than 204 billion yuan, suggesting that China had become one of the largest advertising markets in the world.[52] At the same time, there were also many problems with China's advertising industry. For instance, some companies used advertising to promote counterfeit products; some released ads denigrating the products or services of their rivals; and some exaggerated the functioning and effectiveness of their products in advertisements. These kinds of problem arguably impeded the healthy development of the advertising industry, damaged the interests of consumers, and disturbed the market economy. In 1982 and 1987, the State Council successively promulgated the *Interim Provisions for the Administration of Advertising* and the *Administrative Regulations on Advertising*. In addition, some departments under the State Council and some local governments also enacted a number of supplemental regulations to strengthen control over illegal or harmful advertising. In 1994, the NPC Standing Committee passed the *Advertising Law*, which not only established the basic principles for traditional advertising but also constituted a legal basis for regulating online advertising.

Regulating traditional advertising

Advertising can be defined as "the action of calling something to the attention of the public especially by paid announcements."[53] It mainly involves three parties, namely, advertisers, advertising agents, and advertisement publishers. Advertisers refers to individuals or organizations who place ads in order to target customers. Advertising agents refers to individuals or organizations who provide services for designing and producing ads or providing related services on a commission basis. Advertisement publishers refers to individuals or organizations who publish ads for advertisers or for advertising agents entrusted by advertisers. Examples of advertisement publishers include newspapers, magazines, radio, television, the Internet, and other mass media.

Under the *Advertising Law*, when designing, producing, and publishing ads, the involved parties shall comply with a set of basic principles.

These principles can be summarized as follows: (1) the content of an advertisement shall be true. This mainly requires that an ad should not resort to any falsehood in order to deceive or mislead consumers; an ad should make distinct and clear the uses, quality, price, validity period, promises, and other characteristics of the products or services; data, statistics, survey results, excerpts, or quotations used in an ad should be true and accurate, with the sources clearly indicated; if an ad involves patented products or patented methods, the patent number and patent category should also be clearly stated; an ad should not lie about the patent right of any product that has not in fact received patent right; (2) the content of an advertisement shall be lawful. Specifically, this means that an ad should not contain any of the following content: national flag, national emblem, and national anthem of the PRC; the names of government organs or government functionaries; words such as "state level," "highest level," or "the best"; anything that would jeopardize social stability, the public interest, and personal and property safety; anything that would disturb the public order and violate good social conventions; content that is obscene, superstitious, terrorizing, violent, and evil; content that is discriminatory against nationalities, races, religions, and sex; content that is harmful to the protection of the environment or natural resources; content that denigrates the products or services of other enterprises; and other content that is forbidden by laws and regulations; (3) an advertisement shall be recognizable. This means that, based on the ad's form, content, and publication format, a normal person can quickly recognize it as a type of ad, rather than an artistic work, a news report, or other. Mass media should not in any way publish an ad in the guise of a news report. Whenever an ad is published in mass media, there should be a clear indication to distinguish it from non-advertising information, for the purpose of avoiding misleading consumers.

The *Advertising Law* also imposes strict restrictions on advertising related to people's health. It mandates that ads for medicines or medical apparatus should not contain any of the following content: unscientific assertions or assurances in terms of efficiency or uses; statements of treatment efficiency or curative rates; comparisons with other medicines or medical apparatus in terms of efficacy or safety; the titles or images of medical research institutes, academic institutions, medical organizations or experts, doctors or patients; and other content that is prohibited by laws and administrative decrees. The content of medicine ads should be based on the indications approved by the public health department. Ads for therapeutic medicines that must be applied under the guidance of doctors, as required by the government, should include the words "to seek doctor's advice in the purchasing and application." It is prohibited to advertise such special-purpose drugs as anesthetics, psychotropic drugs, toxic drugs, and radioactive drugs in any place. It is prohibited to publish tobacco ads via broadcast, film, television, newspapers, or periodicals. It is also prohibited to post tobacco ads in any waiting rooms, cinemas and theatres, meeting halls, sports sites and gyms, and other public places. All tobacco ads should carry the indication "smoking is harmful to your health." Moreover, the content of ads for goods, wines, and cosmetics should conform to the requirements set by the public health department and not use any medical terms.

To ensure the truthfulness and lawfulness of advertisements, the *Advertising Law* stipulates that advertising agents and advertisement publishers are obliged to review the documents of certification and the content of ads provided by advertisers. To design, produce, and publish ads, advertisers should have or provide the following documents of certification: business licenses and other documents certifying production and management qualifications; certificates for the content of advertisements regarding product quality, issued by quality inspection organizations; and other documents certifying the truthfulness of the content of the ads. In using the names or images of others for advertising, advertisers should have or provide the prior written approval of the persons concerned. Advertising agents and advertisement publishers are legally required to check the authenticity, validity, and lawfulness of these documents of certification. In addition, advertising agents and advertisement publishers are also required to review the content of ads, especially checking whether the content is prohibited by relevant laws and regulations. Where an ad is found to contain false or illegal content, or the relevant documents of certification are found to be incomplete, the advertising agent should not provide services, including design and production, and the advertisement publisher shall not publish the ad.

Regulating Internet advertising

Internet advertising is a form of promotion that uses the Internet to deliver marketing messages to attract customers.[54] Examples of Internet advertising include interstitials, banner ads, button ads, pop-up ads, pop-under ads, e-direct marketing, sponsorship, classified ads, text ads, floating ads, flash multimedia ads, interactive games, paid searching advertising, and so on. Compared to traditional advertising, Internet advertising possesses many competitive advantages. In cyberspace, for example, the message can be published immediately without any time or geographical limitations; the message can be disseminated quickly to a wide range of audiences at very low or no cost; and the message can be interactive and customized enough to meet various special needs. Since the first online ad appeared on Chinabyte.com in 1997, China's online advertising has undergone amazing growth and expansion. In 1998, online advertising sales were 48 million yuan; in 2004, this figure increased to 1.9 billion yuan;[55] and in 2010, the sales of online advertising were estimated to be 23 billion yuan.[56] In spite of the rapid growth of online advertising, China has also been plagued by such problems as the prevalence of false, deceptive, and hidden online advertising, which could fundamentally be attributed to the lack of appropriate legislation in this area.

So far, China relies basically upon the *Advertising Law* to regulate online advertising, but new problems raised by online advertising have rendered this law powerless to a great extent. For example, the boundary between the participants in traditional advertising is so clear that the *Advertising Law* is able to specify the responsibilities of each one (e.g., advertisers, advertising agents, and advertisement publishers). Advertisers often rely on advertising agents for the design and production of ads, which are then released by the advertisement publisher. Both advertising agents and advertisement publishers need to go through the certification process and obtain a permit to operate an advertising business. This mechanism is designed to ensure the truthfulness of traditional advertising, but it became obsolete when applied to online advertising. In cyberspace, an ISP is both an advertising agent and an advertisement publisher; if the ISP promotes its own products or services on its own website, it plays a triple role of advertiser, advertising agent, and advertisement publisher. Where the boundary between different participants becomes blurred, it is inappropriate to apply to online advertising the specific responsibility of each participant as prescribed in the *Advertising Law*, and it is thus difficult to curb the occurrence of false and illegal ads in cyberspace.

The *Advertising Law* prescribes that broadcasting and television stations, newspapers, periodicals, and publishing units shall designate special departments to handle advertising business and go through the procedures for the registration of such business. So far there have been no legal provisions that require ISPs to register for operation as advertising businesses. In practice, due to the huge number of advertising websites, the regulatory authorities would find it impossible to handle all applications for registration. In addition, most websites have not established an advertisement management system to check the identity of advertisers and the authenticity and legality of advertisements. All these factors contribute to the current explosion of deceptive, misleading, and illegal ads on the Internet.

Cyberspace is also plagued with hidden advertising, in which the marketing message is delivered in a non-advertising manner so that consumers will not view it as an advertisement. The *Advertising Law* stipulates that advertisements shall be recognizable to consumers. Internet advertising, as a form of advertising, should abide by this rule. The fact is, however, that unrecognizable, hidden advertising has become widespread and increasingly intricate in cyberspace. Typical examples include publishing advertisements in the guise of news reports, making use of a bulletin board service column to promote products or services in the guise of public discussion, and embedding advertisements in keyword searching procedures. So far there is no law or regulation that addresses the issue of hidden advertising on the Internet.

In March 2011, the SAIC, the national regulator for advertising, released a directive called the *Suggestions on the Specific Administration of False and Illegal Advertisements*, which established some restrictions on Internet advertising. The directive requires the telecommunications regulatory authorities, in cooperation with the industry and commerce administration organs, to shut down those websites that have not obtained a permit to provide commercial Internet services; that have not gone through the archival-filing procedure for providing non-commercial Internet services; or that have not obtained special permission to engage in drugs, medical equipment, and health care information services. Meanwhile, the relevant Internet access service providers should stop providing service to such sites, otherwise, they will be subject to administrative punishment. In fact, in early 2010, the regulatory authorities closed down 10 sites that had released illegal sexual drugs ads as well as eight portal sites that provided linking services to those sites.[57]

In addition, some local governments have enacted specific regulations to ensure the truthfulness and lawfulness of online advertising. A representative one is the *Interim Measures of Beijing Municipality for the Administration of Internet Advertising* (hereinafter referred to as the *Beijing Measures*).[58] The *Beijing Measures* stipulates that the Beijing Administration of Industry and Commerce is charged with the regulation of online advertising and establishing an Internet advertising administration center at www.HD315.gov.cn. To facilitate administration, all websites are divided into commercial and non-commercial. While non-commercial ISPs are prohibited from providing any online advertising services, commercial ISPs must register with the industry and commerce administration organs in order to provide such services as the design, production, and publication of online ads. To register, a commercial ISP must have a license for providing Internet services, a record of filing with HD315.gov.cn, and an online advertising administration department that includes qualified personnel and relevant technology and equipment. When providing advertising services, the ISP must review the advertiser's documents of certification, along with the content of the ads. If the documents are incomplete or the content is false, the ISP should refuse to provide services. If everything is fine, the ISP should act and send the completed ads to the Internet advertising administration center, which, after review, sends the ads to the target site for publication. Moreover, the *Beijing Measures* also establishes many specific restrictions on the content of online ads; such restrictions are basically consistent with those as prescribed by the *Advertising Law*.

Case 3.8   Case of *Mr. Zhou* v. *Jinbao Electronic Publishing Center*: fraudulent Internet advertising[59]

In 2006, Beijing Chaoyang Court tried China's first case of fraudulent Internet advertising, i.e., *Mr. Zhou* v. *Jinbao Electronic Publishing Center, Beijing Sohu Internet Information Service Co., and Beijing Xinwang Internet Co.* In November 2004, the plaintiff saw a digital camera ad of Shenzhen Digital Technology Development Co. on people.com.cn. He then wired 8,600 yuan to the bank account of the advertiser, Shenzhen Digital, to make a purchase. Receiving no response, the plaintiff verified from official sources that both the advertiser and the ad were fabricated. He also learned that people.com.cn was owned by defendant Jinbao, the ad was placed by defendant Sohu, and the ad's link to the website of the fabricated advertiser was enabled by defendant Xinwang. The plaintiff claimed that three defendants had failed to take any

---

measures to verify the truthfulness of the ad, and so they should be responsible for his economic loss. After review, the court held that, to support his claim, the plaintiff should prove three facts: he had seen the ad link on people.com.cn; the ad was deceptive; and because he had believed the ad, he had suffered economic loss. The court continued that since the plaintiff had failed to take appropriate measures to collect valid evidence against the defendants in a timely manner, he himself had to bear the negative consequences of the purchase. On the grounds of the insufficiency of the evidence, the court rejected all of the plaintiff's claims. However, the question of how to define the responsibilities of different participants in online advertising remained largely unaddressed.

Damage to reputation

Protecting one's reputation has become increasingly difficult in the Internet era. This is because people can disseminate defamatory materials easily through the Internet. In recent years, Chinese courts have witnessed a rapid increase in online defamation cases. However, defamation in cyberspace is often complicated, involving multiple relationships among tortfeasors, victims, Internet users, and Internet service providers. While China has applied the basic principles of existing defamation law to online defamation, it has also enacted several new provisions to solve the new problems brought about by the Internet. Against this background, this section will first present the evolution of defamation law and then analyze the establishment and defenses of traditional and online defamation.

Evolution of defamation law

Reputation refers to the overall quality or character of certain individuals or organizations as seen or judged by people in general. The right of reputation means that individuals and organizations have the right to the protection of the law against unlawful attacks on their reputations.

Defamation refers to unjustified damage to one's reputation, as by libel, or slander, or insult. It can be in the form of oral or written statements; disseminated through newspapers, radio, television, or new media; or expressed through insulting physical gestures.

The law against defamation has been established in Western countries for centuries.[60] From the founding of the PRC in 1949 to the reform and opening up in 1978, however, the concept of the right to reputation was largely ignored in Chinese law.[61] During the same period, China experienced the Cultural Revolution and many other nationwide political movements. These movements caused much pain to Chinese citizens, including that resulting from damage to their reputations; and people gradually realized that it was important to have their reputations protected through legislation. In 1979, the NPC passed the *Criminal Law*. Under Article 246 of the law, any act of publicly humiliating another person or inventing stories to defame him, if the circumstance is serious, constitutes a criminal offense. This is considered China's first law on defamation. In 1986, the NPC enacted the *General Principles of the Civil Law*, which also provides protection against defamation. Article 101 of the law clearly stipulates that "citizens and legal persons shall enjoy the right of reputation. The personality of citizens shall be protected by law, and the use of insults, libel or other means to damage the reputation of citizens or legal persons shall be prohibited." These two laws show that defamation can be a criminal or civil charge, depending on the degree of seriousness of the offense. Later, the Supreme People's Court published the *Interpretation on Several Issues about the Trial of Cases Concerning the Right of Reputation* in 1993 and 1998 (hereinafter referred to as the *1993 SPC Interpretation* and the *1998 SPC Interpretation*, respectively), providing specific legal guidelines for dealing with defamation cases.

Case 3.9   *Xi Hong* v. *People's Daily*: an early defamation case[62]

With the introduction of relevant laws, cases involving defamation gradually emerged in China. One early example is *Xi Hong* v. *People's Daily*. On July 20, 1988, the *People's Daily* published an article titled "The Construction Authority of Kashgar City Shows Incompetent Leadership: Xi Hong Who Slacks at Work and Complains without

Justified Reasons Turns into a Special Citizen," which was written by two of its journalists. Plaintiff Xi Hong subsequently sued the defendant, *People's Daily*, for defamation. In this case, the defendant is the primary newspaper of China's ruling Communist Party, while the plaintiff was an average worker. Partially because of the difference of status, the court did not accept the case until 1989. During the following three years, the defendant ignored the court's repeated subpoena, refusing to respond. The case was finally heard in 1992 and settled by mediation in 1997. Spanning almost a decade, this case pioneered China's tort involving defamation.

Since the case of *Xi Hong* v. *People's Daily* (see Case 3.9), defamation cases in China have increased gradually and steadily. According to the *China Law Yearbook*, Chinese courts heard a total of 3,183 defamation cases in 1993; and this number increased dramatically to 6,665 in 2000.[63] A considerable proportion of these cases included news media as the defendant.

With the advent of the Internet age, online defamation is becoming the latest trend in torts involving damage to reputation. Online defamation refers to the act of defaming others through the use of the Internet; the defamatory content can be text, pictures, sound, animation, and other forms of digitalized materials that can be transmitted in cyberspace. With regard to the new problems raised by online defamation, the NPC's *Decision on Safeguarding Internet Security* stipulates that, in order to protect the personal and property rights of individuals and organizations, anyone who makes use of the Internet to insult or to slander other people with fabricated stories shall bear criminal responsibility if his act constitutes a crime. The *Decision* also provides that, to maintain the order of the socialist market economy and social administration, anyone who make use of the Internet to damage other people's business reputation and product reputation shall be investigated for criminal responsibility if his act constitutes a criminal offense. This law thus provides legal support and guidelines for Chinese courts to criminalize online defamation in serious circumstances.

It has been well observed that a number of features unique to the Internet have distinguished it from any other media. These features have led to the re-examination of existing criminal or civil laws relating to defamation, to allow for their possible extension to cyberspace. One key feature is the ease of access to cyberspace. Compared to traditional print or broadcast media, the Internet enables people to publish content much more conveniently and at a much lower cost. This means that the opportunity for defamation has become exponentially greater. Another feature of the Internet is its extraordinary capacity to disseminate information. On the Internet, information can be delivered much faster to a much wider range of people than through traditional media. With regard to defamation, defamatory content uploaded to the Internet may spread instantly to every corner of the world. This means that online defamation may cause much more harm to the victim. In addition, it is relatively difficult to determine the tortfeasors in the case of online defamation. In many cases, users are not required to reveal their true identity when sending e-mails or posting messages on blogs and bulletin boards. While this feature causes users to be far less inhibited in spreading defamatory materials in cyberspace, it also makes it more difficult for the plaintiff to identify the creators or communicators of the content. In addition to the tortfeasors, Internet service providers may also need to bear legal responsibility for their users' defamation acts. However, the issue of what kind of responsibility Internet service providers should assume remains controversial in China.

From both a historical and a realistic point of view, the key to resolving defamation issues is to establish a case of infringing on the reputation. According to the *1993 SPC Interpretation*, a tort involving defamation shall have at least four components: the reputation of the victim has been damaged; the conduct of the offender is illegal; there is a causal relationship between the conduct of the offender and the damage to the victim; and the offender is subjectively at fault. In Chinese judicial practice, these four elements have been specified respectively as follows: (1) publication—the content has been published; (2) defamation—the content is defamatory; (3) identification—the defamatory content specifically points to the plaintiff; and (4) fault—the defendant is subjectively at fault. The following sections will examine how these four adjusted elements have been applied to online defamation, and what additional adjustments have been made to solve special problems created by the Internet.

Publication

In order to establish a case of defamation, the plaintiff must show that the allegedly defamatory content was made public. In other words, the defendant must have shared such content about another person with at least one other person.[64] In accordance with Chinese law and judicial practice, if the defamatory content has not been published, it will have no social influence and thus be unable to cause harm to the reputation of another person; if the defamatory content has been published, however, it is sufficient for the plaintiff to prove that the reputation of the plaintiff has been damaged.[65] As for the economic damage and/or mental anguish damage to the plaintiff, these can be used by the plaintiff to prove that the damage to his reputation is serious. Even if the plaintiff cannot provide proof of economic damage and/or mental anguish damage, however, the court should not assume that the defamatory content does not constitute a tort.[66]

There are at least two distinct forms in which the publication of defamation may occur in cyberspace. Each of these forms of publication raises distinct problems. The first form is electronic mail. It is argued that e-mail correspondence is often more like spoken conversation than written interaction and people tend to say things that they would normally not say in writing or in face-to-face interaction. In other words, senders of e-mail are more likely to make statements that turn out to be defamatory. Of course, not all e-mails that include defamatory content constitute an infringement of the reputation of others. If the offender sends the e-mail only to the person who is being defamed, his behavior does not constitute a tort, for such e-mail is considered unpublished and unable to damage the social reputation of the recipient. Only when the offender sends the defamatory e-mail to at least one other person may he risk infringing on the reputation of another person. This includes making use of e-mail lists to send the e-mail to many different persons. The system of an e-mail list consists of a list of e-mail addresses, the subscribers receiving e-mails at those addresses, the e-mail messages sent to those addresses, and a single e-mail address which, when designated as the recipient of a message, will send a copy of that message to all subscribers. Within such a system, it is very easy for a careless or inexperienced user to send a defamatory message to every subscriber on the list, even though he intended to reply only to the author of a particular message.

Another form of publication in cyberspace involves online forums, message boards, blogs, home pages, and so on. Since websites normally can be accessed by people around the world, any content posted in such places is presumed to be published; furthermore, expression occurring in these places is often anonymous and interactive, and so Internet users may be less inhibited in attacking other individuals or entities there. This means that defamation may occur much more frequently in these places. A typical example in this regard is the defamation case concerning Hengsheng laptop computers (Case 3.10).

Case 3.10　*Heng Sheng Group* v. *Wang Hong*: defamation via a bulletin board[67]

In 1998, defendant Wang Hong published an article titled "Please See How I Was Badly Cheated when Purchasing a Laptop from Heng Sheng" on the bulletin board system of Sitong Lifang. Plaintiff Heng Sheng Group thus sued defendant Wang Hong for defamation, charging that his article had caused huge damage to the reputation of the Group. The court in the second trial supported the plaintiff's claim, awarding the plaintiff 90,000 yuan.

Republication

Republication refers to the act of republishing certain work, including the reprinting, translation, adaptation, and performance of that work. In the United States, if somebody disseminates defamatory content to a third person, who in turn spreads the same content to other persons, then the third person will also be responsible for defamation; if the third person has a reasonable defense, or has reason to believe that the content he helped to disseminate is true or is not subjectively at fault, however, he will not bear legal responsibility for his act of republication.[68]

In China, legal provisions on republication mainly focus on the act of reprinting. The *1998 SPC Interpretation* provides that for the reprinting of a work by a news medium or publishing agency, if one party files a lawsuit with a court for the reason that the reprinting entity infringes on his right of reputation, the court shall accept the case. This shows that reprinting defamatory works may constitute a tort. In 2000, the GAPP promulgated the *Notice on Further Strengthening the Administration of the Reprinting of Articles in Newspapers and Magazines*. This notice stipulates that when reprinting news articles or documentary works, newspapers and magazines should verify the accuracy of the reprinted works; if they discover an inaccuracy, they should promptly correct it and also take measures to eliminate any negative impact. This provision makes it clear that anyone who reprints a work is required to verify the accuracy of that work.[69]

Republishing defamatory information on the Internet is also prohibited in Chinese law. For example, the *Administration Measures for Internet*

Information Services provides that Internet service providers shall not reproduce any information that insults or slanders a third party. Similarly, the *Administrative Provisions on Internet News Services* stipulates that the news information or the electronic bulletin board services provided by an Internet service provider shall not contain content that defames a third party. Once the content republished on the Internet infringes on the lawful rights of others, the Internet will in fact function as an aggravator of tort damage. At present, Chinese websites have no right to collect news; they are only allowed to republish the news produced by traditional media. The problem is that it is unrealistic for websites to verify the accuracy of every piece of news information.

Case 3.11 Stanley Tong: republication of defamatory content[70]

On February 3, 2004, *Youth Times* first published a news article about film director Stanley Tong and his former girlfriend. This article was later reprinted by *Chengdu Business Daily* and seven other newspapers. Alleging that the article damaged his reputation, plaintiff Stanley Tong sued all these newspapers, including *Youth Times* and *Chengdu Business Daily*. The court held that, in terms of the components of a libel case, both publishing and reprinting defamatory content may constitute a tort; in terms of civil liability, however, there should be some difference between the media that publish the article and those that reprint it. The court determined that all the sued newspapers should stop infringement, make an apology, and take measures to eliminate any negative impact of this article on the plaintiff; in addition, *Youth Times* as the initiator of the article should also pay financial compensation to the plaintiff. All parties in this case concurred with the verdict.

The role of Internet service providers

In the United States, Internet service providers (ISPs) may play two different roles in a defamation case: those of publisher and of distributor. The role of publisher means that the ISP is involved in the creation, editing, or reprinting of the defamatory statement. Like a normal author or editor, the ISP may be subject to tort liability for the defamatory statement published on its website. The role of distributor means that an ISP functions only as a platform or channel for people to exchange information, rather than participating in the production or editing process of the defamatory statement. Like such traditional information distributors as libraries and bookstores, the ISP in this situation does not assume legal responsibility for the defamatory statement displayed on its website. These principles on the role of ISPs have been gradually accepted by the international community.

Chinese law creates similar obligations and protection for ISPs. Article 36(1) of the recently enacted *Tort Liability Law* stipulates that ISPs should bear tortious liability in the event that they infringe upon the civil rights or interest of an individual through the Internet. This provision mainly focuses on the role of publisher that ISPs may play. It means that if an ISP directly provides its users with content that is created, edited, supplied, or controlled by itself, then it should be responsible for the accuracy of the content; if the content infringes on another person's right to reputation and no reasonable defense can be raised, the ISP should bear tortious liability. For example, for an ISP providing such services as online forums and chat rooms, it often has direct control over the information exchanged in those places. If somebody intends to post obviously defamatory content there, the ISP should reject such a posting; otherwise, it may be subject to tort liability.[71]

Also, Article 36(2) of the *Tort Liability Law* provides that where an Internet user engages in tortious conduct through the Internet, the injured party shall have the right to notify the ISP and request that it take necessary measures, such as deleting content, screening content, or denying service to the offending individual. Where an ISP fails to take necessary measures in a timely manner after being notified of such offenses, it shall be jointly and severally liable with the Internet user for additional damage. The provision gives ISPs a "safe harbor" from defamation claims if they implement certain notice and take-down procedures. It also reflects the will of legislators to strike a balance between facilitating Internet development and protecting individual rights.[72] Generally speaking, if ISPs only provide a platform for their users to exchange information, and all of their information services are carried out by an automatic technical process, then they function only as distributors and thus do not bear liability for the infringing activities of their users. Only after the injured party has provided notice to the ISP regarding the allegedly infringing material, the ISP then has a legal obligation to take prompt and necessary action to take down such material. Chinese law currently does not require the ISP to inform the individual responsible for the material before it is taken down, but it does require notification after the material has been taken down. If the individual provides a "counter-notice" claiming that the material does not infringe on another person's right to reputation, the ISP must then promptly inform the claiming party of the individual's objection.

In addition, Article 36(3) of the *Tort Liability Law* provides that where an ISP knows that an Internet user is infringing upon another person's rights or interests through its services, and fails to take necessary measures, it shall be jointly and severally liable with the Internet user for any additional harm. The emphasis of this provision is on the "knowing" principle. If the ISP has discovered the infringing activity of its user and failed to take necessary measures to stop such activity, it will be considered as having an indirect intention to infringe upon another person's rights and thus should be subject to tort liability. The *Administrative Measures for Internet Information Services* previously promulgated also stipulates that if an ISP discovers information transmitted through its website that obviously falls within the scope of content prohibited by law, including obviously defamatory content, it shall immediately stop the transmission, save the relevant records and make a report to the relevant authority. The term "obviously falls" refers to the situation whereby a reasonable man can recognize without doing any research that the transmitted information includes defamatory content.[73] In practice, many defamatory statements in cyberspace can be readily identified. If an ISP has discovered obviously defamatory content and fails to take necessary measures in a timely manner, it may have tort liability in accordance with Chinese law.

Case 3.12 *Ginde Possession Group* v. *Baidu, Inc.*: infringement of right to reputation[74]

Baidu, Inc. is China's largest search engine, and Ginde Possession Group is a large-scale manufacturer of plastic pipe equipment in China. Plaintiff Ginde found that when users searched with such keywords as "Ginde," "Ginde Possession," and "Ginde Recruitment", there would be a lot of information containing "Ginde Swindler," "Ginde Possession Cheater," "Ginde Recruitment Hoax" at the top of the results pages. In November 2008, Ginde sued Baidu for infringing on its right to reputation. The court held after the hearing that Ginde Possession Group was a company that mainly produced plastic pipe equipment; that its products, under the trademark "Ginde," were appraised as famous Chinese branded products; and that its trademark "Ginde" has also been identified as a well-known trademark. The court continued that, as a legal entity, Ginde Possession Group had the right to reputation, which should not be infringed upon through the use of insults and libel by others. In this case, when typing keywords related to Ginde Possession Group into Baidu's search engine, users would see such words as "Ginde Swindler," "Ginde Possession Cheater," and "Ginde Recruitment Hoax." These words caused real damage to Ginde's social reputation. The plaintiff Ginde had informed the defendant Baidu of the infringing information, but the defendant did not delete the content until it was sued by the plaintiff. The court thus held that the defendant Baidu had failed to fulfill its obligation; its behavior was subjectively at fault and objectively harmful to Ginde's reputation, thus constituting an infringement of the defendant's right to reputation. The court determined that Baidu must immediately stop infringement and also post a written apology on its website.

One important issue in this case is how to define the role of search engines like Baidu in defamation disputes. Search engines are often driven by automated search algorithms, or a mixture of algorithmic and human input. If Baidu operated algorithms and did not intervene in the search results, it would be considered as having no control over the content, and thus be immune from any tort liability. The problem was that it was technically hard for the plaintiff to prove that Baidu had committed the act of intervening in the searching process. In addition, plaintiff Ginde previously requested defendant Baidu to delete the allegedly defamatory statements. The problem was that the involved parties had very different understandings as to what content could be considered as defamatory. That was why Baidu refused to take further action after being requested to do so. It is thus necessary to clarify what is defamatory content.

Defamation

To be actionable, a challenged statement must be defamatory. Generally speaking, a defamatory statement is "that which tends to injure 'reputation' in the popular sense; to diminish the esteems, respect, good will or confidence in which the plaintiff is held, or to exercise adverse, derogatory or unpleasant feelings or opinions against him."[75] Under Article 7 of the *1993 Supreme Court Interpretation*, an act of insulting or slandering a person in written or verbal form and consequently causing damage to his reputation should be recognized as infringing on his right to reputation. Inaccurate or false news reports, if causing damage to the reputation of another person, should also be handled as defamation cases. Article 8 of the *1993 Supreme Court Interpretation* provides that for reputation disputes caused by the writing and publishing of critical articles, each one should be handled differently, based on its different circumstance, by a court: if an article is basically true and does not insult the dignity of others, it should not be considered infringement of reputation; if an article is basically true but insults the dignity of others and subsequently causes damage to their reputation, it should be considered infringement of reputation; and if an article is basically false and causes damage to the reputation of others, it should be considered infringement of reputation. These provisions have been applied to news articles that criticize or make comments on the products or quality of service of manufacturers, operators, or distributors, as specifically stipulated in Article 9 of the *1998 Supreme Court Interpretation*. Based on the above-mentioned judicial interpretations and Chinese judicial practice, we can argue that there are mainly three types of defamation: false statements of fact, improper comments, and insulting expression.

False statements of fact

Disseminating false statements of fact is arguably the most common way to infringe on a person's right to reputation. It is also a crucial element of defamation. If the plaintiff cannot prove the falsity of the content, he then cannot sue the defendant for defamation. Falsity can be further divided into two categories: that which the defendant is able to foresee and that which the defendant is unable to foresee. Under the principle of fault liability in China's tort laws, only the former may cause the defendant to bear tort liability.[76]

In Chinese judicial practice, false statements of fact involve at least five different situations: (1) the article is seriously false. This mainly refers to the fabrication of fact. If disseminated, the fabricated fact is highly likely to damage a person's reputation and thus constitutes a tort; (2) the article is basically false. The case of *Li Guyi* v. *Radio & TV Weekly* in 1991 is an example (Case 3.13); (3) the fact concerning the injured party is false. An article may have no error in its main part. In its minor part, however, it may include false facts about another person, for whom the article is basically false. This situation may also result in a tort case; (4) the fact that determines the nature of the problem is false. An example is the 1989 case involving *Family and Life* magazine (Case 3.14); (5) the identity of the involved party is false. This mainly refers to a situation whereby a mistaken identity occurs in an article, as in the case *Xie Weiping* v. *Tang Guoji* (Case 3.15).

Case 3.13   *Li Guyi* v. *Radio & TV Weekly*: publication of a basically false article

This case was caused by an article published in *Radio & TV Weekly*. The article presented 10 facts among which the court found 8 to be false. Based on this finding, the court determined that the article was basically false and thus constituted a tort.

Case 3.14   *Liu Xiaoqing* v. *Family and Life Magazine*: publication of false information

In 1989, *Family and Life* magazine published an article claiming that film star Liu Xiaoqing had evaded over 1 million yuan in taxes. Liu then filed a lawsuit for defamation. The court verified that Liu's tax evasion was in fact less than 10,000 yuan. According to Chinese law, tax evasion of over 1 million yuan constitutes a crime but tax evasion of less than 10,000 yuan is an offense. The court held that since the most important fact revealed in the article was false, the magazine should bear tort liability.

Case 3.15 *Xie Weiping* v. *Tang Guoji*: a case of mistaken identity

In 2001, freelance writer Tang Guoji published an article about Xie Weiping, sports star Liu Xuan's mother, in the magazines *Modern Women* and *Female World*. This article was supplemented with a picture of Xie and Tang, which, however, was mistakenly marked as a group photo of Xie and her husband. Xie thus sued Tang and the two magazines for defamation and appropriation. The court determined that the two magazines should compensate the plaintiff for mental anguish, but freelance writer Tang was immune from any liability because he was not at fault.[77]

Improper comments

A comment is a statement that expresses a personal opinion based on a fact, but is not a proven fact. In terms of whether they imply some underlying facts or not, comments can be divided into two categories: non-pure comments and pure comments.[78] The former imply some underlying facts while the latter do not. In accordance with Chinese judicial practice, non-pure comments may infringe on the reputation of others. It is not because they express some unfavorable opinions, but because they imply some underlying facts, such as suggesting that someone is a criminal, an incompetent leader, or a corrupt official. If the underlying facts turn out to be false, such comments may constitute defamation. In the trial, the court may first request the defendant to reveal the underlying facts, and then check whether such facts are true or false.

Pure comments do not imply any underlying facts, but are often made based on certain facts. The questions thus are whether the facts on which pure comments are based must be true, and if such facts are not true, whether reviewers should bear legal responsibility. It is argued that reviewers should have no obligation to verify the facts on which their comments rely because otherwise many comments could be suppressed or could not be completed. If reviewers have sufficient reason to know that the facts are false but still include them in their published comments, however, they should be considered as disseminators of false facts and thus subject to tort liability.[79] Another important question is whether pure comments themselves constitute a tort. Some people argue that if comments made on a true or false fact are seriously improper and cause real damage to the victim, they should be treated as a tort. This argument is not supported by Chinese law.[80] In fact, Chinese law protects the use of hyperbole and extreme statements when it is clear that these are rhetorical ploys. For example, Article 9 of the *1998 SPC Interpretation* stipulates that consumers and news media may be subject to legal liability only when their comments include false underlying facts or insulting expression. In other words, if neither false underlying facts nor insulting expression are involved, reviewers should not bear legal liability for their improper comments.

Insulting expression

An insult is "an offensive or contemptuous remark or action" which is designed to "lower or hurt the dignity or pride of a person."[81] Like comments, insults can be divided into non-pure insults and pure insults.[82] Non-pure insults suggest some underlying facts, while pure insults do not. Regarding non-pure insults, the court may require the defendant to reveal the underlying facts. The case can then be judged on the basis of whether the facts are true or false. If the facts are false, the insult may constitute a tort; otherwise it may not. "Pure insults" mainly refers to the direct use of foul or abusive words or acts, and they do not imply any underlying facts. In most cases, pure insults can easily be identified. However, the meaning of the allegedly insulting words or acts may vary in different circumstance or cultures. The court thus has to consider the specific circumstance and culture in which the insults are expressed. In judicial practice, when determining whether certain pure insults damage another person's reputation, the court mainly considers whether the use of insulting words has lowered his dignity or pride. For example, if a reporter calls a government official a "fat pig" only because of his obesity, his statement may lower the dignity of the official and thus be considered insulting. If he calls a corrupt official a "moth," however, his statement may not be considered insulting because it is the corrupt action of the official rather than the statement of the reporter that truly lowers the dignity of the official.[83]

Defamatory content in cyberspace

Regarding online communication, should the standard for determining what constitutes defamatory content be different? It is argued that statements in chat rooms, bulletin boards and other areas of cyberspace are often casual, emotional, and imprecise, so that the strict application of defamation law to statements made in such contexts will impose a burden of constant vigilance that will greatly offset the benefit of the Internet as a public sphere.[84] It is also argued that, since the Internet affords the offended a readily accessible opportunity to rebut offensive speech and, furthermore, the general public usually do not attribute much credence to that speech, liability for defamation in cyberspace is unnecessary.[85] In China, defamation law generally applies to statements made in cyberspace, but the standard for determining whether a statement is defamatory seems to be much lower.

Case 3.16 *Tang Chunxiang* v. *Huang Zhangjin*: reasonable criticism is not an infringement of reputation[86]

On September 26, 2004, defendant Huang Zhangjin published an article titled "One suggestion—Please eliminate the ID 'Chunxiang' yourself" in the Internet Criticism column of the KDNET website. This article suggested that the article "A Young Girl and a Coffin in front of the Higher Court," which had previously been published on the KDNET by plaintiff Tang Chunxiang, was entirely fabricated; so that the plaintiff had better eliminate his ID so as to save his reputation. The plaintiff claimed that the defendant, as Editor of *China Youth Daily* and Moderator of the Youth Reference Forum of China Youth Online, had so much influence on Internet users that the article published by the defendant on the KDNET incited numerous users to humiliate him. The plaintiff thus sued the defendant for defamation. The court verified that the main reason for the defendant to claim that the plaintiff's article was fabricated was that the plaintiff had failed to provide pictures in a timely manner to prove the authenticity of the facts mentioned in his own article. The court held that speech in cyberspace is different from that published in traditional media like newspapers and magazines, and the former should enjoy more freedom when criticizing somebody or something. The defendant's article and subsequent user responses to his article should be treated as reasonable criticisms and did not violate Chinese law. In addition, after the plaintiff uploaded relevant pictures, the defendant made a public apology and also deleted his article. Based on these facts, the court determined that the defendant's act did not constitute an infringement of the plaintiff's reputation. The plaintiff's request for financial compensation was rejected.

Identification

The allegedly defamatory content must be of and concern a specific person, that is, the injured party can be identified and named by the public. If the content does not point to a specific person, then there can be no victim. It is thus argued that identification can help to build up the causal relationship between the defamatory content and the damage to the victim. Such a causal relationship is an element of a tort in Chinese civil law.[87] Identification includes two situations: first, the author directly points out the victim's name and identity in the work; second, the audience can infer the identity of the victim, based on the content of the work. In the second case, although the author does not use the real name of the victim, such information as background, situation, and specific time and location provided in the work would be sufficient for people to identify the character in the work with the victim. This is also regarded as a type of identification.

The concept of identification applies not only to news reports and commentary but also to such literary works as memoirs, biographies, and novels. According to the *1993 SPC Interpretation*, if a published literary work does not depict a specific person in real life as its prototype, and there are only some similarities between the plot of the work and the person's real situation, such a work shall not constitute infringement of reputation; if a literary work depicts real persons and real events, and includes content that defames a specific person, such a work shall be treated as an infringement of reputation; if a literary work depicts a specific person or the facts about a specific person without explicitly revealing his true identity, and includes content that insults or humiliates the person, such a work may constitute infringement of reputation.

Case 3.17 *Lu You* v. *Huang Jianxiang*: infringement of reputation[88]

On June 6, 2008, sports commentator Huang Jianxiang published "Speaking out Something Nasty in Advance" in his Sina blog. The article mentioned that the former Chinese men's soccer coach Duyi had caused a female Chief Men's Soccer Correspondent's "ectopic pregnancy." Lu You, a female journalist of CCTV, thought Huang was talking about her in this article and making use of her privacy to fabricate a scandal between Duyi and herself. Therefore, she sued Huang for defamation, requesting a public apology and compensation of 500,000 yuan for her mental anguish damage. The court thought that the issue focused on whether the public could conclude that the plaintiff was the journalist depicted by Huang in his article, even though Huang had not mentioned the journalist's real name. The court pointed out that a title like "Chief Men's Soccer Correspondent" was not used only by CCTV, and the plaintiff's title was used only within her company, rather than being announced to the public. Besides, it was hard to prove whether other female reporters who covered men's soccer had experienced ectopic pregnancy because it was too private a matter to investigate. The court thus held that the evidence was not adequate to prove that the defendant's article referred exclusively, specifically, and only to the plaintiff, and the public could hardly conclude that the plaintiff was the journalist discussed in the article. In other words, the evidence could not prove that there was a direct causal relationship between Huang's article and the damage to Lu's reputation. The court rejected all of the plaintiff's claims. The plaintiff appealed to a higher court, which upheld the ruling of the first trial court. However, the higher court held that Huang's article had negative influence on the reputation of the plaintiff to some degree, and his inappropriate speech hence deserved criticism.

In cases involving reputation disputes, the identified party may be not only an individual but also a company. The reputation of a company consists of business reputation and product reputation, which are the invisible assets of an enterprise and are protected by both tort law and unfair competition law. If what has been spread online or offline has damaged the business reputation or business credit of an enterprise, it could be regarded as an infringement of reputation. The case of *Ginde Possession Group* v. *Baidu, Inc.* discussed above is a typical example (see Case 3.12). Another example is the lawsuit between two online shoe stores, Letao and Okbuy, in 2010 (Case 3.18).

Case 3.18   *Letao* v. *Okbuy*: damage to reputation constitutes unfair competition[89]

The court verified that defendant Okbuy had released online ads which included such content as "wanna buy athletic shoes? Okbuy is a better choice than Letao," and these ads could be easily found on the Google search page using such keywords as "Letao" or "乐淘." The court determined that the defendant's promotional action had damaged the reputation of the plaintiff and constituted unfair competition. The defendant was required to make a public apology and compensate the plaintiff for economic loss.

It is a controversial issue whether government departments and agencies might also enjoy the protection of defamation law. China's *General Principles of the Civil Law* only include a general provision that legal entities have the right to enjoy the right of reputation, but there are neither regulations nor judicial interpretations that clearly stipulate that "legal entities" referred to in the civil law include government agencies. It is believed that defamation law is essentially to protect the reputation of a citizen or a legal entity, and a state organ should be excluded from the scope of its protection. Article 41 of China's Constitution states that a citizen has the right to criticize and give suggestions to any state organ and its functionaries. Some commentators argue that this means that state organs should not possess the right of reputation. Others point out that, even if a government agency was wrongly criticized or blamed, this wrongness would not cause economic loss or material loss to the agency.

Besides, a government agency often has a good opportunity to rebuke wrong criticism and can establish or improve its reputation through actions, and thus does not need to seek the protection of defamation law. In judicial practice, there have been several state organs that sued news media for defamation, and in some cases the court awarded economic compensation and mental anguish compensation to state organs.[90] This arguably shows the shortcoming of giving state organs the right of reputation, since the agency may use this right to discourage criticism of its performance and policies.[91]

Group defamation

One special problem with identification is group defamation, that is, speech or other communication that defames a particular group on the basis of its ethnicity, gender, geography, occupation, sexual orientation, or other characteristics. Article 101 of the *General Principles of the Civil Law* declares that a citizen or a legal entity has the right to reputation, and the dignity of a citizen should be protected by law. In addition, Article 108 of the *Civil Procedure Law* provides that to establish a case, the plaintiff must be a citizen or a legal entity that is directly involved in the case. These provisions indicate that the right of reputation applies only to a specific person and a tort must involve a specific victim. "The specific person" includes the following situations: (1) the specific person is directly identified; (2) the information supplied by the author is sufficient enough for the public to locate a specific person even though his name is not mentioned; and (3) the statement points to a very small group, such as a sole proprietorship or partnership. In this situation, each member of the group should be deemed as a specific person.[92] Overall, if the allegedly defamatory statement refers only to a broad group of people, it may not be considered tort, and neither the group nor its individual members may claim compensation. Regarding how to determine whether the reputation of an individual member is damaged in the case of group defamation, the courts in the United States have proposed two criteria: first, the size of the group involved must be small enough that every member can be recognized; second, the defamatory content concerns every member of the group. When these two criteria are met, each member of the group can sue for infringement of reputation.[93] In China, it seems that the courts have not formulated certain criteria to evaluate group defamation, as is shown in the following two cases.

Case 3.19 *Mongolian Doctors* v. *China International Broadcasting Publishing House*: group defamation upheld by the court[94]

In the case of *Mongolian Doctors* v. *China International Broadcasting Publishing House*, the court supported a defamation claim by a relatively large group. In 1989, defendant China International Broadcasting Publishing House published 10,000 copies of a dictionary compiled by Lin Xingguang, who had died. On page 203 of the dictionary, the term "Mongolian doctors" was defined as "doctors with poor medical skills, doctors frequently making medical errors." As a result, 189 Mongolian doctors jointly sued the defendant. The court judged that when the reputation of a group was damaged, every member could become a victim, and every member could thus file a lawsuit as an individual. The court determined that the defendant should compensate each plaintiff with 1,000 yuan for mental anguish.

Case 3.20 *Liu Min* v. *Long Yongtu*: denial of a group defamation claim[95]

In the Long Yongtu case, however, the courts denied a plaintiff's group defamation claim indirectly through jurisdiction objection. In June 2008, Long Yongtu, the secretary-general of Boao Forum for Asia, said in a public meeting: "The government should get tough with unruly people, instead of being held hostage by them." Long also argued that people or households who refused to move while bargaining for unreasonably high compensation when their land was requisitioned for a construction project should not be tolerated by the government. Long's statement soon triggered off a hot debate on "unruly people" in cyberspace. Liu Min, a Shenzhen citizen, felt that Long's statement on "unruly people" insulted him, given his own experience with land requisition. He thus wrote a letter to the Secretariat of the Forum, requesting an apology from Long. After getting no response, Liu filed a suit at a local court in Shenzhen. The case was tried first by the Shenzhen Futian People's Court and then by the Shenzhen Intermediate People's Court. The latter delivered a final verdict: since the plaintiff could neither prove that the infringing activity of the defendant had occurred in Shenzhen nor show that his interests and rights were directly damaged by the defendant, the case could not be established.

The creator of online content

"In cyberspace, nobody knows you are a dog." The anonymity of online communication results in a problem involving reverse identification, that is, how to identify the creator of defamatory content on the Internet. If the creator cannot be identified, the victim may not be able to receive any legal remedy even if the content has caused true damage to his reputation.

Case 3.21   Mr. Xiao: failure to prove damage to reputation[96]

On June 12, 2002 Mr. Xiao received several calls from strangers, asking him whether he needed sexual services. He learned from the callers that there was a message publicized on the website 263.com. The message said that "I am lonely, longing for a girl who can stay with me during the whole day or just at night"; it also included Xiao's cell phone number for contact purposes. At Xiao's request, the website promptly deleted the message. But Xiao found himself misunderstood and blamed by his friends and family members because of this embarrassing and insulting message. He thus sued the website, requesting a written apology, 1,500 yuan of economic compensation, and 5,000 yuan of emotional distress

> compensation. The court held that the defendant, after being informed by the plaintiff, had deleted the message in a timely manner, thus having fulfilled its legal duty; and that the plaintiff had failed to prove that the message had lowered his dignity and damaged his social reputation. Therefore, the court rejected the plaintiff's claims.

In Case 3.21, the ISP involved was immune from legal liability, thanks to its timely deletion of the message, while the victim had to seek compensation from the sender of the message. The problem was that the creator of online content was anonymous, so the victim found it hard to obtain legal remedy. It is argued that anonymity is not absolute in cyberspace. In China, Internet users are often required to register with ISPs when using the latters' services. An ISP is obliged to keep private its users' information, but when an infringing activity occurs, the ISP has the duty to provide the information of relevant users. Under Article 65 of the *Civil Procedure Law*, the court has the right to investigate and collect evidence from relevant units or individuals, and such units or individuals may not refuse to provide evidence. This means that, in a case of infringement, the ISP shall report the true identity of the tortfeasor to the relevant judicial organs. Furthermore, Article 14 of the *Administrative Measures for Internet Information Services* stipulates that Internet information service providers shall keep a record of the information that users disseminate, the times of dissemination, the URLs, and the domain names; Internet access service providers shall keep a record of such information as the times online subscribers are online, the subscribers' account numbers, the URLs and the domain names, and the callers' telephone numbers; and both Internet information service providers and Internet access service providers shall keep copies of such records for 60 days and shall provide them to relevant government authorities upon the lawful request of the latter. These legal provisions obviously give judicial organs the power and right to acquire a user's personal information. The question is whether or not the injured party also has the right to ask the ISP to provide the offender's personal information. So far, Chinese law and regulations have not made specific stipulations in this regard. Notwithstanding, if an ISP provides a person's information to the injured party without verifying the facts of infringement, it may violate the former's right to privacy.[97]

Fault

Fault refers to a type of liability in which the plaintiff must prove that the defendant's speech or conduct was either intentional or negligent. Fault-based liability is the opposite of strict liability, which is the absolute legal responsibility for damages or injury that can be imposed on a defendant without proof of fault or negligence. In China, the law of tort adopts the principle of fault-based liability: the person who is subjectively at fault bears tort liability, while the person who is not subjectively at fault bears no tort liability, except as otherwise stipulated by law. This principle applies not only to the tortfeasor but also to the mass media publishing the infringing content. In addition, this principle applies to the reputation disputes occurring not only to traditional media but also to new media. If the law requires ISPs to bear strict liability, this may significantly limit the development of the Internet industry.[98]

Fault can take the form of either negligence or intent. Negligent fault arises if, when a reasonably prudent person would foresee the possibility of his conduct injuring another, and would take necessary steps to guard against such occurrence, a person continues with that conduct. Simply stated, negligence implies the failure to exercise reasonable care. Negligent fault may be attributed to a person only when he has the mental capacity to understand the consequences of his conduct and also has the physical ability to control that conduct accordingly. In judicial practice, the common reasons why news media as a defendant might be found negligent include: "reliance on an untrustworthy source; not reading or misreading pertinent documents; failure to check with an obvious source, perhaps the subject of the story; and carelessness in editing and news handling."[99] The key question for the court is whether the defendant made a good faith effort to determine the truth or falsity of the matter.

Intentional fault is also referred to as actual malice. In *New York Times Co. v. Sullivan*, Justice Brennan defines actual malice as "knowledge of falsity or reckless disregard of whether the material was false or not."[100] This definition has been basically adopted by China's legal scholars and professionals. Knowledge of falsity is nothing more than lying. It means when the defamatory material was published, the communicator knew that the material was false. If the plaintiff can prove that the defendant lied, actual malice has then been shown. Reckless disregard means that the communicator published the defamatory material with reckless disregard for truth or falsity, that is, with serious doubt that the material was true. To determine whether the defendant exhibits reckless disregard, the court often takes into account the urgency of a story, the reliability of a story's source, and the believability of the information.[101]

In Chinese judicial practice, an offender may bear different liabilities for his defamatory statement, depending on whether such statement is negligent or intentional and whether the circumstance is serious or not. If the statement is negligent, he may bear civil liability. If the statement is intentional and the circumstance is not serious, he may bear civil liability; if the statement is intentional and the circumstance is serious, he may bear criminal liability. It can be seen that whether the offender has actual malice is a key criterion for determining whether he shall bear criminal liability. In accordance with Chinese law, cases concerning the crime of defamation are "tried only after being told," unless involving national security and public order. Thus, to a great extent, it is the plaintiff who determines whether the defamation shall be handled as a civil case or a criminal one.[102] In most cases, the plaintiff would opt to resort to a civil procedure that emphasizes compensation. If he wins his civil suit, the plaintiff may regain his reputation and also receive material compensation. On the other hand, Chinese criminal law emphasizes criminal punishment of the offender rather than material compensation to the victim, which is often a very small amount. That is why in China a vast majority of defamation cases are handled as a tort and few end up being handled as a crime.[103] With regard to online defamation, the *Decision of the NPC Standing Committee on Guarding Internet Security* stipulates that defaming others via the Internet may constitute a crime, but most relevant cases so far have been handled as a tort, for the above-mentioned reason.

Concerning public persons

Determining which category of fault shall apply to a particular defamation case can be a difficult but critical process. Whether the plaintiff must show actual malice on the defendant's part, or just negligence, is a determination that often will ordain the ultimate outcome of a defamation lawsuit.[104] In the United States, this critical determination is based on whether the plaintiff is a public or a private person.[105] If the plaintiff is a public person, either a public official or a public figure, he is required to prove the actual malice of the defendant in order to win the case. In the case of *New York Times* v. *Sullivan*, the Supreme Court held that the First Amendment protects the publication of all statements, even false ones, about the conduct of public officials except when statements are made with actual malice. In the United States, the principle of "actual malice" in fact renders it difficult for the plaintiff to win the case, thus helping news media to get rid of the threat of defamation. It has been found that in nearly 30 years, the U.S. news media as a defendant overall lost 9% defamation cases; specifically, when the plaintiff was a public person, the news media lost only 4% of such cases.[106]

Article 41 of China's Constitution provides that a citizen has the right to make criticisms and suggestions to any state organ or its functionaries as long as he neither deliberately fabricates nor distorts facts. This provision is very close to the "actual malice" standard proposed by the U.S. courts. This means that, in terms of the Constitution, it should be hard for government officials to win a defamation lawsuit against news media, given the difficulty of proving the actual malice of the defendant. Many legal scholars in China have also reached a consensus on actual malice, arguing that if the defamatory content concerns public persons as well as public interests, then the court should judge in favor of freedom of speech; and the communicator shall be immune from civil or criminal liability unless it is proved that he has the actual malice to defame others.[107] In Chinese judicial practice, however, the court adopts the general principle of fault liability. The communicator may bear legal liability for the allegedly defamatory statement, no matter whether intentional or negligent, no matter whether the plaintiff is a public person or a private person. In other words, a public person can sue an individual or organization for defamation and the plaintiff does not have to prove the actual malice of the defendant. This has led to the frequent failure of Chinese news media in defamation cases. Yale University Professor Chen Zhiwu collected 210 defamation cases that occurred in China from 1987 to 2003, all involving news media or journalists as the defendant. He found that the news media or journalists lost 63% of cases; furthermore, among the cases in which the plaintiff was a public official, the news media or journalists lost 65%.[108] This indicates that China may need to undermine the reputation protection of public figures in order to strengthen its protection of free speech.

Case 3.22 *Fan Zhiyi* v. *the Oriental Sports Daily*: news reports serving the public interest are protected by law[109]

One influential case concerning public persons is *Fan Zhiyi* v. *the Oriental Sports Daily*. Soon after the match between China and Costa Rica at the 2002 Football World Cup, a rumor spread that one player of China's soccer team was involved in soccer gambling. From June 16 to 21, the *Oriental Sports Daily* published a series of related articles, including "Fan Zhiyi Involved in Soccer Gambling on the Match China v. Costa Rica," "Fan Jiulin: My Son Did not Participate in Any Soccer Gambling," "Sober Announcement of Fan Zhiyi," and "Truth Has Been Revealed: Fan Zhiyi Did Not Gamble." Fan Zhiyi therefore sued Wenhui-Xinmin United Press Group, the parent company of the *Oriental Sports Daily*, for defamation. The court, after investigation, held that the source of information of the *Oriental Sports Daily* was not fabricated, and the structure and content of the articles showed that the newspaper intended to reveal the truth about a gambling scandal. Regarding the plaintiff's claim that the newspaper had damaged his reputation by identifying his name, the court responded that the plaintiff, as a public figure, should bear some minor damage caused by the supervision of public opinion. The news coverage seemed to concern only the private affairs of the plaintiff, but when those private affairs related to the World Cup and the Chinese soccer team, they should be considered a matter of public concern, which certainly deserved investigation by the news media. The court concluded that the defendant was not at fault, and that news reports serving the public interest should be protected by law. The court thus rejected all of the plaintiff's claims.

Case 3.23   Xie Jin: actual malice in the online defamation of a public figure[110]

On October 18, 2008, China's famous film director Xie Jin died at a hotel prior to the centenary ceremony of his mother high school—Chunhui High School in Shangyu, Zhejiang. After Xie's death, Song Zude and Liu Xinda wrote blog articles like "Don't Die Like Xie Jin," "Xie Jin and Liu Xiaoqing Had an Illegitimate Child Named Xie Yuqing Who Lived Overseas and Got Serious Cerebral Palsy." The first article announced that Xie's sudden death was caused by sexual activities, while the second one claimed that Xie and actress Liu Xiaoqing had an illegitimate child with serious cerebral palsy. Xu Dawen, Xie's widow, thus sued Song Zude and Liu Xinda for defamation at a local court. The court verified that the two defendants had disseminated fabricated facts about Xie and proactively encouraged others to republish their articles. The articles were published on the day following the death of Xie. Afterwards, the two defendants continually damaged Xie's reputation in public, claiming that they had relevant photos, recordings, and other evidence to prove the authenticity of their articles. In addition, the defendants used the Internet to spread the infringing information so that the damage to Xie's reputation could be enlarged to the greatest extent. Holding that the defendants had the actual malice to defame Xie, the court adjudged that the defendants should compensate the plaintiff for all kinds of loss, as well as make an open apology in the newspapers.

Retractions and clarifications

As for traditional news media, if what they have published has been found to be an infringement on another's right of reputation, they must publish a correction statement or take other measures to eliminate the negative effects on the injured party; otherwise, they may bear tort liability. However, even if the media make such retractions or take clarification measures, they still cannot completely exempt themselves from liability; instead, they may be partially relieved of the liability. It is argued that retractions or corrections are only remedial measures taken after the defamation; if the media have allowed the release of infringing materials without fulfilling their obligation to conduct prior examination of the content for accuracy, they shall bear responsibility for being subjectively at fault. For the ISPs, however, to verify all information before release is a burden that they cannot afford, and a practice that is fundamentally against their growth. This concern has been addressed in the recently enacted *Tort Liability Law*. According to this law, where an ISP was previously not aware of the infringing information, but promptly takes such necessary measures as deletion, blocking, or disconnection after being informed by the injured party, it shall be completely immune from liability; if the ISP fails to take necessary measures in a timely manner, it shall be jointly and severally liable with the tortfeasor for any additional harm.

Case 3.24 "Rotten People Lousy Textbook": ISP subject to tort liability[111]

In November 2005, Chen Tangfa, an associate professor of communication at Nanjing University, sued Hangzhou Blog Information Technology Co. for reputation infringement. The cause of the lawsuit was that an Internet user named "K007" had published a blog article titled "Rotten People Lousy Textbook" on blogcn.com, which was owned by the defendant. The article reproached the plaintiff as "a wretched man" and "a hooligan." After finding the article, the plaintiff called the website, requesting the latter to delete the article. The website asked the plaintiff first to provide materials to prove his identity, otherwise it would not delete the article. Due to a lack of consensus between the plaintiff and the defendant, the infringing content was retained until the lawsuit started. The court, after hearing the case, held that the article "Rotten People Lousy Textbook" contained content insulting and humiliating to the plaintiff; when the plaintiff called the defendant and requested the deletion of the content, it can be assumed that the defendant knew of the infringement at that time; however, the defendant merely kept asking the plaintiff to provide identity information and took no measures to stop the infringement. The court concluded that the defendant had failed to exercise the due care of a prudent administrator, and should be subject to tort liability. The court demanded that the defendant should post an apology to the plaintiff on the home page of its website and also compensate the plaintiff 1,000 yuan for economic loss. The verdict was affirmed by a higher court upon the plaintiff's appeal.

Defense strategies

When a case of defamation is established, the defendant is supposed to bear civil and even criminal liability. However, Chinese law allows the defendant to defend for the purpose of reducing or eliminating his liability. In the defense process, the defendant may provide proof that the plaintiff's charges are unfounded, partially or completely. In China, defense is an integral part of procedural law. The purpose of giving the defendant the right to defend is to ensure procedural justice as well as the fairness and appropriateness of the verdict. Specifically, the *1993* and *1998 SPC Interpretations* and other laws and regulations have formulated the following defense strategies concerning reputation disputes, and these strategies apply to online defamation cases.

Truth

Truth is the most important defense against the charge of infringement of reputation. It means that when an action for defamation arises, the defendant may defend by proving the truth of his statement.[112] The truth defense focuses on whether the statement is one of fact or opinion. If a false statement is presented as fact, then a case of defamation may be established; otherwise it may not. In accordance with the *1993* and *1998 SPC Interpretations*, the degree of truth concerning a statement can be divided into four levels: completely true, largely true, largely false, and seriously false. After receipt of the claims from a litigant, the court may determine not to accept the suit if it verifies that the allegedly defamatory statement is completely true or largely true. The court will only accept a case in which the involved statement is found to be largely false or seriously false. Therefore, if the defendant can prove the truth of his statement, he can successfully defend himself against the plaintiff's libel charges. In this defense process, it is the duty of the defendant to prove that the statement is true. The defendant must, based on the relevant facts, substantially prove the authenticity of the statement. If the statement implies some underlying facts, the defendant must also prove the truth of such underlying facts. Therefore, whether or not a defendant can defend successfully depends on how he presents and interprets the facts, including underlying facts, implied in a statement.

Fair comment

Another defense used in defamation cases is fair comment. This defense is often regarded as a protection for robust publicized opinions about public persons. For something to constitute fair comment, the comment must be on matters of public interest, based on known facts, and with no actual malice underlying it. First, the comment must be on matters of public interest. The key issue is how to define the scope of matters of public interest. It is argued that since news reports have come into the public view, they should be considered related to the public interest; therefore, any comment based on news reports that have been published should be identified as being on matters of public interest.[113] This broad definition of "matters of public interest" has been largely accepted by Chinese courts. Second, the defendant must prove that his comment is based on known facts rather than fabricated facts. The facts must exist before the defender publishes his statement. The defendant is not required to prove the truth of the facts; otherwise, there would be no difference between fair comment and truth defenses. Therefore, where the facts cited in the comment come from reliable news sources, the comment should be considered fair even if such facts are later proved to be false. That is because the commenter has no obligation to verify the truth of the cited facts.[114] Third, the defendant must prove that his comment has no actual malice. Obviously, if the defendant's comment was made with actual malice, it could not qualify as fair comment. Actual malice means that the defendant intentionally made a false statement of asserted facts, or showed reckless disregard for whether the alleged facts were false or not. If the defendant was found to have intentionally made a false statement of facts, then any comment based on those facts would be considered as being made with actual malice.

Privilege

Privilege means that in order to protect the public interest or their own legal rights and interests, citizens and organizations may make defamatory statements without taking legal responsibility. In accordance with the U.S. common law, there are two types of privilege: absolute privilege and qualified privilege. Absolute privilege refers to the situation whereby even defamatory statements made maliciously are exempt from liability. This type of privilege applies to defamatory statements made in a court or in a governmental session. Qualified privilege provides a defense as long as the statement was not made with actual malice. It is often given to journalists where the statement concerns the public interest, such as news reports related to public meetings, public entities, or government documents.

Many Chinese laws protect the legitimate exercise of rights, which is similar to the concept of privilege in the United States. The so-called legitimate exercise of rights means that a citizen is allowed to damage others' reputation when exercising his right according to the relevant laws and regulations. Part of legitimately exercised rights can be treated as absolute privilege. For example, the members of national or local people's congresses have the freedom to discuss public affairs in public meetings, regardless of whether their statements cause harm to others' reputations. In addition, the administrators of state organs have the right to make comments on their staff, based on certain facts. As long as the exercise of such right is within the scope of their duties, even unfair comments would not be deemed as violating others' reputations. There are some legitimately exercised rights that can be seen as qualified privilege. For example, China's Constitution stipulates that a citizen has the freedom to make criticisms and suggestions to state organs and their functionaries. Even if the citizen's statement is derogatory, he can still be immune from legal liability. But he is not allowed to fabricate or distort facts in this process. In addition, the *1998 SPC Interpretation* prescribes that news reports based on public documents and government activities are immune from infringement of reputation claims, unless they include false statements of fact. This suggests that news coverage of official documents and official activities can also be considered as enjoying qualified privilege. Therefore, when exercising their right to speech, both Chinese citizens and the news media possess the weapon of privilege to defend against the charge of infringement of reputation.

Notes

1. They include the 1954 Constitution, 1975 Constitution, 1978 Constitution, and the current 1982 Constitution.
2. Yongzheng Wei (2006) *Lectures on Journalism and Communication Law*, 2nd edition, Beijing, China: Renmin University of China Press.
3. Yongzheng Wei (2006) *Lectures on Journalism and Communication Law*, 2nd edition, Beijing, China: Renmin University of China Press.
4. See Paul Siegel (2008) *Communication Law in America*, 2nd edition, New York: Rowman and Littlefield.
5. See 505 U.S. 377.
6. W. Wat Hopkin (ed.) (2003) *Communication and the Law*, Northport, AL: Vision Press, p. 59.
7. See the *Regulations Regarding Strengthening the Administration of Publications Describing Major Party and National Leaders* that was promulgated in 1990.
8. It refers to the *Measures on the Filing of Important Topics of Books, Periodicals, Audio/Visual Productions, and Electronic Publications* which was promulgated in 1997 by the GAPP.
9. Refer to Chapter 2 for detailed information about administrative licensing of Internet services.
10. W. Wat Hopkin (ed.) (2003) *Communication and the Law*, Northport, AL: Vision Press.
11. John D. Zelezny (2011) *Communication Law: Liberties, Restraints, and the Modern Media*, 6th edition, Boston, MA: Wadsworth.
12. W. Wat Hopkin (ed.) (2003) *Communication and the Law*, Northport, AL: Vision Press.
13. John D. Zelezny (2011) *Communication Law: Liberties, Restraints, and the Modern Media*, 6th edition, Boston, MA: Wadsworth, p. 50.
14. John D. Zelezny (2011) *Communication Law: Liberties, Restraints, and the Modern Media*, 6th edition, Boston, MA: Wadsworth.
15. Erwin Chemerinsky (2006) *Constitutional Law: Principles and Policies*, 3rd edition, New York: Aspen Publishers, p. 941.
16. Erwin Chemerinsky (2006) *Constitutional Law: Principles and Policies*, 3rd edition, New York: Aspen Publishers.
17. Erwin Chemerinsky (2006) *Constitutional Law: Principles and Policies*, 3rd edition, New York: Aspen Publishers.
18. Erwin Chemerinsky (2006) *Constitutional Law: Principles and Policies*, 3rd edition, New York: Aspen Publishers, p. 941.
19. Raymond S. R. Ku and Jacqueline Lipton (2010) *Cyberspace Law: Cases and Materials*, New York: Aspen Publishers, p. 116.
20. Raymond S. R. Ku and Jacqueline Lipton (2010) *Cyberspace Law: Cases and Materials*, New York: Aspen Publishers, p. 117.
21. See Article 13 of the current Criminal Law.
22. Several administrative regulations including the *Administrative Measures for Internet Information Services* provide that if the offender's act of producing, reproducing, or disseminating information involving national

security is insufficient to constitute a criminal offense, he shall be subject to administrative penalty; only when his act constitutes a criminal offense shall the offender be investigated for criminal responsibility.

23. Jun Wang (2000) *Judicial Guideline on the Criminal Law*, Beijing: The Law Press.

24. Jun Wang (2000) *Judicial Guideline on the Criminal Law*, Beijing: The Law Press.

25. Eric Barendt (2001) *Freedom of Speech*, New York: Oxford University Press, p. 153.

26. John D. Zelezny (2011) *Communication Law: Liberties, Restraints, and the Modern Media*, 6th edition, Boston, MA: Wadsworth, p. 88.

27. Eric Barendt (2001) *Freedom of Speech*, New York: Oxford University Press, p. 153.

28. Erwin Chemerinsky (2006) *Constitutional Law: Principles and Policies*, 3rd edition, New York: Aspen Publishers, p. 999.

29. In accordance with relevant laws and regulations, if the offender's act of disclosing state secrets is insufficient to constitute a criminal offense, he shall be subject to administrative penalty instead of criminal punishment.

30. See S. 2533, the State Secrets Protection Act.

31. U.S. Department of State Foreign Affairs Handbook Volume 5 Handbook 3 – TAGS/Terms Handbook: 5 FAH-3 H-700 E.O. 12958, AS AMENDED, TELEGRAM CLASSIFICATION MARKING, U.S. Department of State, 14 July 2009, retrieved March 15, 2011 from http://www.state.gov/documents/organization/89254.pdf.

32. It is generally considered China's supreme military policy making body and its Chairman is the commander-in-chief of the armed forces.

33. Yijun Wang (2007) "Experts interpreting the Law on the Disclosure of Government Information," *China Youth Daily*, April 25.

34. Xinhua News Agency (2010) "Experts' opinion on Liu Xiaobo case," Xinhuanet.com, retrieved March 10, 2011 from http://news.xinhuanet.com/world/2010-10/25/c_12698346.htm

35. The source of the case is Chengdu Immediate People's Court of Sichuan Province Criminal Verdict Chengdu Immediate Criminal Division First Trial Case No. 49 (2001) [Chinese]. An English translation of the criminal judgment, by William Farris, can be retrieved from http://www.feichangdao.com.

36. The source of the case is Changsha Immediate People's Court of Hunan Province Criminal Verdict Changsha Immediate Criminal Division One First Trial Case No. 29 (2005) [Chinese]. The English translation was published by Global Voices (http://www.globalvoicesonline.org/wp-content/ShiTao_verdict.pdf), a website that translates and reports on blogs from around the world, and is used under Creative Commons Attribution-Only license http://creativecommons.org/licenses/by/2.5.

37. Denying this verdict, the defendant Shi Tao filed an appeal to the Higher People's Court of Hunan Province, which upheld the verdict.

38. See the *Interpretations of Several Issues on the Specific Application of Law in the Handling of Criminal Cases about Producing, Reproducing, Publishing, Selling, and Disseminating Pornographic Electronic Information via the Internet, Mobile Communication Terminals and Sound Message*

Stations (2010), which can be retrieved from the official website of the Supreme Court: http://www.court.gov.cn/qwfb/sfjs/201002/t20100223_1741.htm.

39. For a crime to be constituted, different offenders need to meet different requirements for the minimum amount or quantity of involved pornographic publications, which can be found in the *2010 Interpretation*.

40. See the *Interpretations of Several Issues on the Specific Application of Law in the Handling of Criminal Cases about Producing, Reproducing, Publishing, Selling, and Disseminating Pornographic Electronic Information via the Internet, Mobile Communication Terminals and Sound Message Stations* (2010), which can be retrieved from the official site of the Supreme Court, http://www.court.gov.cn/qwfb/sfjs/201002/t20100223_1741.htm.

41. See the article the "Supreme People's Court Publicized 6 Typical Cases Involving Internet Pornography and Mobile Phone Pornography," which can be retrieved from the official site of the Supreme Court, http://www.court.gov.cn/spyw/xssp/201011/t20101110_10923.htm.

42. See the *Interpretation of the Supreme People's Court and the Supreme People's Prosecutorial on the Concrete Application of Law on Handling the Cases of Committing Crimes by Organizing and Using Cult Organizations* (1999), available at http://www.people.com.cn/item/flfgk/gwyfg/1999/113102199903.html.

43. In China, there have been at least 15 organizations that were banned as cults, among which the most influential is Falun Gong.

44. The source of the case: Dongying Immediate People's Court of Shandong Province Criminal Verdict, Dongying Court Criminal Division One Final Trial Case No. 5 (2006).

45. Located in Shandong Province, Shengli Oil Field is the second-largest oil field in China.

46. Merriam-Webster Dictionary, "Superstition," retrieved August 10, 2010 from http://www.merriam-webster.com/dictionary/superstition.

47. For example, a survey of middle and high school students in Beijing revealed that 40% were addicted to online fortune-telling. Sun Xupei (2008) *The Study on the Law of Journalism and Communication*, Shanghai, China: Fudan University Press.

48. The source of the case: Qingxiu People's Court of Nanning, Guangxi Criminal Verdict, Qingxiu Court Criminal Division First Trial Case No. 375 (2008).

49. 163.com is one of the largest commercial websites in China.

50. The source of the case: Zhuzhou People's Court of Hunan Province Criminal Verdict, Zhuzhou Court Criminal Division First Trial Case No. 230 (1997).

51. Fangyan Wang and Dishu Zhu (2008) "An Investigation on the Blue-chip Shares Refinancing Event," *21st Century Business Herald*, February 28, retrieved July 21, 2010 from http://finance.cctv.com/20080228/101252.shtml.

52. China Advertising Investment Analysis and Forecast Report, 2011–2015, retrieved October 10, 2010 from http://www.ocn.com.cn/reports/2006370guanggao.htm.

53. Merriam-Webster Dictionary, retrieved May 20, 2011 from http://www.merriam-webster.com/dictionary/advertising?show=0&t=1308728297.

54. See Wikipedia (2011) *Online Advertising*, retrieved June 22, 2011 from http://en.wikipedia.org/wiki/Online_advertising.

55. See reportbuyer.com (2006) *China Online Advertising Development Report, 2005–2006*, retrieved December 4, 2011 from http://www.reportbuyer.com/business_government/advertising_marketing/china_online_advertising_development_report_2005_2006.htm.

56. See "The Status of China's Internet Advertising Market," retrieved March 10, 2011 from http://www.chinasigns.cn/Artichttp://www.chinasigns.cn/Article/flcs/wlmt/200703/20615.htmlle/flcs/wlmt/200703/20615.html.

57. See the website of the SAIC: http://www.saic.gov.cn/.

58. This regulation was promulgated by the Beijing Administration of Industry and Commerce in 2001.

59. Yan Shi (2008) "Sohu Sued for Deceptive Ads, The Consumer's Claims Rejected due to Insufficient Evidence," retrieved February 12, 2011 from http://china.findlaw.cn/info/jingjifa/guanggao/anli/67788.html.

60. See John D. Zelezny (2011) *Communication Law: Liberties, Restraints, and the Modern Media*, 6th edition, Wadsworth: Cengage Learning.

61. Lixin Yang (2008) *The Expansion of and Restriction on the Right of Reputation*, October 1, retrieved July 16, 2010 from http://www.yanglx.com/dispnews.asp?id=726.

62. Xinbao Zhang and Changqing Kang (1997) "The Status, Problems, and Strategies of Handling Defamation Cases," *Modern Legal Studies*, 3.

63. Yongzheng Wei (2006) *Lectures on Journalism and Communication Law*, 2nd edition, Beijing, China: Renmin University of China Press.

64. Robert Trager, Joseph Russomanno, and Susan D. Ross (2010) *The Law of Journalism and Mass Communication*, 2nd edition, Washington, DC: CQ Press.

65. Xupei Sun (2008) *The Study on the Law of Journalism and Communication*, Shanghai, China: Fudan University Press.

66. Xupei Sun (2008) *The Study on the Law of Journalism and Communication*, Shanghai, China: Fudan University Press.

67. The source of the case: Beijing No. 1 Immediate People's Court Civil Verdict Beijing No. 1 Immediate Civil Division Final Trial Case No. 1438 (2000).

68. Xinbao Zhang (1997) *The Legal Protection for the Right of Reputation*, Beijing, China: China University of Political Science and Law Press.

69. Yongzheng Wei (2006) *Lectures on Journalism and Communication Law*, 2nd edition, Beijing, China: Renmin University of China Press.

70. The source of the case: Shanghai No. 1 Immediate People's Court Civil Verdict Shanghai No. 1 Immediate Civil Division One First Trial Case No. 13 (2004).

71. Deliang Liu (2010) "The Freedom to Information and the Information Monitoring Obligation of Internet Service Providers," January 25, http://blog.china.com.cn/liu_deliang/art/2840734.html.

72. Yu Liao (2010) "How to Establish the Legal Liability for Online Defamation," http://www.chinanews.com/cul/2010/10-14/2587158.shtml.

73. Yongzheng Wei (2006) *Lectures on Journalism and Communication Law*, 2nd edition, Beijing, China: Renmin University of China Press.

74. Yi Zhao (2009) "Baidu Website Link Raises Reputation Disputes," http://bjgy.chinacourt.org/public/detail.php?id=79757&k_w=金德

75. W. Page Keeton, Dan B. Dobbs, Robert E. Keeton, and David G. Owen (eds.) (1984), *Prosser and Keeton on Torts*, 5th edition, West Group, s 111 at 773.

76. Yongzheng Wei (2006) *Lectures on Journalism and Communication Law*, 2nd edition, Beijing, China: Renmin University of China Press.

77. Qiaochu Yang (2001) "Thanks to Wrong Notes with Her Picture, Liu Xuan's Mother Intends to Launch a Defamation Suit and Request One Million Compensation," *Tianfu Morning Daily*, December 4.

78. See Jian Hou (2011) "Comments and Insulting Words in Reputation Disputes," January 31, retrieved March 10, 2011 from http://www.acriticism.com/article.asp?Newsid=12375&type=1001.

79. See Jian Hou (2011) "Comments and Insulting Words in Reputation Disputes," January 31, retrieved March 10, 2011 from http://www.acriticism.com/article.asp?Newsid=12375&type=1001.

80. See Jian Hou (2011) "Comments and Insulting Words in Reputation Disputes," January 31, retrieved March 10, 2011 from http://www.acriticism.com/article.asp?Newsid=12375&type=1001.

81. See the definitions of "insult" and "humiliate" in the Free Dictionary at http://www.thefreedictionary.com.

82. See Jian Hou (2011) "Comments and Insulting Words in Reputation Disputes," January 31, retrieved March 10, 2011 from http://www.acriticism.com/article.asp?Newsid=12375&type=1001.

83. See Jian Hou (2011) "Comments and Insulting Words in Reputation Disputes," January 31, retrieved March 10, 2011 from http://www.acriticism.com/article.asp?Newsid=12375&type=1001.

84. Madeleine Schachter and Joel Kurtzburg (2008) *Law of Internet Speech*, 3rd edition, Carolina Academic Press.

85. Mike God (1996) "Libel Law: Let It Die," *Wire* 4(3) (March), http://www.wired.com/wired/archive/4.03/letitdie.html.

86. The source of the case: Linqing Immediate People's Court of Shandong Province Civil Verdict Linqing Civil Division One First Trial Case No. 393 (2005).

87. Yongzheng Wei (2006) *Lectures on Journalism and Communication Law*, 2nd edition, Beijing, China: Renmin University of China Press.

88. The source of the case: Beijing No. 2 Immediate People's Court Civil Verdict Beijing No. 2 Immediate Civil Division Final Trial Case No. 12807 (2009).

89. Xinhua News Agency, "Letao Sues Okbuy, also Considering Suing Google Overseas," http://news.xinhuanet.com/fortune/2010-11/25/c_12816457.htm.

90. Such as the case of *Futian People's Court of Shenzhen* v. *The Democracy and the Rule of Law Magazine*.

91. Xupei Sun (2008) *The Study on the Law of Journalism and Communication*, Shanghai, China: Fudan University Press.

92. Lixin Yang (1996) *On the Law of Personal Rights*, Beijing, China: China Procuratorate Press.
93. Liming Wang and Lixin Yang (1995) *Personal Rights and News Media Tort*, Beijing, China: China Fangzheng Press.
94. The source of the case: Fuxin Mongolian People's Court of Liaoning Province Civil Verdict Fuxin Mongolian Civil Division First Trial Case No. 1095 (2002).
95. Tao Yang (2009) "'Unruly People' Sued Long Yongtu: The Case Rejected by the Court," *Southern Metropolis Daily*, March 11, http://gd.nfdaily.cn/content/2009-03/11/content_4976570.htm.
96. Zhongpeng Zhao and Ruyin Li (2003) "Who Used My Cell Phone Number for Seeking Sex Service on the Internet?" *Beijing Morning Post*, January 23.
97. Refer to Chapter 4 for detailed discussion of the issue of infringement of the right of privacy.
98. See article "A Study on the Right of Reputation in Cyberspace," which can be retrieved from http://china.findlaw.cn/info/minshang/minfa/minshiquanli/renshenquan/mingyuquan/62893.html.
99. Don R. Pember and C. Calvert (2007/2008) *Mass Media Law*, New York: McGraw Hill, p. 220.
100. 376 U.S. 254 (1964).
101. Robert Trager, Joseph Russomanno, and Susan D. Ross (2010) *The Law of Journalism and Mass Communication*, 2nd edition, Washington, DC: CQ Press.
102. Yongzheng Wei (2006) *Lectures on Journalism and Communication Law*, 2nd edition, Beijing, China: Renmin University of China Press.
103. Xupei Sun (2008) *The Study on the Law of Journalism and Communication*, Shanghai, China: Fudan University Press.
104. John D. Zelezny (2011) *Communication Law: Liberties, Restraints, and the Modern Media*, 6th edition, Wadsworth: Cengage Learning, p. 147.
105. Public people include public officials and public figures. According to the U.S. Supreme Court, "public officials" refers to government employees who have substantial responsibility for or control over the conduct of government affairs. "Public figures refers to those who have assumed special prominence in the resolution of public issues or the character of public events."
106. Xupei Sun (2008) *The Study on the Law of Journalism and Communication*, Shanghai, China: Fudan University Press.
107. See *The New Interpretation on News Media Torts against Reputation and Privacy (Draft Suggestion)*, http://media.people.com.cn/GB/8251154.html; Wei Yongzheng (2002) *The New Study on Journalism Law*, Beijing, China: China Customs Press, p. 301; and Zhang Xinbao (1997) *The Legal Protection for the Right of Reputation*, Beijing, China: China University of Political Science and Law, p. 107.
108. Zhiwu Che (2004) *The Legal Dilemma of Journalistic Speech*, Chinese Legal Professionals.
109. The source of the case: Jingan People's Court of Shanghai Municipality Civil Verdict Jinan Civil Division One First Trial Case No. 1776 (2002).
110. The source of the case: Jingan People's Court of Shanghai Municipality Civil Verdict Jinan Civil Division One First Trial Case No. 779 (2009).

111. The source of the case: A. Ying (2007) "China's First Case Again, This Time It Involves Blog," *People's Court Daily*, April 27.
112. In China, disclosing another person's private affairs is deemed an act of infringement of his right to reputation, even if such private affairs are true. This is arguably a drawback of China's defamation law. The issue of privacy is discussed in detail in Chapter 4.
113. See *The New Interpretation on News Media Torts against Reputation and Privacy (Draft Suggestion)*, http://media.people.com.cn/GB/8251154.html.
114. Fengchang Dou (2001) "How Can Commentary Be Fair," *Legal Daily*, July 2.

Privacy interests

Abstract: This chapter first introduces the concepts of privacy and the right to privacy, and the development of privacy law. It then examines how traditional invasion of privacy claims have been applied to speech in cyberspace. In the final section, the chapter focuses on several specific issues crucial to the protection of online privacy, including data collection, online profiling, and data protection paradigms.

Key words: privacy, privacy law, appropriation, intrusion on seclusion, disclosure of private facts, data collection, data protection, online profiling

With the rapid development of information technology, human society has entered into an era of unprecedented information explosion. People avail themselves of the Internet to communicate and connect with one another; meanwhile, the collection of personal information has become easier than ever before, due to the abundance of such information in cyberspace. As long as one's personal information is available on the Internet, it will spread around the world rapidly, and can be downloaded and copied without limit. Therefore, while the Internet provides numerous and substantial benefits to individuals, it also imposes a huge challenge for the protection of their privacy. This chapter begins with a brief introduction to privacy law, including the definition of privacy, the definition of the right to privacy, and the development of privacy law. It then investigates how existing laws on invasion of privacy have been applied to the Internet. Finally, it examines the numerous ways that courts, legislatures, regulators, and businesses have attempted to protect individuals from threats to privacy imposed by online data collection and disclosure.

Introduction to privacy law

Privacy and the right to privacy

Privacy can be defined as personal secrecy unrelated to matters of public interest. It includes the three aspects of private information, private activities, and private space.[1] Private information refers to all data and information about a person, such as his name, pictures, domiciles, weight, height, income, life experience, phone numbers, and medical records. Private activities refers to all individual activities that a person is reluctant to publicize, such as his/her daily schedule, social interaction, sexual life with spouse, and extramarital sexual life. Private space refers to the secret space of a person, such as the secret parts of his/her body, his/her habitation, diaries, correspondence, travel luggage, and nowadays virtual space.

The right to privacy refers to the right of a person to keep private his personal information, personal activities, or personal space that is not of legitimate public interest or concern. The purpose of protecting the right to privacy is to ensure that everyone has a right to live in society without being disturbed. The core of the right to privacy arguably lies in a person's right to determine how to deal with his privacy. Therefore, it is an invasion of privacy to spy on or publicize the personal secrecy of any person, if such an act is against his will.

Generally speaking, the right to privacy includes the following four aspects: (a) the right to live a quiet and peaceful life. Everyone shall have the right to live quietly and peacefully. For instance, his personal life should be free from illegal prying and harassment; and his house should be free from illegal surveillance, monitoring or photographing; (b) the right of control over personal information. Everyone shall have the exclusive right to collect, store, protect, and disseminate his personal information, such as about his health, life experience, religious beliefs, marital status, financial status, and social relations; (c) the right to privacy of communication and correspondence. Everyone shall have the right to privacy of correspondence, telephone communication, mail, e-mail, cable, and other communications; and (d) the right to make use of one's own privacy. Everyone shall have the right to make use of his privacy for commercial or non-commercial purposes, unless otherwise prohibited by law. For instance, he may use his life experience to create literary works in order to obtain economic benefit. However, the use of his own privacy shall not violate the law or harm the public interest.

For example, he is not allowed to take make use of his body to produce obscene works for dissemination; such an act will constitute a criminal offense in serious circumstances.

In accordance with Chinese law and social norms, Chinese citizens have at least nine specific rights related to privacy. They include: (a) citizens have the right to keep their names, portraits, addresses, home telephone numbers, and other personal information private. Such information shall not be spied on, publicized, or disseminated without their permission; (b) citizens' personal activities, especially in their houses, shall not be monitored, spied on, or pried into, except as monitored in accordance with law; (c) citizens' residences shall not be unlawfully entered, pried into, or harassed; (d) citizens' sexual lives shall not be intervened into, pried into, investigated, or publicized; (e) citizens' savings and property conditions shall not be investigated or publicized, except as required by law; (f) citizens' correspondence, dairies, and other personal documents (including private information stored on computer) shall not be pried into or publicized; citizens' personal data shall not be unlawfully gathered, transmitted, processed, and utilized; (g) citizens' social relationships, including friendships and family relationships, shall not be unlawfully investigated or publicized; (h) citizens' archival materials shall not be unlawfully publicized or made known to people who have no right to know; and (i) citizens' previous or current personal experience shall not be collected or disclosed, even if it has already been publicized elsewhere.[2]

Development of privacy law

The concept of privacy was first put forward in 1890 by two American scholars, Samuel D. Warren and Louis D. Brandeis, in their article "The Right to Privacy," which was published in the *Harvard Law Review.* Mainly concerned with the news media's invasion into personal privacy, they argue that news reporters sometimes make great efforts to create rumors so as to cater to the poor taste of their readers, and that these rumors often cross the sacred boundary of personal privacy and violate social norms. In their view, everyone has a right to live undisturbed, i.e., "the right to be let alone." Any infringement on this right shall be considered an invasion of privacy. With the advance of human society, the concept of privacy was gradually expanded to include many other personal aspects such as property, genes, health, and physiological information. But the right to privacy was still considered a defensive and passive right, which was felt only after being violated. In the current information era, personal details are not merely exposed by the news media; they may be also gathered, provided, or publicized by private or public entities. Therefore, legal scholars have proposed an alternative concept of privacy, namely, "the right to control one's own privacy," and they argue that individuals should have the right to determine whether and how to publicize and utilize their own private information. From this perspective, the right to privacy can be considered a positive right.[3] Over time, it has become much easier for individuals or organizations to obtain access to personal information because of the development of information technology, and the scope of privacy protection is expected to be expanded accordingly.

Although Chinese law has not established privacy as an independent right, many laws suggest the recognition and protection of privacy. Article 38 of the current Constitution stipulates that the personal dignity of citizens is inviolable; Article 39 stipulates that the residences of citizens are inviolable: unlawful searching of, or intrusion into, a citizen's residence is prohibited; Article 40 provides that the freedom and privacy of citizens' correspondence are protected by law: no organization or individual may, on any grounds, infringe upon citizens' freedom and privacy of correspondence, unless otherwise stipulated by law. These constitutional provisions provide the basis for the protection of privacy in other law sectors.

In the field of civil law, the NPC passed the *General Principles of the Civil Law* in 1986. Since law makers lacked understanding of the concept of privacy at that time, this civil law established only such personal rights as the right of name, portrait, reputation, honor, and life and health, and left out the right of privacy. This defect in the legislation was corrected to a certain degree in two subsequent judicial interpretations. In 1988, the Supreme Court issued the *Opinions on Several Issues Concerning the Implementation of the General Principles of the Civil Law (for Trial Implementation)*. This judicial interpretation stipulated two types of privacy-related tort, i.e., infringement of a citizen's right of portrait, and the act of unlawfully disclosing a citizen's private facts in oral, written, or other forms. In 1993, the Supreme Court promulgated the *Interpretation on Several Issues about the Trial of Cases Concerning the Right of Reputation*, of which Article 7 provides that acts of disclosing or disseminating a person's private materials without his consent shall be handled as an infringement of the right of reputation. This provision clearly includes the disclosure of private facts as an infringement of privacy. In 2009, the NPC Standing Committee passed the *Tort Liability Law*, of which Article 2 explicitly stipulates that privacy is a civil right and the invasion of one's privacy shall bear tort liability. This means that privacy as a fundamental human right has been officially written into Chinese law.

In accordance with Chinese criminal law, anyone who intentionally violates others' right to privacy and thereby causes serious consequences shall be criminally punished. Specifically, Article 245 of the *Criminal Law* states that "a person who unlawfully subjects another person to a bodily search or a search of his residence or unlawfully intrudes into another person's residence shall be sentenced to a fixed term of imprisonment of not more than three years or criminal detention"; Article 252 provides that "a person who conceals, destroys or unlawfully opens another person's letters, thus infringing upon the citizen's right to freedom of correspondence, shall be sentenced to a fixed term of imprisonment of not more than one year or criminal detention if the circumstance is serious"; and Article 253 stipulates that "a postal worker who opens, conceals or destroys mail or telegrams without authorization shall be sentenced to a fixed term of imprisonment of not more than two years or criminal detention." This shows that China's criminal law mainly focuses on preventing a citizen's residence and correspondence from being trespassed on or intruded into, while many other serious invasions of privacy have not yet been criminalized.

Chinese procedure law also provides protection for citizens' right to privacy. Article 152 of the *Criminal Procedure Law* clearly stipulates that cases of first instance in a court shall be heard in public, but cases involving citizens' private affairs shall not be heard in public. In a similar vein, Article 120 of the *Civil Procedure Law* provides that civil cases in a court shall be heard in public but civil cases involving citizens' private affairs shall not be heard in public; Article 66 provides that evidence shall be presented in the court and cross-examined by the parties but evidence that involves citizens' private affairs shall not be presented in an open court session. As far as the *Administrative Procedure Law* is concerned, Article 45 states that administrative cases in a court shall be tried in public, but those that involve the private affairs of individuals shall be an exception. Article 30 proposes that a lawyer who serves as an agent may consult materials pertaining to the case, and may also investigate among, and collect evidence from, relevant individuals and organizations; if the information involves individuals' private affairs, he shall keep it confidential; and the involved parties may consult the materials relating to the court proceedings of the case, but shall not consult the involved individuals' private affairs.

Other Chinese laws, such as the *Administrative Reconsideration Law*, the *Administrative Punishment Law*, the *Law on the Protection of Minors*, the *Law on the Protection of Women's Rights and Interests*, the *Law on the Protection of Disabled Persons*, the *Law on the Protection of Rights and Interests of the Aged*, and the *Law on the Protection of Consumers' Rights and Interests* have also provided protection for privacy. All of the above-mentioned laws provide a framework for us to understand China's protection of privacy in cyberspace. The next section will explore how these laws are used to deal with the issue of Internet privacy.

Invasion of privacy claims

American legal scholar William L. Prosser divided all cases concerning invasion of privacy into four categories: (1) "appropriation, for the defendant's advantage, of the plaintiff's name or likeness"; (2) "intrusion upon the plaintiff's seclusion or solitude, or into his private affairs"; (3) "public disclosure of embarrassing private facts about the plaintiff"; and (4) "publicity which places the plaintiff in a false light in the public eye."[4] The four categories of invasion of privacy have been adopted by U.S. tort law, and by most of U.S. state laws. In China, the first category involves the issue of infringing on one's rights to name and portrait, which have been individually protected by law. In fact, the right to personal name and portrait is closely related to the right to privacy, so that the former is discussed as an integral part of the latter in this chapter. The second and third categories are widely recognized as invasion of privacy by Chinese law, and so both of them are examined in detail in this chapter. The last category is often treated as an infringement of reputation, which has already been covered in Chapter 3.

Appropriation

Appropriation of name or portrait occurs when a person uses the name or portrait of another person without permission and for personal gain or commercial purposes. In China, Article 99 of the *General Principles of the Civil Law* provides that citizens shall have the right of personal name and shall be entitled to determine, use, or change their personal names in accordance with relevant provisions. Article 100 provides that citizens shall have the right of portrait, and the use of a citizen's portrait for profit without his consent shall be prohibited. These articles arguably recognize appropriation of name or portrait as a form of invasion of privacy.

Appropriation of name

A name is a word or a symbol by which a person is commonly and distinctively known. The right of name refers to a citizen's right to choose, use, and change his name. The *General Principles of the Civil Law* prohibits interference with, usurpation of, and false representation of personal names, which can be viewed as three forms of appropriation of names. Interference herein refers to the act of interfering with another person's choosing and use of his names, which can be real name, pseudonyms, and stage names. Usurpation of personal names refers to the act of using another person's name without his consent. False representation refers to the act of engaging in economic and civil activities in the name of others. All these acts are conducted without the consent of the name holder, and probably for commercial benefit.

Case 4.1   The Luo Caixia case: appropriation of personal name[5]

An influential case involving appropriation of personal name is the Luo Caixia case. In 2004, Luo Caixia of Shaodong County, Hunan Province failed to enter college after the college entrance examination, but her classmate Wang Jiajun was admitted to Guizhou Normal University under her name. Luo studied for another year and then enrolled in Tianjin Normal University. She was supposed to graduate in 2009. Since her name had been appropriated, however, she encountered a series of problems with graduation, and her certificate of qualification as a teacher was also cancelled. The court found that Wang's father was a senior official at the Police Department of Shaodong County and he had unlawfully managed to get his daughter into college under Luo's name. The case was eventually mediated. Both Wang and her father were required to bear tort liability. Luo also graduated successfully with her teaching certificate.

In addition, Chinese civil law provides protection for enterprise names equal to that provided for personal names. Like individuals, enterprises are also entitled to choose, use, and change their names. However, commentators point out that the protection of personal names should be treated differently from the protection of enterprise names. The purpose of protecting personal names is to ensure that a citizen's personal rights cannot be infringed, while the purpose of protecting enterprise names is to preserve an enterprise's economic interests and also to maintain fair competition. The right of personal name essentially concerns the protection of citizens' privacy, and the right of enterprise name is mainly to do with the protection of intellectual property rights, which will be covered in detail in Chapter 5.

Appropriation of portrait

Portrait refers to a likeness of a person that is created by a photographer, painter, or sculptor and fixed on certain materials such as photographic paper, paper, wood, stone, mud, and electronic media. One important feature of a portrait is its distinctiveness. A person is often distinctively recognized according to his portrait, especially his facial image. Thus, as long as an image or picture can help to distinguish one person's appearance from another person's, it should be considered a portrait.[6] Another feature of portrait is its exclusivity. A portrait directly originates from a particular person. No matter where he is, whether he is still alive, or whether he has assigned his portrait to another person for ownership purposes, he is always the subject of his portrait. Nobody can transform the subject of his portrait into that of another person.[7] The third feature of portrait is its property value. A portrait can be produced, used, sold, or transferred for economic profit. This is particularly evident for the portraits of celebrities, which often have a high market value.

The right of portrait mainly refers to the right of a citizen to produce and use his portrait. The right to produce means that a citizen has the right to produce his portrait according to his will, including the right to determine whether and how to produce his portrait, and who can produce his portrait and who cannot. Similarly, the right to use means that a citizen has the right to use his portrait according to his will, including the right to determine whether and how to use his portrait, and who can use his portrait and who cannot. It should be noted that currently only the right to use a portrait is protected by Chinese civil law.

Article 100 of the *General Principles of the Civil Law* clearly stipulates that the use of a citizen's portrait for profit without his consent shall be prohibited. In other words, an invasion of a citizen's right of portrait consists of two elements: one is to use his portrait without permission, and the other is to use his portrait for profit. While it is easy to determine the first element, it is relatively hard to identify the second. In judicial practice, whether the defendant intends to pursue economic profit by appropriation of the plaintiff's portrait is often a key factor in determining whether or not the defendant's act constitutes a tort. The most commonplace appropriation of portrait occurs in marketing activities. Focusing on this problem, Article 130 of the *Opinions of the Supreme People's Court on Several Issues Concerning the Implementation of the General Principles of the Civil Law (for Trial Implementation)* mandates that using one's portrait to produce advertisements, trademarks, window dressing, etc. for profit without his consent shall be considered an infringement of his right of portrait (Case 4.2).

Case 4.2 *Zhuo Xiaohong* v. *Sun Dexi and Chongqing Dairy Product Company*: infringement of right of portrait[8]

A representative case in this regard is *Zhuo Xiaohong* v. *Sun Dexi and Chongqing Dairy Product Company*. Defendant Sun was a photographer working for a photography company. In April 1983, he took a photo of the plaintiff, based on their agreement that the photo would be used only as a sample inside the sales counter. Without the plaintiff's permission, however, Sun and Chongqing Dairy Product Company later edited the picture and used it as a trademark for the company's bottled products. The plaintiff therefore filed a lawsuit for portrait infringement. The court ruled that the two defendants had used the plaintiff's portrait for commercial purposes without the plaintiff's permission, thus infringing on the plaintiff's right of portrait. The court determined that defendant Chongqing Diary Product Company should immediately stop using the trademark and pay the plaintiff compensation of 300 yuan for economic loss; and defendant Sun compensated the plaintiff 150 yuan for economic loss.

It should be pointed out that using a citizen's portrait for matters of public interest is not regarded as an infringement in China. This includes at least the following situations: (1) using a citizen's portrait for protecting his own interest. For example, public security organs publicizing and disseminating the portrait of a lost child; (2) using a citizen's portrait for protecting public interests. For example, public security organs using the portrait of a criminal in a "wanted" poster, judicial organs taking pictures of criminal suspects for the compilation of relevant evidence, and university professors using the portraits of other people in their research and teaching activities; and (3) using a citizen's portrait in news coverage. In many cases, news articles inevitably involve the use of others' portraits. As long as such use is related to the content of news and is beneficial to society, it does not constitute any tort. Some kinds of news report do not concern public welfare but can attract public attention, such as reports about entertainment and sports celebrities. Due to the ambiguity of the concept of public interest, these kinds of report can easily spark off controversy and lead to lawsuits.[9]

Appropriation in cyberspace

The rapid development of the Internet and related information technology has imposed new challenges on the protection of citizens' rights of portrait and name. For instance, many Internet users post pictures of their friends or favorite public figures on their own home pages or blogs without permission. Does this infringe upon the portrait right of those people? As discussed above, an infringement of the right of portrait must meet both of the following two conditions: one is "without consent"; the other is "for commercial use." As long as one of the conditions is not met, it does not constitute infringement. This leads to the conclusion that if Internet users do not use others' images for commercial purposes, they shall not be subject to an infringement charge. The question is how to define the commercial use of Internet activities. For example, posting film stars' portraits on personal online space may not generate direct income, but it may help to increase the popularity of the space among Internet users, which can eventually lead to social or economic gain. In this situation, portraits are used indirectly for commercial purposes, and they are often uploaded without permission. If this kind of action is considered as an infringement, the circulation of public figures' images in cyberspace will be significantly limited, and the advantage of openness inherent to the Internet will not be fully realized. One possible solution is to provide a strict definition of the scope of "commercial use." It has been proposed that a portrait can be considered for "commercial use" only when it is used directly for commercial purposes. In cyberspace, many people in fact post others' portraits for non-commercial purposes, but they may still risk infringing on others' rights. This may occur when the owner of the portrait asks the poster to delete the picture for reasons of privacy, but the poster refuses to do so.

Under Article 36 of the *Tort Liability Law*, Internet users or Internet service providers (ISPs) should bear tortious liability in the event that they infringe upon the civil rights or interests of an individual through the Internet. This provision confirms that Internet users or Internet service providers should not post others' portraits online for commercial profit without their consent; otherwise they will be subject to an infringement charge. Article 36 states that where an Internet user engages in tortious conduct through the Internet, the injured party shall have the right to notify the ISP and request that it take necessary measures. Where an ISP fails to promptly take necessary measures after being notified, it shall be jointly and severally liable with the Internet user for additional damage. Therefore, if a citizen asks an ISP to delete his picture which has been posted on the ISP's website by others, the ISP should act upon the request, no matter whether or not the posting is for commercial use; otherwise the ISP will be subject to tort liability. In addition, these two provisions of the *Tort Liability Law* basically apply to the protection of the right of name. No one is allowed to infringe on the right of a citizen's name; and ISPs must take effective measures in a timely manner when they are informed of infringing activities on their websites.

Case 4.3   *Zhao Benshan* v. *Hainan Tianya Company and Google China Company*: infringement of right of portrait[10]

In May 2009, Hainan Tianya Company and Google China Company released a flash ad on the website Tianya Community to promote their joint web-based product Tianyan Q&A. This ad used a cartoon portrait of Chinese comedy star Zhao Benshan without Zhao's consent. Zhao sued both companies for infringing on his right of portrait. The court found that, without Zhao's consent, Hainan Tianya and Google China had publicized a cartoon image that was highly similar to Zhao's portrait, as well as a complementary narrative from *No Lack of Money*, which came directly from Zhao's performance work. The court held that as long as a cartoon portrait can distinguish a person's appearance from that of others, it should enjoy equal protection to that enjoyed by a portrait. In this case, Hainan Tianya had used Zhao's cartoon image for commercial purposes without his permission, thus infringing upon Zhao's right of portrait; Google China was mainly engaged in technical support for the website involved. It was not at fault, so it did not assume tort liability. The court determined that defendant Hainan Tianya should cease its infringing activities and publish a statement of apology in "Tianya Community," and pay plaintiff Zhao compensation of 120,000 yuan for economic loss.

Intrusion on seclusion

Intrusion on seclusion refers to the intentional interference with a person's solitude or private concerns in a manner that would be highly offensive to a reasonable person. The intrusion may be physical, such as entering unlawfully into someone's property, or technological, such as using a miniature camera. Intrusion is arguably an information gathering tort; legal wrong occurs at the time of intrusion; no publication is required.[11] The purpose of the intrusion tort is "to preserve individuals' dignity by preventing unwanted encroachment into their physical space and private affairs."[12]

A typical intrusion is to trespass, steal, or intrude by electronic means into the precincts of another's home. Chinese criminal law stipulates that anyone who unlawfully intrudes into another's home may commit a crime. Chinese administrative law provides that intrusions which are insufficient to constitute a crime may be subject to administrative penalty. According to early Chinese civil law, the home is a type of property, and the freedom of the home should be protected by property law. Under modern civil law, however, the home is considered a private living space, and so it should be protected by privacy law. In terms of property law, intruding into another's home usually causes little actual damage to property, and so the legal remedies awarded to the victim could be negligible. Under privacy law, the victim could claim mental anguish compensation, thus obtaining much more and better remedies. Commentators thus argue that the change to privacy law protection against intrusion into one's home signifies the increasing respect of Chinese law for personal dignity; it also reflects the development of Chinese legal culture.[13]

With the progress of human society, the protection of privacy has expanded from the home to public space. Commentators point out that when a person appears in public he is assumed to give up some of his privacy. Thus, taking a picture of a person in a public meeting cannot be considered an invasion of his privacy. Even in public space, however, a person has not completely abandoned his privacy, such as his bodily secrecy and private activities in public places.[14] For instance, it is not permitted to put a camera in public toilets or in the fitting rooms of clothing stores. It is thus argued that citizens can have claims to privacy even in public space, as long as such expectation of privacy is reasonable.

The emergence of the Internet has given rise to the concept of private cyberspace, which refers to the private space that is built on computers or cell phones, has functionality for information storage and exchange, and remains subject to human control.[15] This so-called private cyberspace includes but is not limited to the computer memory of end users and the server space of ISPs that are used or occupied by Internet users, such as personal websites, home pages, blogs, and online accounts.[16] From 2006 to 2007, China witnessed a nationwide prevalence of two computer viruses, Worm Nimaya and Grey Dove, which unlawfully intruded into the virtual space of millions of Internet users. The chief reason for the frequency of illegal invasion of private cyberspace arguably is that China has not yet established an effective legal system to curb it. Commentators have proposed that China should acknowledge the legal existence of private cyberspace so that the privacy law on traditional "physical space" can be expanded to people's activities in cyberspace. In other words, both kinds of space, physical and virtual, if private by nature, should enjoy the equal protection of privacy law.[17] The intentional intrusion into an Internet user's cyberspace without authorization should constitute infringement of his right of privacy.

Another important intrusion on seclusion is to infringe upon a citizen's freedom and privacy of correspondence. Freedom of correspondence refers to the right of a citizen to correspond with others through all kinds of communication tools. Any organization or individual should not interfere with the exercise of this right, unless the interference is in accordance with the law. Interference herein includes such acts as seizing, concealing, or destroying others' letters; or interfering with the use of communication tools by others. Privacy of communication means that the content of a citizen's correspondence by letter, telephone, telegram, teletypewriter exchange, e-mail, or other tools should be private. Any organization or individual should neither unlawfully open others' letters, telegrams or teletypewriter exchanges, nor eavesdrop on or record others' phone conversations, unless this is performed in accordance with the law. An offender who infringes on others' freedom and privacy of correspondence shall bear tort liability; if the circumstance is serious, he may be subject to criminal liability.

In cyberspace, the matter of infringement upon citizens' freedom and privacy of correspondence is becoming increasingly complicated. For instance, a hacker may use various technological means to steal, change, or destroy the personal information of Internet users, while the injured party can almost never discover the identity of the hacker. An ISP may transfer or close its customers' e-mail accounts, thus causing the loss of customers' e-mails and the disclosure of personal privacy or commercial secrets. What is more, some network owners or administrators may intentionally monitor the computers and e-mail systems operating in local area networks through network centers.[18] All these actions constitute serious infringement of the privacy of Internet users. China has therefore extended the traditional protection for personal correspondence to people's online communication. The *Administrative Measures for Safeguarding the Safety of International Connecting of Computer Information Networks*, enacted in 1997, stipulates that no organization or individual may use the Internet to violate a citizen's freedom and privacy of correspondence. The *Telecommunication Regulations of the PRC*, enacted in 2000, reaffirms protection for the freedom and privacy of telecommunications users, which includes Internet users. Under this law, such acts as deliberately prying into others' correspondence, intruding into others' personal files, or changing/destroying others' data all constitute invasion of privacy. The infringing parties may be Internet users (Case 4.4); they may also be ISPs.

Case 4.4 *Xue Yange* v. *Zhang Nan*: freedom and privacy of e-mail correspondence[19]

China saw its first case of infringement of the freedom and privacy of correspondence via e-mail in 1996. Both plaintiff Xue Yange and defendant Zhang Nan were graduate students in the psychology department of Beijing University. In April 1996, Xue received an e-mail from the University of Michigan informing her that she was being offered a full scholarship to study at its school of education. Upon learning this, defendant Zhang sent a reply to the sender in the name of Xue without her knowledge, stating that plaintiff Xue had decided to turn down the scholarship. Xue thus lost a precious opportunity to further her studies in the United States. In June 1996, Xue filed a lawsuit against Zhang for infringing on her right of name. After mediation, the plaintiff was awarded a certain amount of economic compensation. Although this case was filed for the violation of a citizen's right of name, the infringed object was in fact a citizen's freedom and privacy of correspondence.

In almost all cases, permission is the only defense for intrusion lawsuits. Newsworthiness is not a defense because publishing is not an element of the tort. If the victim permits the offender to collect and disseminate his personal information online, then the offender will not bear any civil liability. The permission should reflect the victim's will, rather than being obtained by force or deception. In addition, permission can be implied. So if a reporter enters a private property and the property owner responds to the reporter's questions, this implies that the interview can proceed.[20]

Spamming

The development of the Internet brings a unique, destructive, and recurring means of intrusion into others' privacy, namely, e-mail spam. According to a survey by the Internet Society of China, from August 2004 to April 2005, Chinese netizens received an average of 16.8 unsolicited e-mails per week; spam e-mails constituted 60.87% of the total number of e-mails they received. China is one of the countries that are most affected by junk e-mail. Responding to this problem, the MIIT promulgated the *Administrative Measures for Electronic Mail Services* (hereinafter referred to as the *Measure*) in 2006. This is an administrative regulation but has arguably paved the way for the future enactment of an anti-spam law by the NPC.

The targets of the *Measure* mainly include senders of e-mail, e-mail service providers, and Internet access providers. This is partially identified in Article 2: the *Measure* shall apply to the provision of Internet e-mail services as well as the provision of access services to Internet e-mail services and the transmission of Internet e-mails within the territory of mainland China. The term "Internet e-mail services" herein refers to the activities of establishing Internet e-mail servers to provide tools for Internet users to send and receive Internet e-mails. One major goal of the *Measure* is to enhance the protection of citizens' privacy of communication. As Article 3 provides, citizens' privacy of correspondence in using e-mail services shall be protected by law. Unless a procuratorial organ or a public security organ is making a legal inspection of the content of correspondence for the purposes of national security or crime investigation, no organization or individual shall infringe upon any citizen's privacy of correspondence on any pretext.

In the view of Chinese law makers, strengthening the administration of e-mail services can be the first step in fighting spam on the Internet. The *Measure* includes: (a) establishment of a permit system for e-mail services. Article 4 of the *Measure* stipulates that whoever intends to provide e-mail services shall obtain a permit for operating value-added telecommunication businesses or go through the record-filing procedure for operating non-commercial Internet services in advance. Without such a permit or record-filing, no organizations or individuals shall provide Internet e-mail services; (b) establishing an IP registration system for e-mail services. Article 6 states that the government is taking the registration-based measure of administering the IP address of ISPs' e-mail servers, asking ISPs to register the IP addresses of their e-mail servers with the MIIT or its local subordinates in advance; (c) strengthening the security settings for e-mail services. Article 7 provides that Internet e-mail service providers shall build up an Internet e-mail service system according to the technical standards of the MIIT, cancel the anonymous forwarding functionality of the e-mail server, and strengthen the safety administration of the e-mail service system; and (d) specifying the obligations of e-mail service providers to their users. Article 8 prescribes that e-mail service providers shall clearly inform users of the contents of the services and rules for use. Furthermore, Article 9 stipulates that e-mail service providers have the obligation to keep confidential users' personal registered information and Internet e-mail addresses; no e-mail service provider or any of its employees is allowed to use or publicize any user's personal information without the consent of the user, unless otherwise prescribed by any law or administrative regulation.

There is no disagreement that spam should be prohibited, but the issue of how to define spam remains controversial. The *Measure* does not offer a definition of spam, but it suggests a list of actions that may be considered to be spamming. These include: sending to a recipient an e-mail containing commercial advertising content without the recipient's clear consent; not marking "advertisement" or "AD" in the title of an e-mail that contains commercial advertising content; and continuing to send e-mails containing commercial advertising content to a recipient who initially consents to receive such e-mails but later declines to continue receiving them. In addition to unsolicited e-mails with commercial advertising content, the *Measure* also prescribes the following actions as spamming: intentionally concealing or forging such important sender information as the sender's e-mail address; using another person's computer system to send e-mails without his authorization; selling, using, sharing, or disseminating another person's e-mail address that has been obtained by automatic online collection, arbitrary alphabetical/ digital combination, or other means; creating, reproducing, publishing, or disseminating e-mails that contain unlawful or harmful content as stipulated by relevant laws; and using e-mails to engage in activities endangering network safety or information safety and prohibited by relevant laws.

Commentators argue that while the *Measure* provides a set of operational standards for identifying and fighting spam, it confuses e-mails that contain unlawful content with e-mails that contain commercial advertising content. The former are directly prohibited by law, while the latter may sometimes be welcomed by consumers. According to the *Measure*, all commercial e-mails sent to a recipient without his consent will be considered spam. The problem is that some commercial e-mails may be exactly what a recipient wants to see and receive. Therefore, it is argued that whether or not an e-mail is spam should be determined by the recipient, i.e., only e-mails sent to a recipient against his wishes can be considered spam.[21] This does not mean that the recipient can freely accuse the sender of sending spam. The recipient must provide proof that the sender deliberately sent the commercial e-mail against the recipient's wishes. Under the *Measure*, any organization or individual who sends spam will be subject to administrative or criminal punishment (Case 4.5).

Case 4.5   Administrative punishment for sending spam e-mail[22]

In August 2006, the Guangdong Communication Administration found that a company was sending bulk e-mails that contained commercial advertising content to a considerable number of Internet users. This regulatory agency therefore implemented administrative punishment pursuant to the *Administrative Measures for Internet Email Services*, ordering the company to immediately stop sending spam and also to pay a fine of 5,000 yuan.

However, spam is increasingly being regarded as a tort, particularly as an infringement of others' privacy. As discussed above, the real problem with spam is that the offender sends messages to the recipient's private cyberspace (i.e. e-mail box) against his wishes. Subjectively, the offender forces the recipient to read the e-mails, so he is infringing on the recipient's right of correspondence; objectively, the unsolicited e-mails occupy the space of the recipient's e-mail box, and the recipient has to spend time deleting those e-mails, thus leading to loss of time and money.[23] Due to these factors, in China a person who sends spam is now more likely to bear tort liability.

Disclosure of private facts

Disclosure of private facts arises where one person publicizes truthful private information that is not of legitimate public concern, and the release of which would be highly offensive to a reasonable person.[24] The tort of private facts aims at protecting a citizen's dignity and peace of mind by discouraging the publication of intimate facts.[25] Unlike defamation, truth is not a defense for invasion of privacy. If private facts are publicized, the victim may receive monetary compensation for the resulting emotional injury.

Private facts

The key consideration in a disclosure of private facts lawsuit is whether the matter being publicized is public or private. If the matter is one of public concern, there is no invasion of privacy. However, if the matter is not one of public concern, and it is one that people would find offensive, there is an invasion of privacy. In reality, "there are many facts a person wants to keep private simply because they are not for public knowledge."[26] Private facts suits can relate to a person's sexual information, domestic difficulties, medical information, financial condition, and similar facts.

"Sex" is private by nature. Publicizing a person's sexual activities, sexual organs, sexual features, sexual psychology, sexual habits, and sexual defects through text or image often constitutes an invasion of privacy. In addition, when reporting sex crimes or sexual harassment, the reporter usually should not disclose the victim's name, identity, address, and other identifying information; otherwise, he may invade the victim's privacy. Unethical practice in one's sexual life, such as adultery and extra-marital sex, should also be regarded as private, as long as such behavior does not cause harm to the public.[27]

Love, marriage, and family situations also fall within the scope of privacy and are legally prohibited from being disclosed (Case 4.6).

Case 4.6   Violation of right to privacy: the case of Mrs. Shi Liling[28]

An influential case in this regard involved Mrs. Shi Liling, who fell in love with Chiang Wei-kuo and had a son with him in 1937.[29] Later, Chiang went to Taiwan, while Shi stayed in mainland China and married another man. Her son with Chiang grew up and also worked in mainland China. In 1995, a book titled *The Secret History of the Chiang Family* published the romance between Shi and Chiang. This caused Mrs. Shi to file a lawsuit. She claimed that the book had disclosed her romance with Chiang without her consent, thus violating her privacy; in addition, the book's statement that she had died in the 1940s was seriously false and damaged her reputation. Her claim was supported by the court.

There are many other types of personal information viewed as private, such as an individual's names, photos, phone numbers, home address, savings and property status, health status, social relations, diaries, and other private information or files that the individual is unwilling to expose to the public. Such personal information has been protected by various laws. For instance, the *Statistics Law* stipulates that survey data concerning any private individual or his/her family should not be divulged. The *Commercial Banking Law* provides that commercial banks should adhere to the principles of voluntary deposit and confidentiality for their depositors. The *Lawyer Law* requires that a lawyer should not divulge the private affairs of the parties concerned in a case. The *Law on Medical Practitioners* requires that patients' private information shall not be divulged. In addition, the *Regulation on the Prevention and Treatment of HIV/AIDS* prescribes that any person or organization shall not disclose the personal information of patients or their families; such information includes the name, address, employment, photograph, medical history, and any information that may identify the person concerned.

In addition, crimes or other misconduct by a minor should also be treated as private facts. Under the *Minors Protection Law* and the *Criminal Procedure Law*, crimes committed by a minor shall not be tried publicly. Furthermore, the *Minors Protection Law* specifies that, with regard to cases involving a minor's crime, the name, home address, photos, and other identifying information of the minor may not be disclosed in news reports, films, TV programs, and in any other publicly circulated documents prior to the judgment. The *Prevention of Juvenile Delinquency Law* goes further and deletes the restrictive term "prior to the judgment," requiring that news reports, television programs, and other publications should not disclose the minor's name, address, photograph or any other information that can be used to discover the minor's identity. This shows that China's judicial protection for the privacy of minors is very strict, mainly in order to create a favorable environment for minors to grow up in.

Defenses

In Chinese judicial practice, most infringement of privacy cases concern the news media. As for defenses in such cases, China has formed the following mechanisms.

Consent

If a person has given his consent to the publication of the information concerned, this consent can be a defense for the media, even if the person later claims that his right to privacy was infringed. In other words, once the person has provided the information, or permitted its publication, the media shall bear no liability for invasion of privacy. However, the following three points should be considered: (a) the subject of the information should give explicit consent for the publication of his private information by news media. Disclosure to journalists, particularly in a private interview, does not equal permission for publication; (b) the person should voluntarily disclose the private information; disclosure under coercion or violence cannot serve as a valid defense; (c) a person only has the right to disclose his or her own private information. News reporting involving a third person's privacy must have the third person's consent; otherwise, it will constitute an invasion of the third person's privacy.[30]

Public records

If the information is obtained from public records, the publication of such information does not constitute an act of infringement. Public records refers to information already available to the public in the form of official documents, notifications, judgments, notices, etc. that are approved for publicity and reference by the Party and state organs. In such cases, the information has been so widely published as to destroy its confidentiality; the citation of such information will not constitute a breach of confidence. However, in closed-door hearings, even if there is a reference to relevant private information in the judgment, the right to privacy shall still be protected.[31]

Public places

Reporting on people in public places shall not be an act of infringement, for there is no expectation of privacy in such places. Once a person appears in a public place, he agrees, by default, to give up some rights to privacy; he shall therefore allow others to observe his demeanor, even to make audio and video recordings. Journalists are free to report on and take photos of traffic accidents, crimes, or even a public kiss. However, it should be noted that a person's rights to privacy are not completely denied in public spaces. Privacy should still be considered in terms of private space in public places, such as toilets in public places. Thus, *public places* as a defense bear restrictions; they are subject to being weighed by the judge on a case-by-case basis.[32]

Public interest

If personal information is somehow related to the public interest, it is no longer a private matter in a general sense, and thus is not subject to privacy protection. News coverage in such cases is, therefore, not an intrusion of privacy. For example, Chinese law generally does not protect private information concerning a crime. A criminal thus cannot claim for invasion of privacy by the media in matters of criminal fact. What is more, for people who have been implicated in a crime, such as the victim of the crime or the family of the criminal, their rights to privacy may also be partially restricted, due to the public interest aspect of the case.[33]

Public figures

Public figures refers to those people "who have assumed special prominence in the resolution of public issues or the character of public events."[34] Public figures can be government officials, writers, artists, film stars, sports stars, scientists, entrepreneurs, social activists, even criminals, defendants, or criminal suspects, and others who have entered the public spotlight. These people often become the focus of public attention and news coverage, and their privacy is much more limited than that of the average person. Therefore, news reports of their personal information do not constitute an invasion of privacy. However, this does not mean that public figures do not have any right to privacy. It is widely accepted that unlawful intrusion into their residences should be prohibited; surveillance or monitoring of their private and family lives should be prohibited; their marriage affairs should not be interfered in; their freedom of communication should not be restricted; and their activities and matters unrelated to the public interest should not be intervened in.

Online dissemination of private facts

Disseminating another person's private facts online without authorization is also considered as an infringement of privacy. However, infringement of privacy in cyberspace seems to be more complicated than in the context of traditional media. The infringer in the traditional media environment often has certain social relations with the infringed person, and is thus easily identified. In cyberspace, anyone can be the sender of information, but he can also be the receiver of information; anyone can be the victim, but he can also be the perpetrator; moreover, there may be no real social relations between the perpetrator and the victim.[35] The infringing parties include not only Internet users but also Internet service providers, and the courts often find it difficult to identify infringers. In addition, web-based communication is particularly rapid and open. This means that the consequences of invasion of privacy in cyberspace can be significant. If an infringement in cyberspace cannot be stopped in a timely manner, it may cause huge damage to the victim.

Based on the *Tort Liability Law* and relevant laws and regulations, where the victim finds that his personal privacy has been violated on the Internet, he has the right to request the related ISP to remove, block, or disconnect the links to the infringing information. If the ISP fails to take such necessary measures in a timely manner after being notified of the infringement, it should bear collateral responsibility for additional damage. A major consideration herein is that if an ISP is required to bear more responsibility, the development of the Internet industry and thus the dissemination of information may be hindered. The *Tort Liability Law* thus adopts the internationally prevailing "notice-delete" mode to protect people's privacy in cyberspace, while reducing the burden on service providers. However, the *Law* also stipulates that if an ISP knows that an infringement on privacy is occurring but fails to take necessary measures, it should still bear tort liability for additional damage. The remaining issue is that there should be a well-established standard for the definition of privacy, and that the standard can be understood and implemented by an ISP.

Case 4.7 Infringement of privacy in cyberspace: the case of "maritime woman"[36]

An influential case of privacy infringement in cyberspace concerns the nude pictures of a "maritime woman." Plaintiff Ms. Yin was a student of Shanghai Maritime University. She broke up with her boyfriend Mr. Zhu, who then uploaded a great deal of private (and even nude) pictures of the plaintiff to the Internet for purposes of revenge. The pictures were then accessible and searchable on Baidu.com, China's largest search engine. The plaintiff claimed that by June 2, 2009, the search engine Baidu.com had not taken any measures to deal with her private pictures; furthermore, its encyclopedia section dedicated a specific entry to her private information under the title of "maritime woman." The plaintiff thus sued Baidu.com for infringement of privacy. The defendant argued that it was functioning only as an index of information; it had not published or disseminated any of the plaintiff's information by itself; and moreover, it had disconnected the links to such information after receiving the plaintiff's complaint. The court determined that the defendant had dedicated an encyclopedia entry to the plaintiff's private information and also kept the infringing information, and so it should be liable for infringement of privacy.

Case 4.8   Infringement of privacy in cyberspace: the Edison Chen photo scandal[37]

Another case involves the scandal of Hong Kong actor Edison Chen's photo. In early 2008, a man named "Kira" distributed over the Internet hundreds of intimate and private photographs of Chen with various women, including actresses Gillian Chung, Bobo Chan, Rachel Ngan, and Cecilia Cheung. According to the investigation, the pictures were originally stored on Chen's laptop; when Chen took his laptop to be repaired, the pictures were illegally copied and then uploaded to the Internet. The scandal shook the Hong Kong entertainment industry and received high-profile media attention both locally and around the world. Following the scandal, the police arrested an IT professional who they suspected might have initially released Chen's sex pictures on the Internet. Later, Chen admitted publicly that the pictures disseminated on the

Internet were his, and apologized to all the actresses involved and to the public.

In terms of privacy protection in cyberspace, the Chen photo scandal raised the following critical issues: whether Chen had infringed on the privacy of the actresses when he took pictures of them; whether the computer repairmen had infringed on Chen's privacy; and whether the public who helped to spread Chen's sex pictures had infringed on the privacy between Chen and the actresses. It is argued that the first question mainly concerns whether the actresses agreed to be photographed or voluntarily assumed any possible risk. If they agreed or voluntarily assumed risk, Chen would not bear any infringement liability. The second question essentially involves the invasion of privacy in cyberspace. Chen had privacy rights over the pictures saved on his laptop, and he did not want the pictures to be viewed or copied by others. Therefore, commentators argue that the computer repairmen should be considered as having violated Chen's privacy. As for the third question, commentators hold that even if the victims in this case were public figures, such sex pictures had no public value, and so they should not be disclosed to the public. The key to determining whether the public had infringed the privacy of Chen and of the actresses was the scope of the dissemination of information. If a person had sent the pictures only to another person via e-mail, he would not be viewed as committing an infringement. If he had uploaded the pictures to a website or sent them to others via bulk e-mail, however, his acts would constitute infringement.

Specific online privacy issues

The rapid development of the Internet in China has generated a variety of privacy violation cases, and the corresponding establishment of related regulatory mechanisms. This section focuses on three specific online privacy issues: data collection, human-flesh searching, and data protection models.

Data collection

As society enters the information age, personal information is becoming increasingly valuable. It can bring the users of such information not only tangible economic benefits but also intangible social capital. Meanwhile, the development of the Internet makes it much easier for people to collect and use data. As long as the data are uploaded to the Internet they can, theoretically, be shared by all users of the resource. Indeed, online data collection has become a focus of public concern. Various business organizations, government agencies, and even individuals are trying to collect, process, and manage online data for commercial or other purposes. In practice, the most common ways to collect personal data via the Internet include the following.

The first way is to obtain personal data through user registration. When Internet users apply for online accounts, personal home pages, free e-mail, and other services, Internet service providers often require them to provide personal information, such as home address, e-mail address, age, phone numbers, credit card numbers, and work unit. While service providers can legally collect such information, they should be obliged to keep the information confidential. In late 2005, a website named UCLOO was publicly selling the personal information of 90 million people. This immediately became the focus of attention and criticism nationwide. China's media later disclosed that the personal information came from China's largest student portal site, 5460.net, which requires its registered users to provide the said information. After the incident, 5460.net claimed that it had not intentionally sold such information to UCLOO; instead, it was the vulnerability of the data management that had caused the disclosure of user information.[38]

The second way is obtain users' personal data is through cookies. This refers to a technology that allows the web server to store small amounts of data on a client's computer hard drive or memory, or to read data from a client's hard disks. It means that when a user visits a website, the web server may place a small text file on the user's hard disk; the text file is often used to record the user's ID, password, viewed pages, downloaded information, and other information related to the user's online activities. The web server can then use the information collected through cookies to build a large database. When the user again visits the site, the site will read the cookies, retrieve the user's previous information, and then make corresponding responses, such as allowing the user to log in without providing his ID and password. It is acknowledged that cookies may facilitate people's online activities. The problem is that cookies involve a great deal of personal information; once such information is stolen by or transferred to another person, it may constitute a violation of users' privacy. Therefore, some countries, such as Sweden, have legislation on cookies, requiring web servers to state the properties of cookies used and also to provide instructions on how to disable cookies.

The third way is to use search engines to collect information. A search engine is a website that specializes in providing searching services; it automatically searches for and processes information available on the Internet. The results are presented in the form of an information database and an index database. With these databases, the search engine then responds to different requests and provides the needed information. The searching methods include full-text search, keyword search, and classification search. Among these, the most popular and effective method is keyword-based retrieval. Users type in keywords and then give a search command; the engine will find all information containing the keywords in its database and display a list of hyperlinks for the search results. According to a report released by the China Internet Network and Information Center (CNNIC) in 2006, over 30% of cyber-users surveyed used search engines to search for their own names. Among these users, nearly 30% succeeded in finding their personal information, which could be phone number, address, e-mail address, and other private information. Such information was often stored in and retrieved from personal blogs, podcasts, alumni databases, online forums, and other sources.

Finally, personal data can be obtained via information collecting devices installed in computer software or placed in hardware. For instance, Intel has included the processor serial number (PSN) in its new processors. A PSN is a series number that is used to identify the user of the computer concerned; indeed, it is often used to monitor the information received or sent by the user. Intel claimed that this effort was to enhance e-commerce security. But critics pointed out that, due to the uniqueness of a PSN, a person who is using a processor with a PSN installed is in fact inviting Intel to track and monitor all of his online activities. A similar problem has also occurred with Qihoo 360, a leading Internet security software company in China. Many users accused this company of using its software to collect clients' private information without authorization. According to a media report, for example, a user was recorded 268 times in 23 of the company's logs from December 8 to 26, 2010. All the activities of this user, such as visiting QQ space, downloading software, and watching online movies, had been recorded in great detail; moreover, all online buyers' names, mail boxes, phone numbers, delivery destinations, delivery fees, order quantities, order times, and so on had all been recorded with great precision.[39]

From the perspective of privacy protection, the concerned person has the right to control his private information. It means that he can choose whether and how to use or process his private information. Without legal authorization, any individual, business organization, or government agency has no right to collect, process, and administer others' personal information. With the popularization of computers and the development of Internet technology, however, the gathering of private information is becoming easier than ever before. In particular, Internet service providers are able to access a huge amount of personal data about their users. Indeed, all the online activities of an Internet user may be subject to direct or indirect monitoring by his service providers without his knowledge. Furthermore, the collected data may be used for commercial purposes or against the interests of the information owner. According to Chinese law, any people or parties who breach others' right to privacy should bear relevant civil and even criminal liability.

Case 4.9   Protection of online privacy: the Qihoo 360 and Tencent QQ dispute[40]

The dispute between Qihoo 360 and Tencent QQ occurred in 2010. In essence, the dispute was about identifying, collecting, and protecting private information through software. In February 1999, Tencent, one of the largest Internet companies in China, introduced Tencent QQ, which has become the most popular instant messaging tool in China. As of July 11, 2011, active user accounts for QQ instant messaging totaled 812.3 million.[41] However, many users accused Tencent of privacy infringement for scanning personal data stored in their hard drive on a large scale. Users also raised doubts about QQ's recording and monitoring of their chat and other online activities, and its right to ban their online accounts. Qihoo is the largest security software company in China. In July 2006, the company released the anti-virus software 360 Safeguard. About one year later, 200 million people were using this software.[42]

In September 2010, Qihoo released Qihoo 360 Privacy Protector and Qihoo Koukou Guard, claiming that these new products could be used to protect the privacy of QQ users. Qihoo declared on its official website that Qihoo 360 Privacy Protector can expose any spyware installed on users' computers. As for Qihoo Koukou Guard, it could provide comprehensive protection for QQ users, including preventing QQ from scanning users' hard drives, preventing QQ accounts from being hacked, disabling unnecessary plug-ins, closing QQ ads, deleting temporary files, deleting QQ-related products such as QQ Media, and so on. It also promised that Koukou Guard would not modify any default QQ settings, so that users would be able to determine the settings for all functions. A few days later, Tencent responded with the rebuttal that QQ did not breach users' privacy, and alleged that Qihoo was defaming QQ by conducting an unfair competition.

A core issue of the dispute was how to define online privacy. To sign up for a QQ account, users are required to agree to such terms as the following: "We will ask you to provide your identifying information or allow us to contact you … personal information collected by Tencent is usually limited to your name, gender, age, birthday, ID number, address, educational level, employer, occupation, hobbies and so on." According to these terms, the information related to users' online activities will not be considered private, and can be collected, processed, and used by the website without users' consent. This is what caused the dispute in which Qihoo 360 charged QQ with privacy infringement but QQ denied any such charge.

As the situation was getting worse, Tencent issued a letter to QQ users, stating that it would stop providing services to those users who were using any of Qihoo 360's software. In other words, users had to choose between Qihoo 360 or QQ. In response, on the next day Qihoo released an open letter announcing the withdrawal 360 Koukou Guard.

The battle between the two companies continued for several weeks. In the end, the Chinese government stepped into the dispute. It ordered Tencent to stop asking users to make a choice between QQ and Qihoo 360, while requiring Qihoo to withdraw its 360 Koukou Guard. Commentators argue that this dispute revealed the fragility of the current laws for protection of people's online privacy and their right to choose services, thus calling for an intensification of efforts to protect the rights of Internet users.

Human-flesh searching

In recent years, Chinese Internet users have created the so-called human-flesh search engine. The searching method is so called because it makes use of human power to filter information that is available online. This is fundamentally different from traditional machine-driven engines such as Google and Baidu. Human-flesh searching first appeared on mop.com, a social networking site. On this site, a user can pose questions and reward the answers with mp—a virtual currency of the site. When another user sees the post, he may actively look for clues. If he succeeds, he will post his findings and claim a reward. This process is called human-flesh searching. When hundreds and even thousands of Internet users work together to collect information about a specific person, using various methods, almost everything about that person may soon be revealed.[43]

Since its inception, human-flesh searching has become a highly controversial issue. Opponents believe that such searching disrespects the privacy of the people concerned and is an abuse of freedom of speech. Moreover, the participants in the searching process may become Internet mobs who may violate state laws and rob the searched-for person of his dignity. Many Chinese are therefore opposed to human-flesh search engines. According to a survey by *China Youth Daily*, nearly two-thirds (64.6%) of the interviewees agreed that human-flesh searching may infringe on people's right to privacy and deprives people of their sense of safety. This has been confirmed by many real cases (Cases 4.10 and 4.11).

Cases 4.10 and 4.11   Two instances of abuse of human-flesh searching

In June 2010, Ping Qijun, deputy director of Jiangxi Flood Control and Drought Relief Office, failed to give a direct answer to questions about "the safety of the people living in the down-stream" in a CCTV interview; he instead repeated "the important instructions" of officials at higher levels. Ping was criticized on the Internet for speaking in a bureaucratic tone, and a human-flesh search campaign was then launched against him. Soon, personal information concerning Ping's family, spouse, and son was made public. His family information was dug up to such an extent that his son dared not go to school.[44]

A similar case happened on December 27, 2007, when CCTV broadcast a news item about curbing violence and pornography in cyberspace.[45] In the news item, a Beijing student named Zhang Shufan spoke to the reporter, and stated: "Last time when I was surfing the Internet, a window popped out all of a sudden, and it was very pornographic and very violent. I closed the window immediately." After the news was broadcast, many posts appeared on the Internet, attacking Zhang's comment "very pornographic and very violent." Some posts even used pornographic cartoon figures to make insinuations against Zhang. These two cases show that although the human-flesh search engine can be a useful tool for aggregating information, it can also be abused, and escalate into Internet violence.

Advocates of human-flesh searching argue that it is an effective tool for people to exercise freedom of speech and supervision of public opinion. The subjects of human-flesh searching are often wrongdoers, or events against social norms or state laws. To some extent, it provides a platform for people to freely express their opinions and vent their anger. Commentators thus argue that human-flesh searching, when properly used, can promote social progress and protect the public interest (Case 4.12).

Case 4.12　The case of Zhou Jiugeng: a typical human-flesh searching case[46]

A typical case concerns Zhou Jiugeng, director of Real Estate Administrative Bureau of Jiangning District in Nanjing. On December 10, 2010, Zhou appeared on TV, saying that real estate developers were selling houses below cost, and so they would soon be investigated. Zhou's claim deeply enraged those citizens who were plagued by soaring house prices. A human-flesh search campaign was then launched against Zhou and received an immediate response. One post revealed that the cigarette Zhou was seen smoking at a public meeting was worth 1,500 yuan, which was equal to three months' allowances for a laid-off worker. Another post said that the watch Zhou wore was a Vacheron Constantin that cost 100,000 yuan. Some even disclosed that Zhou's younger brother was a real estate developer and Zhou's son was a vendor of building materials. All of this personal information was exposed to the public and later proved to be true. Within one month, Zhou was removed from office and subjected to a judicial investigation. On October 10, 2010, the court decided that Zhou was guilty of accepting bribes, sentenced him to 11 years in prison, and confiscated his illegal property of 1.2 million yuan.

Whether human-flesh searching should be legally allowed is a rather complex issue. Commentators argue that an important factor in determining the legitimacy of human-flesh searching is whether or not it involves the public interest. They hold that where the person or event being searched relates to the public interest, human-flesh searching should be allowed; otherwise, it should not be allowed. According to this principle, an action of maliciously launching human-flesh searching on the basis of purely private issues constitutes a breach of privacy, and the victims have the right to request the offender to assume legal liability. In addition, commentators point out that human-flesh searching often involves multiple parties, including the search initiators, the information providers, the participants in the discussion, and the Internet service providers; and different parties should bear different liability. This has been shown in the case of *Wang Fei* v. *Zhang Yile, Daqi.com, and Tianya.com* (Case 4.13).

Case 4.13   *Wang Fei* v. *Zhang Yile, Daqi.com, and Tianya.com*: China's first human-flesh searching case[47]

On December 29, 2007, Jiang Yan, 31, killed herself by jumping from the 24th floor of an apartment building. Her suicide was arguably caused by the infidelity of her husband. Later, Jiang's college classmate Zhang Yile opened a website called Migratory Bird Flying Northward (http://orionchris.cn), claiming it to be a place to pay tribute to and seek justice for Jiang. Jiang's relatives and friends and numerous netizens began publishing articles about the event on Zhang's website. These articles were then republished by two mainstream websites, Daqi.com and Tianya. com. In these articles, Jiang's husband, Wang Fei, became the focus of public criticism and even the subject of a hate campaign. Exhausted by this harassment, Wang sued Zhang, Daqi.com, and Tianya.com at a local court. It was the first case in China related to human-flesh searching.

The court held that, under Chinese marriage law, a husband and a wife should be faithful to each other. Plaintiff Wang's confession in the court and the consensus between Wang and Jiang's parents proved Wang's infidelity. Also, Jiang's diary proved that she had suffered a tremendous trauma in consequence of the infidelity. The plaintiff's infidelity did not violate state law, but it was against social norms. The court thus condemned Wang for his infidelity.

The court also held that defendant Zhang had intentionally disclosed the plaintiff's affair, name, employer, and other personal information on the Internet. The disclosure had led to large-scale human-flesh searching for the plaintiff's identity; and the search had eventually escalated into an intensive, long-lasting personal attack against the plaintiff and his family. The court found that the influence of the disclosure had gone beyond virtual space, as the plaintiff and his parents had been personally harassed and defamed in real life. The court concluded that, by intentionally disclosing the plaintiff's private facts, Zhang had infringed on his right of privacy. The court adjudicated that Zhang should stop the infringement and delete three infringing articles ("Totally Disheartened", "Quietly", and "In the Heart of the Moon") and one photo of Wang and his alleged lover, Dong, from the website; Zhang should also apologize to the plaintiff in an open letter on the website and compensate the plaintiff with 5,000 yuan for mental damages.

The court found that when it covered this event, defendant Daqi. com did not delete the plaintiff's personal information such as his name and photographs, and thus risked the plaintiff's privacy and reputation. The court determined that Daqi.com should stop violating Wang's privacy, delete the column concerning Jiang's suicide from its website, make an open apology to the plaintiff, and compensate the plaintiff with 3,000 yuan for mental damages. In addition, the court found that Tianya.com had deleted posts relating to Jiang's suicide before the plaintiff filed the lawsuit; it had fulfilled its legal obligations, and thus was not subject to any legal liability.

Data protection models

While online privacy is becoming the focus of public discussion, the Chinese government and relevant industries have taken certain measures to strengthen the protection of Internet privacy. These measures can be divided into three categories: legal regulation, industry self-regulation, and technical protection. Among the three categories, legal regulation has become the major type, while industry self-regulation and technical protection have played an ancillary role.

Legal regulation

China has established a series of laws and regulations to protect personal data that is available online. The *Decision of the NPC Standing Committee on Safeguarding Internet Security* enacted in 2000 provides that anyone who intercepts, tampers with, or deletes another person's e-mails or other data will be investigated for criminal responsibility if his act constitutes a crime. Also, the *Criminal Law* revised in 2009 stipulates that the actions of selling or illegally providing others' personal information and illegally obtaining others' personal information constitute a crime, and the offender will be subject to criminal investigation. In addition, the *Tort Liability Law* enacted in 2009 explicitly includes the right to privacy as one of the civil rights, and clearly defines the liability of Internet users and Internet service providers. To sum up, these laws provide a legal basis for protecting people's privacy in cyberspace.

In January 2011, the MIIT promulgated the *Interim Measures for Supervision and Management of Internet Information Service Market (Draft Memoranda for Comment)*, which clearly defines ISPs' responsibility for the protection of online privacy. First of all, the *Draft* stipulates how ISPs should collect and process users' data. Article 12 states that ISPs should respect the privacy of their users, assure the security of users' data, and standardize the procedures for processing users' data. Without legal authorization, ISPs shall not collect and process the personal information of their users. In cases of necessity, the personal data collected should be directly associated with the services provided, and users should be clearly informed about the data collection behavior and purposes of data collection. Moreover, Article 14 provides that ISPs should assure the security of users' data and preserve users' right to modify and delete their own data. Unless otherwise specified by laws and regulations, ISPs are not allowed to modify or delete users' data, or to provide users' data to a third party.

The *Draft* also stresses that ISPs have the obligation to keep users' data confidential. Article 13 states that ISPs should keep users' information confidential; unless otherwise specified in laws, no individuals or organizations may review users' information for any reasons. Article 12 states that in the case of disclosure of personal information, the ISP concerned should immediately inform the relevant regulatory agencies; meanwhile, it should not publicize any unconfirmed information.

In addition, the *Draft* provides specific regulations on the operation of end-user software by network service providers. Article 9 stipulates that where ISPs need to install, run, upgrade, or uninstall software on subscribers' computers, they should provide clear and unambiguous reminders to subscribers and also obtain the consent of subscribers. Article 10 prescribes that where ISPs bundle end-user software with other software, they should explicitly inform subscribers of such bundling and allow subscribers to decide whether to install it or use other such software.

In April 2009, the MIIT also promulgated the *Mechanism for Monitoring and Handling Trojans and Botnets* to respond to the security risks caused by Trojans and botnets. A Trojan is a remotely controlled program installed on the victim's computer by a hacker in order to steal the victim's information. A botnet is a collection of compromised computers connected to the Internet, controlled via standard-based network protocols such as IRC and HTTP. Both Trojans and botnets constitute substantial threats to network information security, and they are the major causes of the disclosure of private information, the wide spread of spam messages, and the massive dysfunction of Internet services.

According to the *Mechanism*, CNCERT is responsible for monitoring the activities of any malicious software within China.[48] Specifically, it collects, verifies, analyzes, and publishes Trojan- and botnet-related information, such as the scale, type, and consequences of the infection. It also provides Internet security service and technology support for handling the problems caused by Trojans and botnets, such as malicious IP addresses and domain names. The *Mechanism* also stipulates that telecommunications service providers are responsible for monitoring the activities of Trojans and botnets within their network systems and also for handling all Trojan and botnet issues reported by CNCERT. The administrative organizations for Internet domain names are responsible for handling the malicious domain names reported by CNCERT. In addition, all organizations related to Internet services should inform users of the responsibility for Internet security on the users' side and also include this information in their contracts with users. Through the above-mentioned measures, the MIIT hopes to establish a comprehensive system for effectively handling Trojan and botnet problems.

It should be added that there are several other laws and regulations that also provide direct or indirect protection for people's privacy in cyberspace. These mainly include: the *Telecommunications Regulations*, the *Administrative Measures for Internet Information Services*, the *Administrative Measures for the Security of International Connecting of Computer Information Network*, and the *Implementation Measures for the Reporting of Internet Security Information*, and so on.

Industry self-regulation

While enhancing legal regulation, China also advocates the strengthening of industry self-regulation for the protection of online privacy. First of all, industry self-regulation is demonstrated by the privacy policy statement published by network service providers. Many websites set up a link to their privacy policy statement on the home page. The statement usually includes the following: the definition of personal information; the basic principles for collecting and processing personal information; the obligation to inform users before the website gathers, discloses, and transfers users' information; the use of cookies; how to adjust the privacy settings and update personal information; the contact information of the network operator, and so on.

For example, the privacy statement of Baidu states: "In the following circumstances, Baidu will disclose your personal information according to your wishes or in accordance with the law, and any possible liability should be borne by you, with your authorization in advance; the requested products and services can only be received with disclosure of your personal information; the disclosure is required by the law and regulations; the disclosure is requested by the relevant government authorities; the disclosure is to safeguard Baidu's legitimate interests; you consent to sharing the information with third parties; any breach of our service terms on your side; and we need to provide information to companies that provide our products or services."[49]

In addition, the privacy policy of Tencent states: "Tencent will not disclose users' private information to any third parties other than its cooperators, except with users' consent or as required by the law. However, when a user registers for an account, if he consents to disclose his private information, or agrees to the disclosure of users' private information in the contract between users and Tencent or Tencent's collaborating parties, the user should assume any risks that may arise. Meanwhile, in order to improve its service, Tencent will collect users' non-personal information for its own use and may also provide such information to a third party."

The problem is that there are too many ambiguities and loopholes in these privacy statements, and such problems are very disadvantageous to the protection of user privacy. For example, the privacy statements often contain the following two mandatory elements: first, no matter whether the user consents or not, the ISP can provide the user's personal information to any of its collaborating parties; second, as long as the user agrees to the privacy policy when registering for an account, his personal information can be disclosed to any third party. These mandatory terms do not appear only in Baidu's and Tencent's privacy statements; they occur in the privacy statements of most other Internet companies that require users to register for services. When users register for an account, they tend to ignore such privacy terms, allowing the ISP to infringe on their privacy without bearing any liability.

China's Internet companies have also followed practice in Western countries[50] and established the Internet privacy certification program. In March 2009, six of China's largest Internet companies (Baidu, Tencent, Sina, Sohu, Netease, and Phoenix) and the Internet Society of China jointly established the ITRUST, an organization that is devoted to promoting the credibility of Internet companies in China. The ITRUST will review and verify the chief information about a website, such as its authenticity and legitimacy, the phone number for customer service, and assess user privacy protection and the level of user satisfaction. After this review and verification, the website can obtain an electronic Web Trust Certificate issued by the ITRUST. The website can then post the certificate on its home page so that users can identify it as a trusted site. So far, nearly 200 Internet companies have obtained this certificate, which arguably helps to strengthen users' confidence in the privacy protection provided by the website.

In addition to the privacy certification system, China is also trying to establish industry guidance to improve the protection of online privacy. In 1998, more than 80 global companies and associations jointly founded the Online Privacy Alliance with the aim of fostering the protection of individuals' privacy online and in electronic commerce. The Online Privacy Alliance issued an industry guideline which stated that: "upon joining the Alliance, each member organization agrees that its policies for protecting individually identifiable information in cyberspace will address at least the following elements ... adoption and implementation of a privacy policy ... notice and disclosure ... choice/ consent ... data security ... data quality and access."[51]

China has a similar industry association, i.e., the Internet Society of China. In June 2004, this society issued the *Public Pledge of Self-Regulation and Professional Ethics for China Internet Industry*, which states: "we pledge to respect the lawful rights and interests of consumers and we shall protect the confidentiality of their information. We pledge not to use the information provided by users for any activity other than those as promised to users, and no technology or any other advantage may be used to infringe upon the lawful rights and interests of the consumers or users." However, commentators argue that this guideline may be too general to guide the privacy protection practice of China's websites.

Technical protection

Technical solutions have also been used to enhance users' control over their private information. One of the most common technical measures is encryption, which refers to the conversion of data into a form that cannot be easily understood by unauthorized persons. Encryption consists of two elements: algorithm and key. An algorithm is the process of combining general information with a string of numbers (keys) to produce a cipher text that cannot be understood. A key is the algorithm used for data encoding and decryption. In many cases, encryption can be an effective tool for protecting individuals' privacy online. However, hackers have improved their skills, and nowadays they can easily decode and steal data by invading other computer systems and obtaining relevant transaction information. Many users have thus adopted firewalls to reduce the possibility of being hacked. Firewalls are the most important security technology developed in recent years; their main function is to check information coming from the Internet and then to block it or allow it to pass through to the computer concerned.

Also, more and more users are adopting software with privacy preferences to enhance the protection of their private information. With this type of software, users can identify websites that meet the online privacy protection requirements and then decide whether to visit them or not; users can also browse a website anonymously so as to avoid the possible leakage of personal information during the browsing process; in addition, users can learn what information they have to provide when conducting transactions online and ensure that the provision of such information will not lead to the infringement on their privacy by others. Currently, the major software in this regard is the Platform for Privacy Preferences Project, or P3P. It was a protocol developed by the World Wide Web Consortium (W3C), designed to provide privacy protection for Internet users. The problem is that some application software may be able to bypass the P3P platform when collecting and processing users' personal information.

In addition, such technologies as access control, information flow control, software protection, virus detection and removal, content classification and filtering, and system security monitoring can also help to enhance the protection of individuals' personal information in cyberspace. But no technology is perfect. Technical solutions to the problem of privacy infringement are, essentially, supplementary means, and cannot replace the leading role of legal regulation. Also, many commentators argue that if users can raise their awareness about self-protection, the possibility of privacy violation will be much reduced.

Notes

1. Xupei Sun (2008) *The Study on the Law of Journalism and Communication*, Shanghai, China: Fudan University Press.
2. Xingwu Feng, Dengqiao Liu, and Jing Zhang (2011) "The Legal Analysis of China's Privacy Rights," retrieved March 15, 2011 from http://china.findlaw.cn/jingjifa/fuyoubaohufa/nvxingquanli/yinsiquan/20110312/68845.html.
3. Xupei Sun (2008) *The Study on the Law of Journalism and Communication*, Shanghai, China: Fudan University Press.
4. William L. Prosser (1960) "Privacy," *California Law Review* 48(3), 383–423, p. 389.
5. The case information was obtained from the website http://news.sina.com.cn/z/gajzwnemmdt/index.shtml.
6. See Yongzheng Wei (2006) *Lectures on Journalism and Communication Law*, 2nd edition, Beijing, China: Renmin University of China Press.
7. See Yongzheng Wei (2006) *Lectures on Journalism and Communication Law*, 2nd edition, Beijing, China: Renmin University of China Press.
8. See the case of Zhuo Xiaohong vs. Sun Dexi and Chongqing Dairy Co., published in the first issue of the Gazette of the Supreme People's Court in 1987.
9. See Yongzheng Wei (2006) *Lectures on Journalism and Communication Law*, 2nd edition, Beijing, China: Renmin University of China Press.
10. See "Zhao Benshan Compensated 120,000 yuan for Picture Infringement, and the Disgruntled Website Appealed to a Higher Court," *Legal Evening News*, March 3, 2011.
11. See Paul Siegel (2008) *Communication Law in America*, 2nd edition, Lanham, MD: Rowman & Littlefield Publishers.
12. Robert Trager, Joseph Russomanno, and Susan D. Ross (2010) *The Law of Journalism and Mass Communication*, Washington, DC: CQ Press, p. 241.
13. See Liming Wang (2009) "The New Development of Privacy Rights," *The Law Review of Renmin University*, 1.
14. See Liming Wang (2009) "The New Development of Privacy Rights," *The Law Review of Renmin University*, 1.
15. See Deliang Liu (2009) "The Infringement in Cyberspace and the Responses of the Civil Law System," retrieved January 10, 2011 from http://www.yadian.cc/paper/63221/.
16. See Deliang Liu (2009) *The Infringement in Cyberspace and the Responses of the Civil Law System*, retrieved January 10, 2011 from http://www.yadian.cc/paper/63221/.
17. See Liming Wang (2009) "The New Development of Privacy Rights," *The Law Review of Renmin University*, 1.
18. For example, some Chinese institutions recently introduced a so-called Network Access Authentication Management System, which could be used to strengthen the monitoring of Internet activities in network terminals, including controllable ones (e.g., desktops, laptops, network servers) and non-controllable ones (e.g., external visitors, the networks of partners and

customers). This system has been heavily criticized for intruding into Internet users' privacy.

19. The case is adapted from Xiuping Li (1997) "China's First Electronic Mail Case," *Law and Life*, 9.

20. Robert Trager, Joseph Russomanno, and Susan D. Ross (2010) *The Law of Journalism and Mass Communication*, Washington, DC: CQ Press.

21. See Deliang Liu (2008) *New Perspectives on Civil and Commercial Law in the Internet Era*, Beijing, China: The Court Press.

22. The case is adapted from: Wu Wei and Liu Quan (2006) "Guangdong Publicly Punished Spam Senders," *Nanfang Daily*, August 15, retrieved December 8, 2010 from http://tech.sina.com.cn/i/2006-08-15/14521086829.shtml.

23. See Deliang Liu (2009) "The Infringement in Cyberspace and the Responses of the Civil Law System," retrieved January 10, 2011 from http://www.yadian.cc/paper/63221/.

24. Restatement (Second) of Tort § 652D (1977), The American Law Institute.

25. Robert Trager, Joseph Russomanno, and Susan D. Ross (2010) *The Law of Journalism and Mass Communication*, Washington, DC: CQ Press.

26. Robert Trager, Joseph Russomanno, and Susan D. Ross (2010) *The Law of Journalism and Mass Communication*, Washington, DC: CQ Press, p. 248.

27. See Yongzheng Wei (2006) *Lectures on Journalism and Communication Law*, 2nd edition, Beijing, China: Renmin University of China Press.

28. See Xuelu Ren (1998) "A Dispute Caused by 'The Secret History of the Chiang Family,'" *Law and Life*, 2.

29. Chiang Wei-kuo is an adopted son of Chiang Kai-shek, who was a political and military leader of 20th-century China. He is known as Jiang Jieshi in Mandarin.

30. Fei Wu (2004) "The Cause of Lawsuits for Media Invasion of Privacy," *Journalistic Practice*, 11.

31. See the article "A Discussion on the Breach of Privacy by News Media," which can be retrieved from http://www.chinalawedu.com/news/16900/174/2004/7/ma121916383418740022 1456_123015.htm.

32. See the article "A Discussion on the Breach of Privacy by News Media," which can be retrieved from http://www.chinalawedu.com/news/16900/174/2004/7/ma121916383418740022 1456_123015.htm.

33. See Yongzheng Wei (2006) *Lectures on Journalism and Communication Law*, 2nd edition, Beijing, China: Renmin University of China Press.

34. John D. Zelezny (2011) *Communications Law: Liberties, Restraints, and the Modern Media*, Wadsworth: Cengage Learning, p. 149.

35. See Liming Wang (2009) "The New Development of Privacy Rights," *The Law Review of Renmin University*, 1.

36. The case is adapted from Li Hongguang and Zhou Kai (2010) "'Maritime Woman' Won the Lawsuit against Baidu," *China Youth Daily*, retrieved January 12, 2011 from http://zqb.cyol.com/content/2010-07/01/content_3303306.htm.

37. Kai Wang (2008) "On the Protection of Privacy Rights and the State Regulation of Indecent Speeches: The Case of the Edison Chen Photo Scandal," *Today's Media*, 5.

38. Li Meng (2006) "From 'Rob Privacy' to See the Lack of the Protection for Personal Data Online," *China Economic Weekly*, January 19.

39. Xiaoping Xie (2011) "Qihoo v. Jinshan: Revealing the Underlying Rules Governing the Internet Industry," *National Business Daily*, January 15.

40. The case information is adapted from Sina.com (2010) "The Qihoo 360 and Tencent dispute," retrieved March 1, 2011 from http://tech.sina.com.cn/z/qihuvsqq/.

41. Tencent.com (2010) "About Tencent," retrieved August 20, 2010 from http://www.tencent.com/en-us/at/abouttencent.shtml.

42. 360 Safeguard (2011) "The Major Events of 360," retrieved September 11, 2011 from http://www.360.cn/about/history.html.

43. Human-flesh searching is basically similar to the term "online profiling" used by the international community. The startling phrase was coined by Chinese users.

44. The case information is adapted from Xinhuanet.com (2010) "A Jiangxi Official Was Human-Flesh Searched for His Speech on CCTV," retrieved May 15, 2011 from http://news.xinhuanet.com/politics/2010-06/29/c_12274924.htm.

45. The case information is adapted from Baidu.com (2007) "Zhang Shufan," retrieved July 18, 2010 from http://baike.baidu.com/view/1342320.htm.

46. The case information is adapted from Xinhuanet.com (2008) "Zhou Jiugeng, Director of Nanjing Jiangning Housing Administration, Dismissed," retrieved December 12, 2010 from http://news.xinhuanet.com/newscenter/2008-12/28/content_10572187.htm; and Xinhuanet.com (2009) "Zhou Jiugeng, Director of Nanjing Jiangning Housing Administration, Sentenced to 11 Years in Jail," retrieved December 12, 2010 from http://news.xinhuanet.com/politics/2009-10/10/content_12207171.htm.

47. The case information is mainly adapted from Yan Shi (2008) "The First Case of Internet Violence: Plaintiff Wang Fei Compensated 8,000 yuan for Mental Damage," retrieved May 1, 2010 from http://www.chinacourt.org/public/detail.php?id=336347.

48. Founded in 1999, CNCERT is a national-level organization mainly responsible for the coordination of activities among all computer emergency response teams within China relating to incidents on national public networks. It provides Internet security services and technology support in the handling of security incidents for national public networks and major national Internet application systems.

49. Baidu, Inc. (2011) "Baidu Privacy Protection Statement," retrieved September 27, 2011 from http://www.baidu.com/duty/yinsiquan.html.

50. For example, the United States has long ago established the online privacy certification program. The most influential organizations granting certificates include TRUSTe and BBBonline.

51. Online Privacy Alliance, "Guidelines for Online Privacy Policies," retrieved December 7, 2011 from http://www.privacyalliance.org/resources/ppguidelines.shtml.

Proprietary interests

Abstract: This chapter focuses on China's protection of three types of intellectual property: copyright, trademarks, and patents. It is particularly concerned with how existing intellectual property laws have been applied to the Internet and also with how new laws and regulations have been created to address new problems caused by various online activities.

Key words: copyright, trademarks, domain names, patents, computer software, Internet business methods, Internet service provider liability

Intellectual property (IP) refers to "creations of the mind," such as literary and artistic works, inventions, and "symbols, names, images, and designs used in commerce."[1] It is generally divided into three categories: copyright, trademark, and patents. In China, each of these is protected by civil law, criminal law, administrative law, and other laws. Furthermore, such protection has been applied to proprietary interests in cyberspace. This chapter mainly examines three types of IP infringement, namely, copyright infringement, trademark infringement, and patent infringement. It is particularly concerned with how these infringements have emerged in cyberspace and how they have been addressed by Chinese law and regulations.

Copyright

Copyright refers to "the exclusive legal rights to reproduce, publish, sell, or distribute the matter and form of something (as a literary, musical, or artistic work)."[2] The primary purpose of copyright protection is not to make writers and artists rich, but to encourage creative production for the ultimate benefit of society at large by giving individual writers, artists, and media organizations control over how and when their works will be exploited commercially. Without this legal protection, creators would be discouraged from producing because anyone else could copy and market the original creators' works and usurp their rightful profits. Also, publishing and production companies would hesitate to invest in major projects, knowing that their creations could be pirated, without restraint, by their competitors. The theory of copyright law, then, is to give creators an economic incentive so that society will benefit from creative production.[3]

China's copyright protection has undergone a long process of development. Its roots can be traced back to the Chinese Constitution adopted in 1982. Under Article 47, citizens have the freedom to engage in scientific research, literary and artistic creation, and other cultural pursuits; the state encourages and assists creative endeavors that are conducive to the interests of the people and made by citizens engaged in education, science, technology, literature, art, and other cultural work. In 1986, the NPC passed the *General Principles of the Civil Law*, in which Article 94 stipulates that citizens and legal persons shall enjoy copyright and be entitled to sign their names as authors, issue and publish their works, and obtain remuneration in accordance with the law. In 1990, the NPC Standing Committee enacted the *Copyright Law*. This is China's first copyright law; it also provides a legal basis for protecting the right to online dissemination on information networks. In November 2000, the Supreme Court issued the *Interpretation on Several Issues concerning the Application of Law in the Trial of Cases in Relation to Copyright Disputes over Computer Network*, which clearly states that the provisions on copyright and other related rights in the *Copyright Law* shall be applicable to digitalized copyright. In October 2001, the NPC Standing Committee passed the *Amendment to the Copyright Law*, which proposed for the first time "the right to online dissemination of information" and also integrated it within the scope of copyright protection. Due to the rapid development of network technology and the increasing complexity of the issue of the right to online dissemination of information, however, the *Amendment* does not explicate this new right; instead, it states that "the measures for protecting the right to online dissemination of information shall be established separately by the State Council." Five years later, the State Council promulgated the *Regulations on the Protection of the Right to Online Dissemination of Information*, which provide clear and systematic stipulations on the action of infringing upon the right to online dissemination of information. In addition, China has also joined such international conventions as the *Universal Copyright Convention*, the *Berne Convention for the Protection of Literary and Artistic Works*, and the *Agreement on Trade-Related Intellectual Property Rights* (TRIPS), thus becoming a crucial part of the world's intellectual property protection system.

In the following, we first present some basic concepts about copyright, including the object of copyright, the subject of copyright, and the specific rights granted under copyright law. We then examine the issue of copyright infringement, the relationship between copyright protection and public interests, and the legal liability of Internet service providers in a copyright infringement.

Copyright basics

The object of copyright

Under the *Copyright Law*, the object of copyright refers to works, including literary works; oral works; music, drama, opera, dance, and acrobatic works; works of fine art and architecture; photographic works; cinematographic works and works created in similar photographic method; drawings of engineering designs and product designs; maps, sketches, and other graphic and model works; computer software; and other works as provided for in laws and regulations. In order to enjoy copyright protection, a work must meet the following four conditions: it must be original; it must be replicable; it must be a creation of literary, artistic or scientific work; it must not be a work whose content is prohibited by laws and regulations.

First, the object of copyright must be original. The work referred to by copyright law must be an original work rather than being copied from someone else's work. Originality means that the author creates the work. Creation refers to a creative activity where the author selects, refines, and processes materials obtained through personal observation, experience, and analysis of political, economic, cultural, and social life, and combines such materials, using the author's own ideas and skills, to produce literary, artistic, or scientific works.[4] The originality required by copyright law is not of the kind of unprecedented novelty, but only of the quality that can distinguish it from other works. With a unique form of expression, an original work can be distinguished from other works, and therefore it can be regarded as having exclusiveness.[5]

It should be noted that copyright law protects only the expression of a thought, rather than the thought itself. The thought expressed in a copyrighted work does not have to be original. The thought can be shared and borrowed. However, the expression of the thought should be original, rather than being copied or borrowed from other sources. This is a basic principle of copyright that has been accepted internationally. Both the TRIPS and the WIPO *Copyright Treaty* prescribe that "copyright protection shall extend to expressions and not to ideas, procedures, methods of operation, or mathematical concepts as such." Similarly, the *Interpretation of the Beijing High People's Court on Several Issues about the Trials of Cases Concerning Copyright Disputes* emphasizes that "the Copyright Law protects the expression and presentation of the themes, thoughts, emotions, and scientific principles, not the theme, thoughts, emotions, and other scientific principles themselves." The main consideration here is that if a thought or idea is protected, it will become an exclusive property of the author. This may lead to an ideological monopoly on the part of the author. As a result, the exchange of ideas may be hindered, and so also may be the development of human civilization.

The originality of online works has demonstrated some different characteristics. The WIPO *Copyright Treaty* provides that "compilations of data or other material, in any form, which by reason of the selection or arrangement of their contents constitute intellectual creations, are protected as such." Similarly, the *Copyright Law* in China stipulates that "a work created by compilation of several works, parts of works, data or other materials that do not constitute a work and having originality in the selection or arrangement of its contents is a work of compilation" which is under the protection of copyright. Therefore, such online works as web page layouts, web link settings, and compilations of data and files, as long as they are original, can be regarded as compiled works and thus subject to copyright protection. Similarly to the protection of offline works, however, this protection does not extend to the data or the material itself, and does not allow infringement or damage of original rights associated with such data or materials.

Second, the object of copyright must be replicable. Replication refers to the duplication of an original work in numerous copies by printing, photocopying, or other physical means. If a work can be copied, it must exist in a physical and tangible format. For instance, written works are fixed on paper; photographic works are fixed on film; television programs, movie, and video works are fixed on film and videotape. Only through those means can such works be appreciated and copied by the public. Thoughts exist only in minds; without some fixed forms of expression, they cannot be accessed by others and thus cannot be called works. Oral works, except for well-known ones, must have a property that can be fixed on certain physical things, such as paper or tape; otherwise, they can hardly be protected by copyright law. Works can be replicated in different forms. For instance, oral works can be duplicated into literary works printed on paper, and such printed works can be changed into broadcast works when released over radio waves.[6] In addition, under the *Interpretation of the Supreme People's Court on Several Issues Concerning the Laws Applicable to the Trial of Copyright Disputes Involving Computer Networks Interpretations* (2006), the digital format of a work is also protected by copyright law. This is largely because the materials uploaded to the Internet can be digitalized and fixed in the computer's hard drive, and then can be read, copied, downloaded, or printed out by readers. Therefore, works transmitted over the Internet can be considered as digitalized expressions of thoughts, which are indisputably replicable.

Third, the object of copyright must be the creation of literary, artistic, and scientific works. Intellectual creation includes a wide variety of activities, while literature, artistic, and scientific creation are just a part of intellectual activity. Such intellectual activity as taking advantage of personal experience and wisdom to improve the efficiency of a production process, or adopting a new line-up and strategy to beat opponents in sports competitions, can also be considered intellectual creation. However, where an intellectual work has not been expressed in text, graphics, or other specific forms, it does not come under the scope of literary, artistic, and scientific creation, and thus cannot be considered as copyrightable work. Furthermore, where an intellectual work is a literary, artistic, or scientific creation, it still cannot enjoy copyright protection if it concerns public affairs or the public interest. Examples include laws; administrative rules and regulations; other documents with a legislative, administrative, or judicial nature; official translations of laws, regulations, and government documents; news on current affairs; calendars; formulas; numerical tables; and forms of general use.

Finally, the content of copyrightable works must not be prohibited by laws and regulations. Under the *Regulations on Publication Administration*, no publication should contain anything that goes against the basic principles determined by the Constitution; that endangers the unification, sovereignty, and territorial integrity of the country; that endangers national security, reputation, and interests; that instigates national separatism, infringes on the customs and habits of minority nationalities, and disrupts the solidarity of nationalities; that discloses state secrets; that insults or slanders others; or that disseminates pornography and superstition, or incites violence, or endangers social ethics and cultural tradition. In addition, the *Decision of the NPC Standing Committee on Safeguarding Internet Security*, the *Telecommunications Regulations*, the *Administrative Measures for Internet Information Services*, the *Regulation on Film Administration*, the *Regulation on Radio and Television Administration*, and so on all set up similar prohibitions. Works including the above-mentioned content are neither allowed to be disseminated nor protected by copyright laws.

The subject of copyright

According to the *Copyright Law*, the subject of copyright is the author of a work, that is, the natural person who directly creates works by means of abstract thinking and the objective expression of such abstract thoughts. The copyright holder may also be other citizens, legal entities, or other organizations which obtain copyright through inheritance or according to relevant laws. Many works involve multiple participants in the creation and dissemination process. Accordingly, the *Copyright Law* has prescribed six types of copyright ownership.

Copyright owner of derivative works

A derivative work is a work based upon or derived from one or more pre-existing works. In practice, a work resulting from adaptation, translation, annotation, or arrangement of pre-existing works can be considered a derivative work. Adaptation refers to switching the original expression type of a work to another expression type, without changing the original content. Translation refers to converting the original expression language of a work to another language. Annotation refers to making comment, interpretation, and clarification on the original work. Arrangement refers to making abridgment, combination, composition, and revision of original scattered works for their readability. Under the *Copyright Law*, where a work is created by adaptation, translation, annotation, or arrangement of a pre-existing work, the copyright of the work is enjoyed by the adapter, translator, annotator, or arranger. But the author of a derivative work must first obtain consent from and make remuneration to its original creator; also, the exercise of the copyright of a derivative work is not allowed to prejudice the copyright of the original work.

Copyright owner of joint works

Where a work is created jointly by two or more co-authors, the copyright in the work is enjoyed jointly by those co-authors. Co-authored works include dividable and undividable works. If a work of joint authorship can be separated into independent parts and exploited separately, each co-author is entitled to independent copyright in the parts that he has created, provided that the exercise of such copyright does not prejudice the copyright in the joint work as a whole. Where a joint work cannot be used when it is divided, the copyright is owned jointly by the co-authors and will be exercised after the co-authors have reached a consensus through consultations. If the co-authors fail to reach a consensus and there is no proper reason for independent use, no party may prevent any of the other parties from exercising any right other than the right of assignment; however, the gains derived should be reasonably distributed among all the co-authors.[7]

Copyright owner of compilation works

Examples of compilation works include encyclopedias, dictionaries, anthologies, complete works, periodicals, newspapers, web page layouts, electronic databases, and so on. As long as a work's content selection or arrangement reflects originality, it can be considered a work of compilation. If the selection and arrangement of the content is simply to put together pre-existing works or materials and does not reflect originality, such selection and arrangement are not new products and thus do not constitute a work of compilation. The compiler enjoys the copyright of compilation works as a whole. The compiler, when compiling others' works, should obtain permission of the copyright owners of original works, pay remuneration to the original authors, and respect the original copyright owner's personal rights. In exercising the copyright of compilation works, the compiler should not prejudice the copyright of the original works. In addition, if compilation works can be separated into independent parts and exploited separately, each original author is entitled to independent copyright in the parts that he has created.

Copyright owner of cinematographic works

Examples of cinematographic works include television programs, video works, and online video works. The copyright of this type of work is held by the producer of the work, but the scriptwriter, director, cameraman, lyricist, composer, and other authors enjoy the right of authorship in the work, and have the right to receive remuneration pursuant to the contract concluded with the producer. In addition, the authors of the screenplay, musical works, and other works that are incorporated into a cinematographic work or a work created by virtue of an analogous method of film production and that can be exploited separately are entitled to exercise their copyright independently. Therefore, the screenplay writer can publish his screenplay through another publisher, and the lyrics writer can produce his work in an album. In addition, the film producer, when exercising his copyright, should not go beyond the scope of normal commercial operation of the film; otherwise, he may risk violating the rights of other creators involved in the film's production.[8]

Copyright owner of works made for hire

A work created by a person in the fulfillment of tasks assigned to him by his employer is viewed as a work made for hire. General speaking, the copyright of such work belongs to the author. However, the employer has a priority right to exploit the work within the scope of its professional activities. During the two years after the completion of the work, the author cannot, without the consent of the employer, authorize a third party to exploit the work in the same way as the employer does. If the author obtains the employer's consent to allow a third party to use the work in the same way as does the employer within two years after completion of the work, the remuneration so derived should be shared by the author and the employer, according to the ratio agreed upon.[9] In any of the following two cases, the author of a work made for hire enjoys only the right of authorship, while the employer enjoys other rights included in copyright laws and may reward the author: (a) drawings of engineering designs, drawings of product designs, maps, computer software, and other works created in the course of employment mainly with the material and technical resources of the employer and under its responsibility; and (b) works created in the course of employment where the copyright is, in accordance with laws, regulations or contracts, enjoyed by the employer.[10]

Copyright owner of commissioned works

Commissioned works refers to works created by a trustee under a contract of commission signed with a client. The ownership of the copyright in a commissioned work should be agreed upon in the contract between the commissioning and commissioned parties. This means that in the contract, the involved parties may agree that copyright belongs to the commissioning parties, the commissioned parties, or both parties, or that both parties are entitled to part of the copyright. If no such statement is stipulated in the contract, the copyright belongs to the commissioned parties.

Where the copyright of a work belongs to a person who has died, the copyright may be transferred to others during the period of copyright protection. In accordance with relevant laws and regulations, there are at least four forms of transfer: transfer through intestate succession; transfer by bequest; transfer by legacy support agreement; and transfer to the state or judicial organ, if an author's right of exploitation and to receive remuneration has no inheritors or legatees. The transfer of copyright focuses on the transfer of property rights in the work, i.e., the rights to exploit and to receive remuneration. The author's personal right cannot be transferred. Where the copyright in a work belongs to an organization whose legal status has been changed or terminated during the period of copyright protection, such copyright should be enjoyed by the successor organization which has taken over the former's rights and obligations, or, in the absence of such successor, by the government.

Traditionally, the author of a work can be determined based on the authorship of the work. Where there is no authorship or where there is a dispute about authorship, the involved parties can determine the author of the work according to the ownership of the original manuscript. However, it is sometimes difficult to identify the original author of a work that is transmitted on the Internet. This is largely because an original work, after being digitalized and recorded on electronic storage devices, can be easily and quickly copied and spread without authorship. It is argued that, since an Internet user often needs to register an online account in order to publish works online, one common means of locating the original author of a work is to check the registration information of relevant parties.[11]

Personal rights and property rights

Copyright involves two types of exclusive rights: personal rights and property rights. Personal rights refers to the rights to obtain identity and reputation from the creation of a work and also to maintain the integrity of the work. Exclusively belonging to the author, personal rights cannot be transferred and do not involve direct economic interests, under normal circumstances. Property rights, also called economic rights, refers to the right to gain economic benefits through the right use of the work. Unlike personal rights, property rights can be transferred. Personal rights and property rights are closely related, yet they can be mutually independent. Where the property right is transferred, the copyright holder still enjoys the personal right. The receiver of the transferred copyright has no more than the property right.

The *Copyright Law* specifies four types of personal right: the rights of publication, of authorship, of alteration, and of integrity. The right of publication is the right to decide whether to make a work available to the public, in what format, at what time, in what place. The right of authorship refers to the right to claim authorship of the work. The author is entitled not to sign his name, or to sign his real name or a pseudonym. The author is also entitled to prohibit others from signing his work. The right of alteration refers to the right to alter or authorize others to alter one's work. The decision whether to alter, how to alter, or whether to authorize others to alter should be made according to the author's wish and should not be forced upon the author. The right of integrity refers to the right to protect one's work from distortion and mutilation. The author has the right to protect his work from being demonized, abridged, added to, or distorted in other ways against his wish and thoughts.

In addition, the *Copyright Law* provides for twelve kinds of property rights: the rights of reproduction, distribution, rental, exhibition, performance, showing, broadcast, communication of information on networks, making cinematographic work, adaptation, translation, and compilation. The right of reproduction refers to the right to produce one or more copies of a work by printing, photocopying, lithographing, making a sound recording or video recording, duplicating a recording, or duplicating a photographic work. The right of distribution refers to the right to make available to the public the original or reproductions of a work through sale or other transfer of ownership. The right of rental refers to the right to authorize, with payment, others to temporarily use computer software, cinematographic works, or works created by virtue of an analogous method of film production. The right of exhibition refers to the right to publicly display the original or reproduction of a work of fine art and photography. The right of performance refers to the right to publicly perform a work and publicly broadcast the performance of a work by various means. The right of showing refers to the right to show to the public a work of fine art, photography, or cinematography, or a work created by analogous methods of film production through film projectors, overhead projectors or any other technical devices. The right of broadcast refers to the right to publicly broadcast or communicate a work to the public by wireless means, to communicate broadcast work to the public a by wire or relay means, and to communicate a broadcast work to the public by a loudspeaker or by any other analogous tool used to transmit symbols, sounds, or pictures. The right of communication of information on networks refers to the right to communicate a work to the public by wire or wireless means in such a way that people may access these works from a place and at a time individually chosen by them. The right of making cinematographic work refers to the right to fix a work on a carrier by way of film production or by virtue of an analogous method of film production. The right of adaptation refers to the right to change a work to create a new work of originality. The right of translation refers to the right to translate a work in one language into one in another language. The right of compilation refers to the right to compile works or parts of works into a new work by reason of selection or arrangement.

Different copyrights have different terms of protection. A term of protection for rights is the time period during which the rights of the copyright holder are subject to legal protection. During the term of protection, the author or other copyright holders enjoy the copyright of the work; anyone who intends to use the work should obtain consent from the copyright owners and pay them remuneration accordingly. According to the *Copyright Law*, the rights of authorship, alteration, and integrity of an author are unlimited in time. This means that when the term of protection for the author's property rights terminates, individuals are free to use the work by copying, distributing, performing, or other means; however, they do not have the right to change the authorship or the content of the work; otherwise, they will be subject to legal liability for copyright infringement. The term of protection for the right of publication and all types of property rights has a certain time limit, that is, the lifetime of the author and 50 years after his death. In the case of a work of joint authorship, the term of protection should be 50 years after the death of the last surviving author. In the case of a work whose copyright belongs to an organization, the term should be 50 years after the first-time publication of the work. In the case of a cinematographic work or a work created by virtue of an analogous method of film production or a photographic work, the term should also be 50 years after the first-time publication of the work. When the term terminates, all personal rights except publication rights remain valid, while all property rights and the right of publication become invalid.

Apart from exceptional cases, anyone who exploits a work created by others is required to conclude a licensing contract with the copyright owner. A licensing contract should include the following content: the category of right licensed for exploitation of the work covered by the license; the exclusive or non-exclusive nature of the right to exploit the work covered by the license; the geographic area and term of the license; the form of remuneration and the method of payment; the liability in case of breach of the contract; and any other matters that the contracting parties consider necessary.[12] There are two types of copyright license: exclusive licenses and non-exclusive licenses. In the case of exclusive licensing, the copyright holder can only entitle a certain person to use his work. In other words, this person has an exclusive right to use his work; the copyright owner shall not sublicense the same work to a third party within the term of licensing. In the case of non-exclusive licensing, the copyright holder can entitle different persons or organizations to use his work within a certain period of time. The form of exclusive licensing or non-exclusive licensing can be stipulated in the contract. Unless otherwise stipulated by law, the exploiter of a work can only obtain non-exclusive rights if there is no explicit statement about exclusive rights in the contract or there is no written contract. Oral licensing agreement is legally invalid.[13]

The property rights of a copyright holder can be assigned or transferred. Assignment of property rights requires the conclusion of a contract in writing. A contract of assignment shall contain the title of the work, the category and geographic area of the assigned right, the assignment price, the date and manner of payment of the assignment price, the liabilities for breach of the contract, and any other matters that the contracting parties consider necessary. The subject matter of copyright assignment is some or all of the property rights. As a result, the receiver of the assignment becomes the legal owner of part or all of the property rights, while the original author loses part or all of the property rights accordingly. Furthermore, the receivers of copyright assignment can license others to receive assignment. In contrast, the subject matter of copyright licensing is related to the exercise rather than the ownership of property rights. The person who is licensed to use a work is not the legal owner of the work; therefore, he cannot sublicense the same work to a third party and must gain permission from and pay remuneration to the author.[14]

Copyright infringement

The *Copyright Law* lists ten types of copyright infringement. They include publishing a work without permission of the copyright owner; publishing a work of joint authorship as a work created solely by oneself without permission of the other co-authors; having one's name mentioned in connection with a work created by another in order to seek personal fame and gain, where one has not taken part in the creation of the work; distorting or mutilating a work created by another person; plagiarizing a work of another person; exploiting by exhibition, film production or any analogous method of film production, or by adaptation, translation, annotation, or by other means, without permission of the copyright owner; exploiting a work created by another person without paying remuneration as prescribed by regulations; renting a work, sound recording, or video recording without permission of the copyright owner of a cinematographic work, a work created by virtue of an analogous method of film production, computer software, sound recording or video recording or the owner of a copyright-related right; exploiting the typographic arrangement of a book or periodical without permission of the publisher; and broadcasting live a performance or communicating the live performance to the public, or recording his performance without permission of the performer.

In Chinese judicial practice, the above-mentioned provisions on copyright infringement have been applied to cyberspace. This is evident in China's first case involving infringement of the copyright of an Internet home page—*Beijing Ruide Co. v. Sichuan Oriental Information Services Co.* (1999) (Case 5.1).

Case 5.1   *Beijing Ruide Co.* v. *Sichuan Oriental Information Services Co.*: infringement on copyright of an Internet home page[15]

Plaintiff Beijing Ruide claimed that defendant Sichuan Oriental had duplicated its Internet home page, including the layout, color, pattern, columns, column headings, programs, drop-down menu, and other aspects of the home page, as well as the logo and search engine on the website. The plaintiff thus sued the defendant for infringing on the copyright of Internet home pages, requesting 199,900 yuan economic compensation. The court recognized that there were obvious signs of plagiarism with regard to the defendant's imitation of the plaintiff's home page. As a result, the court determined that the defendant had violated the plaintiff's copyright in the home page and should compensate the plaintiff 2,000 yuan. The plaintiff's original claim for a larger amount of compensation was not supported by the court.

Case 5.2   The Wang Antao copyright infringement case[16]

In the Wang Antao copyright infringement case (1999), defendant Wang Antao illegally obtained a copy of computer software developed by Tianli Co., and then asked a third party to make minor revisions to the software source code in order to develop software which later generated more than 20 million yuan of profits. The court held that computer software, as intellectual property, was protected by copyright laws, and that Tianli Co. enjoyed copyright protection for any software product resulting from its independent research and development. The software developed by the defendant proved to be minor changes and modifications of Tianli's software; it was not original, so it could not enjoy copyright protection. Moreover, the defendant, without the permission of the copyright owner, had modified the software source code by changing its text, images and logos. The court decided that the defendant had infringed on the copyright of the plaintiff and sentenced him to four years' imprisonment, a fine of 20,000 yuan, and compensation of 286,900 yuan to be paid to the plaintiff for economic loss.

An online work may also become the object of copyright infringement (Case 5.3).

Case 5.3   The Computer Business Information copyright infringement case[17]

In the *Computer Business Information* copyright infringement case (1999), plaintiff Chen Weihua wrote an article titled "Joking MAYA" and uploaded it to his personal home page "3D Sesame Street" in May 1998. Without the consent of the plaintiff, defendant *Computer Business Information* published this article a few months later. The plaintiff sued the defendant for copyright infringement. The court, after hearing the case, held that the article "Joking MAYA" was an innovative literary description of three-dimensional animation technology; it could be digitalized and fixed in computer hard drives, and uploaded to a website to be accessed and copied by Internet users; the article should therefore be subject to copyright protection. The plaintiff's uploading of his article "Joking MAYA" to the website was in fact an act of sharing and disseminating his work via the Internet. Without the plaintiff's permission, the defendant had published his article in its newspaper for economic purposes; it had thus violated the plaintiff's rights of exploitation and to receive remuneration. The court determined that the defendant had infringed upon the plaintiff's copyright, and required the defendant to stop infringement, make a public apology, and pay reasonable compensation to the plaintiff for economic loss.

Infringement of the right to online dissemination of information

The issue of online copyright infringement is becoming increasingly complex, especially given the emergence of a new web-based copyright, i.e., the right to online dissemination of information. Such a concept is mentioned several times in the *Copyright Law*: Article 10 states that the copyright holder shall enjoy the right to disseminate his work via the Internet; Article 37 provides that a performer shall, in relation to his performance, enjoy the right to authorize others to communicate his performance to the public through the Internet, and to receive remuneration; Article 41 provides that anyone who is authorized to reproduce, distribute, and communicate to the public via the Internet sound recordings or video recordings shall also obtain permission from, and pay remuneration to, the copyright owner and the performer, as presented by regulations. In the *Regulations on the Protection of the Right to Online Dissemination of Information*, the right to provide the works, performance, video/audio products to the public in a wire or wireless manner has been summarized as the right to online dissemination of information. Accordingly, acts of violating the right to online dissemination of information may constitute copyright infringement, which can be divided into three categories as follows.

The first type of infringement is to provide without permission any work, performance, or audio-visual products to the public through the Internet. In China, the copyright holder's right to online dissemination of information is protected by copyright laws. Unless it is otherwise prescribed by laws or regulations, an organization or individual that provides the general public with other people's works, performance, or audio-visual products via the Internet must obtain the owner's permission and pay the relevant remuneration.[18] Without permission from or remuneration paid to the copyright owner, providing others' works via the Internet constitutes an infringement upon the right to online dissemination of information (Case 5.4).

The second type of infringement is to purposely avoid or damage the adopted technical measures. For the purpose of protecting the right to online dissemination of information, copyright owners are legally allowed to adopt technical measures. The term "technical measures" here refers to the techniques, devices, and components that are used to prevent or restrict access to online works, performance and audio-visual products or the provision of works, performance and audio-visual products via the Internet in the absence of the relevant owner's

---

Case 5.4 *Chen Xingliang* v. *China Digital Library Co.*: infringement of right to online dissemination of information[19]

A typical case in this regard is *Chen Xingliang* v. *China Digital Library Co.* (2002). Plaintiff Chen Xingliang is a faculty member at Beijing University and the author of several books, including *New Perspectives on Contemporary Chinese Criminal Law*, *General Principles for the Application of the Criminal Law*, and *On Justifiable Defense*. The defendant set up the website www.d-library.com.cn to collect, compile, and publish the works of others. Without permission from the plaintiff, the defendant uploaded all of the above three books to its website. The plaintiff sued the defendant for copyright infringement. The court held that the plaintiff enjoyed the rights to publish and distribute all of his three works, including the right to license a publisher to publish his works. In the absence of contrary evidence, such licensing is limited to publication on paper. Without permission from the plaintiff, the defendant had published his work on the Internet, thus violating his right to online dissemination of information. The court concluded that the defendant had infringed the plaintiff's right to communicate through information networks; it should immediately stop the infringing activity and also bear corresponding civil liability.

---

permission.[20] Under Chinese law, no organization or individual may purposely avoid or break the technical measures, purposely manufacture, import, or provide the public with devices or components that are mainly used to avoid or break technical measures, or purposely provide such technical services to any other person for the purpose of avoiding or breaking the technical measures.[21] This means that the act of circumventing technological measures must be intentional. Inadvertently breaking technical measures is not subject to this constraint. The act of circumventing technological measures can be either direct or indirect. Direct circumvention refers to the act of decoding encoded works, decrypting encrypted works, or avoiding, removing, breaking, or damaging the technical measures by other means. Indirect circumvention refers to the act of, for instance, uploading, transmitting, or providing measures, devices, methods, or techniques that can be used to circumvent or break technical measures. Unless it is otherwise prescribed by laws and regulations that the relevant technical measures may be avoided, both direct and indirect circumvention of technological measures are subject to legal liability.

In accordance with the relevant laws, however, technical measures may be legally avoided under four situations. These include: (a) where published works, performance, or audio-visual products are provided to a small number of people who engage in teaching or scientific research through the Internet for the purpose of teaching or scientific research, and such products can be accessed only through the Internet; (b) where written works as already published are provided to the blind through the Internet for non-commercial purposes in a unique way as particularly perceptible by the blind, and such works can be accessed only through the Internet; (c) where the state organ exercises its functions according to administrative and/or judicial procedures; and (d) where a party carries out testing of computers, computer systems, or the safety performance of the information network.[22] These provisions purport to prevent an absolute monopoly of works by technical measures, since such a monopoly may have a negative impact on society at large.

The third type of infringement is to purposely delete or change the electronic information on rights administration. The term "electronic information on rights administration" refers to the information detailing the work and the author thereof, the performance and the performers thereof, the audio-visual products and the producers thereof, the information on the rights owners in the works, performance and audio-visual products, as well as the requirements for application and the digits or codes representing the aforesaid information.[23] Common electronic information on rights administration includes the name of the work, the author's name, the names of the copyright holders, the names of the authors, performers, and directors of an audio-visual work, the terms and conditions under which the work is used, and the agreement with users of a website.

The information on rights administration is mainly used to protect the authorship of a work and help the public to verify the authenticity of a work. In the digital environment, electronic information on rights administration can easily be removed or changed, thus posing great risk and damage to copyright holders' interests. Under Chinese copyright law, intentionally deleting or altering the electronic rights management information of a work without the permission of the copyright owner constitutes infringement of the copyright owner's right to communicate through information networks, and the infringer shall be subject to a corresponding legal liability.[24] Where it is impossible to avoid deleting or changing the electronic information on rights administration, however, it is legally allowed to remove or change such information. This includes situations in which such information cannot be saved during the process of digital/analog signal conversion; or the involved works, sound recordings, and video clips are used in advertising or other programs of very short duration.[25]

In any of the above infringements, the offender should cease infringement, reverse the negative effects, make a public apology, and make payment of remuneration. Where the offender has also damaged the public interest, the regulatory authority may force him to stop the infringing activities, confiscate his illegal income, and sentence him to a maximum fine of 100,000 yuan. Under serious circumstances, the regulatory authority may confiscate such equipment as computers that enable network services, and investigate his criminal liability in case the conduct constitutes a crime.

Copyright and public interest

The purpose of copyright laws is to protect the rights of copyright owners and to encourage the creation and dissemination of intellectual products. To prevent abuse of such rights and maintain the interest of society at large, however, there are also certain restrictions on copyright. Indeed, an important part of copyright law is to place reasonable and necessary restrictions on copyright in order to achieve a balance between protecting copyright and preserving the public interest. In China, there are two main forms of copyright restriction, namely, fair use and permissive use.

Fair use

Fair use refers to the situation whereby a person can legally use others' work under certain circumstances without permission from or remuneration to the copyright owner. Fair use must abide by several fundamental principles: there must be a certain legal basis for fair use;

the work to be used must have been published; the purpose of fair use must be justifiable, mainly for personal study and research or for the public interest; the name of the work, the name of the author, and the work's origin must be specified in fair use; and fair use must not violate the interests of the copyright owner.[26] Based on these principles, the *Copyright Law* stipulates 12 circumstances for fair use. Taking into account the characteristics of the network environment, the subsequent *Regulation on the Protection of the Right to Online Dissemination of Information* applies 9 of the 12 fair uses to the Internet, and also includes a separate Article elaborating the fair use of libraries and other similar institutions.[27]

The nine circumstances in which fair use can be used as a defense against online copyright infringement are: (a) where an appropriate portion of a published work is quoted in one's own work for the purposes of introducing or making comments on a work, or demonstrating a viewpoint; (b) where it is unavoidable to reuse or cite, for any reason, a published work in newspapers, periodicals, radio/television programs, or any other media for the purpose of reporting current events; (c) where, in order to support teaching or scientific research, a small quantity of a published work is provided to some people who engage in teaching or scientific research; (d) where a state organ uses a published work, within proper scope, for the purpose of fulfilling its official duties; (e) where a work as already published by Chinese citizens or organizations in Chinese is translated into the language of a minority ethnic group and then provided to such people within the territory of China; (f) where a published work is provided to the blind in a special way particularly perceptible to the blind and not for the purpose of making profits; (g) where a published article on current affairs such as political and economic issues is provided through the information network; (h) where a speech as delivered in a public gathering is provided to the general public; and (i) where libraries and other public cultural institutions provide collection through information networks.[28]

Permissive use

Permissive use refers to the situation whereby an individual may use others' published works without consent. Under permissive use, an individual should make payment to the author or other copyright owners, and should state the author's name, the title, and the source of the work. Both permissive use and fair use allow a person to use others' published works without the consent of copyright holders, but the former involves forced payment of compensation, while the latter does not. The purpose of establishing the permissive use system is to simplify the copyright procedure, enhance the dissemination of works, and enable society to enjoy intellectual achievements in a more convenient way. Permissive use must abide by the following principles: it must be authorized in accordance with relevant laws and regulations; the involved work must have been published; it is subject to the author's statement of reservations regarding use by others; it involves the payment of remuneration to the copyright owner; and it must not violate the legal rights and interest of copyright owners.[29]

The *Copyright Law* provides that, except as the copyright owner has otherwise declared, newspapers or periodicals may reprint or abridge a work that has already been published in the press, but they shall pay remuneration to the copyright owner. This provision on permissive use has been applied to the online dissemination of information. Under the *Interpretation of the Supreme People's Court on Several Issues Concerning the Application of Law in the Trial of Cases in Relation to Copyright Disputes over Computer Network* (2004), except that the copyright owner has otherwise claimed directly or through the press or an ISP, reprinting and adapting a work, when the source is indicated and the remuneration paid, do not constitute infringement. In fact, this provision provides both websites and traditional publishers the same right of permissive use. In other words, websites and newspapers can take advantage of permissive use to reprint or abridge published works from each other. However, some argue that reprinting and abridging works published on the Internet goes beyond the requirements of such international conventions as TRIPS. This kind of provision has thus been deleted in subsequently promulgated laws and regulations.

Regarding online communication, the *Regulation on the Protection of the Right to Online Dissemination of Information* sets up two circumstances in which permissive use may be exercised. One concerns distance education. Article 8 states that where the nine-year compulsory education or state education planning is implemented through the Internet, the owner's permission is not required for using fragments of works, short written works or musical works, a single work of fine art, or photographic works to produce courseware. The long-distance education institutions that have produced courseware or acquired courseware according to law may provide such courseware to registered students through information networks, but shall pay relevant remuneration to the copyright owner. The purpose of this Article is to encourage the use of information technology in distance education, which plays an important role in improving education in China's rural and remote areas. The other circumstance for permissive use concerns poverty alleviation. Article 9 provides that where a work on planting and breeding, disease prevention and cure, disaster prevention and relief, or a work that meets people's basic cultural demands, has been published, the ISP should announce in advance the uploading of such a work to the website. Within 30 days of the announcement, where the copyright holder refuses to provide his work, the ISP should not provide his work. Where 30 days have elapsed since the announcement, and if the copyright holder has no different opinion, the ISP then may provide his work and pay the corresponding remuneration. Primarily designed to help in alleviating poverty in rural areas, this Article also places specific restrictions on the receiver of the exploited works, the scope of the works under permissive use, and the ways to obtain permissive use, in order to prevent abuse of this right.

Internet service provider liability

Copyright infringement in cyberspace involves Internet users as well as Internet service providers. How to define ISPs' liability for online copyright infringement not only concerns the level and quality of copyright protection, but also directly affects the development of the Internet industry and the interests of millions of Internet users. In November 2006, the Supreme People's Court further revised the *Interpretation on Several Issues Concerning the Application of Law in the Trial of Cases in Relation to Copyright Disputes over Computer Network*, which specifies the legal liability of an ISP in online copyright disputes. According to this interpretation, an ISP should bear civil liability in any of the following situations: (a) the ISP makes use of its website to participate in, incite, or assist in copyright infringement by a third party; (b) the ISP is well aware that one person has used its network to infringe upon another person's copyright, or the copyright owner has submitted a substantiated warning regarding infringement, but it fails to take such measures as removing the infringing content in a timely manner; (c) where a copyright owner requests the ISP to provide the infringer's registration information so as to pursue the infringer's liability, the ISP, without justification, refuses such a request; and (d) the ISP is well aware that certain methods, equipment, or materials can be used to circumvent or break the technical measures for protecting others' copyright, but it still uploads, transmits, or provides such methods, equipment, or materials online. As can be seen from these provisions, an ISP is not required to examine whether or not the information transmitted or stored by Internet users is infringing, but it is obliged to prevent the dissemination of infringing information when it is aware or informed of the infringement; otherwise, it will bear civil liability.[30]

In order to avoid imposing excessive burdens on ISPs, legislators have further identified several types of ISP liability exemption for online copyright infringement, as prescribed in the *Regulation on the Protection of the Right to Online Dissemination of Information*. First, an ISP providing access services or transmission services may be exempted from liability if it has met all of the following conditions: having clearly proved that access or transmission services are offered automatically by a pre-designed computer program which follows the instructions of the service objects; having not selected or altered the work, performance, or audio-visual recording provided by the service objects; and having provided the work, performance, or audio-visual recording to the designated service objects, while having prevented others beyond the designated service objects from obtaining access.

Second, an ISP providing system cache services may be exempted from liability. System cache refers to a technological means used by an ISP to improve the efficiency of network transmission and to enable its users to obtain information from other websites more quickly. One of the common means is to analyze other ISPs' information that is frequently browsed by the service objects, and then post such information onto the website in order to inform the objects rapidly.[31] An ISP offering system cache services must meet the following three conditions to exempt itself from liability for storing and providing others' works, namely: having not altered the stored works; having not affected the original ISP of the works in managing the relevant works; when the original ISP alters, deletes, or shields the works, automatically altering, deleting, or shielding them according to the technical arrangement.

Third, an ISP providing information storage space services may also enjoy exemption. Information storage space refers to the network information platform controlled or operated by an ISP where the service objects can provide works to the public via the Internet while an ISP has the right to delete or shield them.[32] As for an ISP providing information storage space services, it specifically involves providing its users with disk space where the users can store all kinds of digitalized information, or create a personal or organization website for disseminating information to the public. To be exempted from copyright infringement liability, an ISP providing information storage space must meet the following five conditions: having clearly mentioned that the information storage space is provided to the service objects, and also having publicized the name, contact information, and web address of the ISP; having not altered the work provided to the service objects; having not known and having no justified reason to know that the works provided by the service objects have infringed upon others' right; having not directly obtained economic benefits from the service objects' provision of the work; and after receiving the notification from the owner, having deleted the work regarded as infringing on the right of the owner.

Fourth, an ISP providing searching or linking services may be exempted. Searching services means that an ISP providing such services copies the real-time web pages of other websites to its own Internet server with the help of searching software, then classifies and indexes them, and finally stores the relevant information in these web pages together with their website addresses in the database of the ISP's website in different categories; when an Internet user makes a search request, the ISP carries out a search automatically within the database and then sends the results to the user online.[33] Linking services means that an ISP places on its own website a website address which stores the detailed content of a piece of information under the title of such information; when an Internet user clicks that title, the ISP will automatically provide the users with the content of the information. The content can be stored either on the ISP's own website or on others' websites.[34] Where an ISP providing searching or linking services has disconnected the link to a work that infringed on others' rights after receiving notification from the copyright owner, it should not be liable for compensation. If it knew or should have known that the linked work has infringed upon another's rights, however, it should bear liability for joint infringement.

In addition, the *Regulation on the Protection of the Right to Online Dissemination of Information* also provides a specific "notice-takedown" procedure for protecting the legitimate interests of copyright owners and also for promoting the sound development of the network industry. Under Articles 14 and 15 of the *Regulation*, as for an ISP that offers information storage space or provides searching and linking services, if the copyright owner believes that any of the works involved in the services has injured his right to online dissemination of information, or that his electronic information on rights administration has been deleted or altered, he may file a written notice with the relevant ISP, requesting it to delete the works or cut off the link to the works. The ISP, after receiving the notice, should immediately delete or disconnect the link to the works suspected of infringing on another's rights, and meanwhile transfer the notice to the service object of the works; if the network address of the service object is not clear and the notice cannot be transferred, the ISP should publicize the content of the notice through the Internet. If the ISP, after receiving the notice from the owner, does not immediately delete or cut off the link to the works, it will be considered to be infringing on another's rights to online dissemination of information. The owner should be responsible for the authenticity of the notice, however. If, due to the notice of the owner, the ISP has wrongly deleted or disconnected the link to the works and thus caused a loss to the service objects, the owner should bear compensation liability.

Given that the notice could be wrong or false, the *Regulation* also establishes an "anti-notice" procedure to protect the legitimate interests of Internet users. In accordance with Articles 16 and 17, where an Internet user receives a notice transferred by an ISP and deems that the works have not infringed on any other person's right, he may submit a written statement to the ISP, requesting it to recover the deleted works. The Internet user should be responsible for the authenticity of this notice. After receiving such a notice, the ISP should recover the deleted works and transfer the written statement from the user object to the owner. The owner should not request that the ISP delete or disconnect the link to the works any more. If the dispute continues, the involved parties may file a lawsuit to seek judicial settlement.

Representative cases

As for an ISP's liability in online copyright infringement, China has obviously been searching for a proper judicial ruling. In 1999, Wang Meng and five other writers sued Beijing Online for copyright infringement. At the time, the case aroused a great deal of controversy, mainly because there was no consensus as to whether the ISP providing information storage space could be exempted from liability (Case 5.5). In the cases of *Liu Jingsheng* v. *Sohu* (2001) (Case 5.6) and *Universal etc.* v. *Baidu* (2005) (Case 5.7), the court delivered a principally consistent verdict on whether ISPs providing searching and linking services could be exempted from liability. The three cases are briefly reviewed here.

Case 5.5 *Wang Meng etc.* v. *Beijing Online*: copyright in digitalized works[35]

On June 15, 1999, Wang Meng and five other famous writers filed a lawsuit against Shiji Internet Communication Technology Co. The plaintiffs accused the defendant's website, Beijing Online, of infringing on their copyrights by publishing their literary works online without permission, and requested compensation for economic and emotional damages. This was China's first dispute over copyright infringement caused by a website's publishing others' works.

The court held that the plaintiffs were the owners of the copyright in their literary works, and thus had the exclusive right to use their works or authorize others to use their works in any manner and form. After being digitalized, a work could be delivered on the Internet but did not turn out to be a new work. Thus, the plaintiffs were still entitled to the copyright in their digitalized works. Without permission, the defendant had stored and uploaded the plaintiffs' works to its website, thus infringing on the plaintiffs' rights to use their works and accordingly receive remuneration. The court ruled that the defendant should stop infringement and make a public apology on its website.

Case 5.6 *Liu Jingsheng* v. *Sohu.com*: infringement of copyright by a linking service[36]

Plaintiff Liu Jingsheng claimed that, without permission, defendant Sohu.com had provided linking services to his translation of *Don Quixote* in three formats so that the public could get access to his translation on other websites through the defendant's searching and linking services. The plaintiff sued the defendant for copyright infringement.

The court held that the plaintiff enjoyed the copyright of the original work as well as the electronic version converted from the original work. The focus of this case was how to determine the liability of an ISP providing searching and linking services. Technically speaking, search engines enable users to quickly find specific content in the ocean of online information, while linking techniques enable users to quickly get access to certain websites or web pages. Both techniques enhance people's use of the Internet, and are beneficial to the public interest. Currently, no law requires an ISP providing searching and linking services to examine whether a linked website commits any infringement. If such a law existed, the ISP might give up providing searching and linking services for fear of bearing infringement liability. This might eventually damage the interests of individuals and of society at large. Therefore, if the linked website contains infringing content, the court should investigate the liability of the content creator. Where an ISP knows that the linked website involves copyright infringement but insists on providing a linking service, it functions as enlarging infringement and thus should bear civil liability.

In the present case, the defendant had no obligation to check whether the linked sites involved infringing activities. But after being informed by the plaintiff, the defendant insisted on providing the linking services to the infringing website. The court thus held that the defendant had in fact enlarged the infringement, so that it should bear civil liability. The court ruled that the defendant should make an apology and pay the plaintiff 3,000 yuan for economic loss.

Case 5.7 *Universal Music Group etc.* v. *Baidu.com*: right to online dissemination not infringed by searching service[37]

In July 2005, seven world-famous music companies, including Universal Music Group, Warner Music Group, and EMI Music, filed a lawsuit against Baidu.com for music copyright infringement. The plaintiffs charged that, without permission, the defendant provided online music playing and music downloading services, which involved more than 100 songs owned by the plaintiffs.

After hearing the case, the court held that the function of search engine services is to help Internet users find the needed information as fast as possible. When providing the MP3 searching service, the defendant was unable to forecast, recognize, and control the legality of the searched-for content. In other words, the MP3 searching service provided by the defendant did not constitute an infringement of the right to online dissemination of information. As for the playing and downloading functions of the defendant, the court also did not find that they infringed on others' right to online dissemination of information. That is because playing is a display of the search results, helping people to recognize and make judgments about the information. In addition, the music works for playing and download were not from Baidu.com but from third-party websites that were not prohibited from being linked. The court said that if a plaintiff thought that a search engine had infringed on his right to online dissemination of information, he could send a written notice to the search service provider, requesting it to cut off the link to his works; after receiving the notice, the search service provider should immediately cut off the link. In this case, the plaintiffs had not performed the duty of informing the defendant. As a result, the court rejected all claims of the plaintiffs.

Trademarks

A trademark is the mark that distinguishes one enterprise's goods or services from those of others. It appeared with commodity production and is the product of a commodity-based economy. A trademark has a variety of functions, such as indicating the source of goods, enhancing the sales and marketing of products, ensuring product quality, and establishing the reputation of products. Therefore, a trademark is considered as a right arising from creative activities and the accumulation of experience in the production process. In other words, a trademark results from an enterprise's intellectual activity. This type of intellectual activity has been recognized and protected by intellectual property laws, ultimately leading to the establishment of the trademark system around the world.

In 1950, the then Government Administration Council promulgated the *Provisional Regulation on Trademark Registration*, which was arguably China's first regulation on trademarks. In 1963, the State Council enacted the *Regulation for Trademark Administration*. In 1982, the NPC Standing Committee passed the *Trademark Law of the PRC*, which became China's most important and comprehensive law on trademarks. The law aimed at "improving the administration of trademarks, protecting the right to exclusive use of trademarks, and encouraging producers and operators to guarantee the quality of their goods and services and maintain the reputation of their trademarks, so as to protect the interests of consumers and of producers and operators."[38] The law was amended in 1993 and in 2001 in order to meet the needs of the times and build a more effective trademark system. In 1993, the NPC Standing Committee enacted the *Law against Unfair Competition of the PRC*, which constitutes an integral part of China's trademark law system.

In this section, some basic concepts of trademarks are presented, including the creation of trademarks, the categories of trademarks, and the registration of trademarks. Acts of infringing on the exclusive rights of trademarks are then discussed, as well as exceptional circumstances. Finally, the issue of trademark protection and Internet domain names is investigated. The application of traditional trademarks to the network environment is of particular concern.

Trademark basics

Creation of trademarks

According to the *Trademark Law*, an application for trademark registration may be filed for any visible mark, including word, design, letter, number, three-dimensional mark, or color combination, or a combination of the elements above mentioned, that can distinguish the commodities of one individual or organization from those of others. This indicates that a trademark should have two features, namely, distinctiveness and visibility. Distinctiveness means that the trademark is distinguishable—it can distinguish the products or services of one enterprise from those of others. Visibility means that the trademark is visible—it is obvious or perceptible to the eye of the public. It can be seen that these two features of a trademark are closely related.

The *Trademark Law* also stipulates that certain marks are prohibited from being used as trademarks. These prohibition provisions are commonly regarded as the standard for the creation of trademarks. Neither registered nor non-registered trademarks may violate such a standard. Specifically, the law provides that all of the following marks should not be used as trademarks: (a) those identical with or similar to the national name, national flag, national emblem, military flag, or medals of the PRC, as well as those identical with the names of the specific sites or the names and designs of the symbolic buildings in the places where the central government agencies are located; (b) those identical with or similar to the national name, national flag, national emblem, or military flag of any foreign country, except with the consent of the government of that country; (c) those identical with or similar to the name, flag, or emblem of any intergovernmental international organization, except with the consent of that organization and those unlikely to mislead the public; (d) those identical with or similar to the official mark or inspection stamp that indicate control and guarantee, except with authorization; (e) those identical with or similar to the name or symbol of the Red Cross or the Red Crescent; (f) those being in the nature of discrimination against any nationality; (g) those constituting exaggerated advertising and that are deceitful; and (h) those detrimental to socialist morality or customs, or having other harmful influences. In addition, the place names of an administrative district at the level of county or above or a foreign place name known by the public may not be used as a trademark.[39] But a place name that has other meanings or is used as part of a collective mark or a certification mark can be an exception; also, a registered trademark that has already used place names remains legally valid.

Categories of trademark

Trademarks can be divided into different categories based on their object of use, purpose, form, and popularity. The diversified classification of trademarks in fact reflects the increasing functions of trademarks and the gradual perfection of trademark laws. In accordance with the *Trademark Law of the PRC*, trademarks can be divided into the following categories.

Commodity marks and service marks

The division of commodity marks and service marks is based on the different objects being marked. While commodity marks show the source of goods, service marks distinguish one service provider from others. Under the *Trademark Law*, individuals or organizations that intend to acquire the right to exclusive use of a trademark for the commodities they produce, manufacture, process, select, or promote should file an application for commodity mark registration with the Trademark Office. Similarly, individuals or organizations that intend to acquire the right to exclusive use of a trademark for the service items they provide should file an application for service mark registration with the same regulatory authority. This provision shows that the most significant difference between commodity marks and service marks is the object of use of trademarks. In practice, insurance, banking, tourism, education, hospitals, advertising, transportation, and telecommunications are considered service industries. But both commodity marks and service marks are subject to the same protection of the trademark law.

Collective marks and certification marks

The categorization of collective marks and certification marks is based on the different purposes for which marks are used. According to the *Trademark Law*, a collective mark refers to a mark that is registered in the name of a group, association, or other organization and then provided to the members of the organization for use in business activity. It is used to indicate that the goods or services belong to a group, so that such goods and services can be distinguished from those of other groups. A collective mark can be used only by members of the group registered under the mark; non-members cannot use it. A certification mark refers to a mark that is registered by an organization with supervisory power over certain types of commodities or services but is used by individuals and organizations outside of the supervisory organization on their commodities or services. The purpose of certification marks is to certify the origin, raw materials, manufacturing methods, quality, or other specific characteristics of the involved commodities or services. Different from the case of collective marks, the registrar of a certification mark cannot use its mark. Both the collective mark and the certification mark serve to enhance the coverage and competitiveness of the trademark. In addition, in accordance with China's trademark laws, any individuals or organizations should be allowed to register geographical marks as their certification marks or collective marks if their goods and services meet the requirements for the use of geographical marks.

Two-dimensional marks and three-dimensional marks

The categorization of two-dimensional marks and three-dimensional marks is based on the marks' forms. A two-dimensional mark refers to a mark that consists of word, design, letter, number, color, or the combination of these elements and that is presented horizontally. However, a three-dimensional mark is made up of three-dimensional symbols, such as the Coca-Cola bottle mark of the Coca-Cola Company. It is permissible to apply for the registration of three-dimensional marks, subject to certain restrictions. The *Trademark Law* of the PRC stipulates that an application for a three-dimensional mark shall not be approved if the three-dimensional figure of the mark originates from the nature of the commodity, is required to solve certain technical problems, or makes the commodity substantially valuable. The purpose of setting up these restrictions is mainly to maintain fair competition and promote technological progress.

Ordinary marks and famous marks

The division of ordinary marks and famous marks is based on the popularity of the marks. Ordinary marks are relative to famous marks. In judicial practice, a court often considers the following factors when determining whether a mark is famous: (a) how well the trademark is known by the relevant public; (b) the period during which that trademark has been in use; (c) the period, extent, and geographic scope of any publicity for that trademark; (d) the record of protection of that trademark as a well-known trademark; and (5) other factors for which that trademark is well known. These basic standards help to distinguish well-known trademarks from other, ordinary trademarks. In China, famous trademarks are protected by law. Article 13 of the *Trademark Law* provides that if a trademark is a copy, imitation, or translation of a well-known trademark for the same or a similar commodity that has not been registered in China, and is likely to cause confusion among the public, it shall not be registered or used; if a trademark is a copy, imitation, or translation of a well-known trademark for a different or dissimilar commodity that has been registered in China, and will mislead the public and lead to possible damage to the interests of the registrant of that well-known trademark, it shall not be registered or used. This means that if a famous mark has not been registered in China, the law only prohibits others from registering and using the trademark for the same or a similar commodity; if a famous mark has been registered in China, however, the law prohibits others from registering and using the trademark for any kind of commodity, no matter whether or not it is the same or similar.

Trademark registration

In China, the registration of trademarks is based on voluntary principles, and thus there are both registered and unregistered trademarks. Both kinds of trademark are legal, but they enjoy different rights. Trademark rights refers to the qualification or ability of an individual or organization to possess, use, profit from, and dispose of a particular trademark. Registered trademarks enjoy the right of exclusive exploitation, which is in fact the focus of Chinese trademark law. Unregistered trademarks, including those well-known trademarks registered in other countries, also enjoy certain rights, which, however, are not exclusive.

In accordance with the *Trademark Law*, an application for trademark registration needs to meet two basic requirements. One requirement is that the trademark should be distinctive and easily identified. This is because the basic function of trademarks is to distinguish one commodity from others. Therefore, the *Trademark Law* stipulates that if a mark has the only generic names, designs, and models of the commodities concerned, or simply directly indicates the quality, main raw materials, functions, use, weight, quantity, or other characteristics of the commodities concerned, it may be considered to be lacking distinctive characteristics and thus may not be registered as a trademark. But this restriction is not absolute. The *Trademark Law* also provides that if such a mark listed above has, through usage, obtained distinctive characteristics and can be easily identified, it is still allowed to apply for registration as a trademark. In short, distinctive features are a prerequisite for trademark registration, but they can be obtained through use.

Another requirement is that a trademark for registration should not conflict with the existing rights of others obtained by priority. Under the *Trademark Law*, "anyone who applies for trademark registration should not damage the existing rights of others obtained by priority, neither may he register, in advance, the trademark that has been used by others and has become influential."[40] This provision establishes the principle of prior registration, while also setting up one exception, i.e., no one is allowed to register another's influential mark, even if that mark has not been registered. The purpose is to ensure that trademark registration abides by the principle of fair competition in a market economy.

In China, the Trademark Office of the SAIC is in charge of trademark registration and administration throughout the country. The SAIC also establishes the Trademark Review and Adjudication Board to handle trademark disputes. In addition, a registered trademark can be assigned. When a registered trademark is to be assigned, the assignor and the assignee should sign an agreement of assignment and also jointly file an application with the Trademark Office. A trademark registrant may, by concluding a trademark licensing contract, authorize another person to use its registered trademark. Similarly, the trademark licensing contract should be submitted to the Trademark Office for archiving purposes.

Trademark infringement

One primary purpose of the *Trademark Law* is to protect the right to exclusive use of trademarks. The *Trademark Law* clearly states that trademark registrants are entitled to the exclusive use of their trademarks. However, this exclusive right is not unlimited. The *Trademark Law* stipulates that entitlement to exclusive use of trademarks must be limited to trademarks that have been approved for registration and to commodities on which the use of a trademark has been approved. In order to effectively protect trademark rights and help to eliminate confusion or misidentification among the consumers, China has enlarged the scope of protection, applying the right to exclusive use of trademarks to similar trademarks and goods. Thus, any use of the same or similar trademarks for the same or similar goods will be protected by the law. According to Chinese trademark law, trademark infringement includes the following situations.

First, a party uses a trademark which is the same as or similar to a registered trademark on the same or similar commodities, without a license from the trademark registrant. This practice is referred to as "passing off." Specifically, "passing off" involves four situations: using a trademark which is the same as another party's registered trademark on the same commodities; using a trademark which is the same as another party's registered trademark on similar commodities; using a trademark which is similar to another party's registered trademark on the same commodities; and using a trademark which is similar to another party's registered trademark on similar commodities. Any of the above uses of trademarks will cause confusion or misidentification among consumers, thus infringing on the rights of both trademark registrants and consumers.

Second, a party sells commodities that infringe upon the right to exclusive use of a registered trademark. When a seller supplies consumers with infringing commodities, he is actually helping the infringer to fulfill the purpose of the infringement. Therefore, the *Trademark Law* regards such acts as infringements of the right to exclusive use of registered trademarks, and it attempts to prevent trademark infringement occurring through the circulation of goods. It should be noted that the original version of the *Trademark Law* established only the "principle of fault liability" for this type of infringement, that is, only when the seller "knows" or "should know" that the commodities he is selling involve infringement can the seller be held liable. This is mainly to reduce the burden on sellers, since it is often difficult for sellers to detect trademark infringement for numerous goods. In judicial practice, however, it is often difficult to determine whether the seller "knows" or "should know" of the infringement activity. The revised *Trademark Law* of 2001 thus deleted the provisions of "know" and "should know," in order to strengthen the protection of registered trademarks as well as to enhance enforcement of the law.

Third, a party forges or manufactures without authorization the marks of another party's registered trademark, or sells the marks of a registered trademark forged or manufactured without authorization. A trademark is a mark that identifies the source of a commodity. Its physical form is the mark or logo by means of which the trademark distinguishes commodities. Marks generally refers to the material entities bearing marks such as automobile logos, manufacturers' labels on clothing, and stickers on beverage bottles. Because marks can be used to express the right to exclusive use of a trademark, forging or manufacturing without permission the marks of another party's registered trademark, or selling such marks, is regarded as a trademark infringement.

Fourth, a party misrepresents the source by removing or obliterating the original trademark. This practice is often termed "reverse passing off." In "passing off," a party associates another party's mark with a good or service. In "reverse passing off," a party removes another party's mark prior to sale. It is argued that there is an inherent connection between trademarks and the commodities they represent. When such a connection is removed, as in "reverse passing off," the trademark's function of distinguishing commodities is terminated and the rights of the trademark registrant are thus infringed. This is why "reverse passing off" is also viewed as a type of trademark infringement.

Finally, there are also several other types of trademark infringement. According to the *Regulation for the Implementation of the Trademark Law* and the Supreme Court's judicial interpretations, among other infringements are: using a sign which is identical or similar to the registered trademark of another party as the name of an identical or similar commodity, or as the decoration of the commodity; deliberately facilitating the actions of others in violation of trademark rights by providing such services as storing, delivering, and concealing the infringing goods; and copying, imitating, and translating all or part of the registered trademark of another party for different or dissimilar goods. All of the above types of action may damage the exclusive right to use registered trademarks and thus are considered to be trademark infringement.

Under the *Trademark Law*, when there is an infringement of the right to exclusive use of a registered trademark, and a dispute arises accordingly, the involved parties shall negotiate to settle it. If any party refuses to negotiate or the negotiation has failed, the involved parties may bring a suit before a court or request the administrative department for industry and commerce to handle the matter. If the administrative department for industry and commerce concludes that an infringement has occurred, it may order immediate cessation of the infringement and may confiscate or destroy the infringing commodities and the tools, and may, in addition, impose a fine. If a party disagrees with the decision, it may bring a suit before a court within a specified period. The above shows that China's handling of trademark infringement involves both judicial and administrative measures to enable the parties to settle trademark infringement disputes according to their own wishes and methods.

Exceptions to trademark infringement

To protect the interests of all parties, Chinese trademark law and regulations have also established restrictions on the exclusive right to use trademarks. In exceptional circumstances, producers and operators may use trademarks identical with or similar to the trademarks of others on the same kind of commodity without this being considered as infringement. Specifically, there are three main exceptions to trademark infringement.

Fair use

Fair use refers to the situation whereby a person can use trademarks identical with or similar to the trademarks of another party on the same or a similar kind of commodity without authorization. Commentators argue that fair use can help regulators to strike a balance between preventing trademark infringement and preserving fair competition. Under the *Regulation for the Implementation of the Trademark Law*, where a registered trademark contains the generic name, shape, or model of the goods, or directly indicates the quality, main raw material, function, use, weight, quantity, and other features of the goods, or contains a place name, the holder of the exclusive right to use the registered trademark has no right to prohibit others from using it. Based on this provision, fair use may include the rational use of descriptive words for goods; the use of registered trademarks of other parties to show the functions and characteristics of goods; and the normal use of personal names (titles) or addresses. It is noted that fair use must be motivated by goodwill, i.e., the user has no intention to conduct unfair competition with the trademark owner. Moreover, fair use must not violate the legitimate rights and interests of trademark owners; when necessary, the user may add marks to distinguish his commodities from those of the trademark holder.[41]

The right of priority

If, prior to the registration of a trademark, others have used a similar or identical trademark in good faith and gained a certain level of reputation, the registrant should allow them to continue to use that trademark. In other words, a claim to the right of priority is based on two conditions: first, the use of a similar or identical trademark by others has occurred prior to the trademark's registration; and second, the similar or identical mark used by others has gained a certain level of reputation. In judicial practice, the right of priority is often used as a defense against trademark infringement, but such a defense is subject to certain restrictions. For instance, anyone applying for trademark registration may not register in advance a trademark that has been used by others and has become influential. Otherwise, his action may constitute malicious trademark squatting, which is clearly prohibited by the *Trademark Law.*

The existing rights of others

These include such rights as copyright, patent, the right to pictures, and the right to personal, enterprise, or geographical names that have existed prior to the application for trademark registration. Under the *Trademark Law*, an application for trademark registration should not damage such existing rights of others obtained by priority. Thus, if a person who is charged with trademark infringement can prove that he has certain existing rights regarding the trademark, he may be exempted from liability.

In cyberspace, the matter of trademark infringement has become much more complicated. It is especially difficult to define the liability of ISPs, as is shown in *Shanghai Dazhong Banchang Co.* v. *Baidu Inc.*, China's first case of online trademark infringement (Case 5.8).

Case 5.8　*Shanghai Dazhong Banchang Co.* v. *Baidu Inc.*: trademark infringement in cyberspace[42]

Plaintiff Shanghai Dazhong Banchang Co. is a company that specializes in providing moving services, while defendant Baidu Inc. is China's largest search engine. In April 2007, the plaintiff found that on the sections of "bid ranking" and "hot zone" of the defendant's website there were a number of fake site links under the plaintiff's name. Without permission, the operators of these sites were using the registered trademark of Dazhong to promote their moving services. The plaintiff claimed that the defendant had failed to fulfill its obligation and was allowing the relevant search results to include the fake websites that violated the plaintiff's trademark rights. The plaintiff charged that the defendant had deliberately facilitated other parties' infringing actions by providing such services as storage and transportation, and so it should bear corresponding liability.

The court remarked that, differently from the normal ranking provided by search engines, "bid ranking" not only charges service fees but also requires the party applying for such a service to

---

submit keywords for its products; so that defendant Baidu, a provider of "bid ranking" service, has an obligation to examine the legitimacy of the keywords. If the keywords submitted by the applicant involve the possibility of trademark infringement, the defendant should further review the relevant qualification documents, such as the applicant's business licenses; otherwise, the defendant will be regarded as being subjectively at fault. In the present case, the court held that the defendant should be aware of the trademark of the plaintiff, which had gained a reputation in the market; however, it had allowed many parties that had no relationship with the plaintiff to use "Dazhong Banchang" or "Shanghai Dazhong Banchang Moving Service Co." as the keywords to apply for its bid ranking service, thus causing various websites with identical business names and business operations to be displayed in the search results. The court recognized that the defendant was subjectively at fault because it had failed to fulfill its obligation to pay appropriate attention to the infringing action; objectively, it had facilitated the third parties' actions of violating the plaintiff's trademark rights and conducting unfair competition, causing harm to the plaintiff. The court thus decided that the defendant's action, along with that of the infringing third-party sites, constituted joint infringement, so that it should be subject to collateral liability.

Issues relating to domain names

In cyberspace, each host or intranet is assigned a unique address, often referred to as the Internet Protocol (IP) address. An IP address is initially a group of 32-bit binary numbers that is converted into the corresponding decimal numbers and then divided into four parts with dots. For example, Baidu's IP address is currently 202.108.22.5. Since it is hard for the public to remember IP addresses, domain names have emerged to enhance the publicity of the Internet. Domain names refers to the hierarchical character identifiers used to identify and locate a computer on the Internet, and they correspond to a computer's IP address.[43] A domain name generally consists of characters, numbers, and symbols; it has two parts separated by dots, as in www.baidu.com. In a complete domain name, the part to the right of the last dot is often referred to as the top-level domain or the first-level domain; the part to the left of the last dot is the second-level domain, to the left of that is the third-level domain, and so on. Since domain names are more convenient for users to memorize, they constitute a fundamental means for users to access the Internet.

With the development of the Internet, a large number of companies have launched websites to promote their products. Each website represents a unique domain name, which has become an important tool for a company to distinguish itself from others in the market. Specifically, a company often uses its name, trademark, or trade name as the central domain, while Internet users often search for and access the company's website by its name or trademark plus ".com". This means that the domain name has become a symbol or a mark of the company. It is a distinct identifier, representing the company's unique value and orientation. It can thus become a key factor in determining the popularity and visibility of the company.

In recent years, domain names have been viewed as closely related to trademarks. Like trademark holders, domain name owners have the right to possess, use, and transfer their domains. Due to the economic value of domain names, companies have witnessed such activities as cybersquatting and the selling, purchasing, loaning, pledging, and licensing of domain names. Many people argue that domain names are the natural extension of trademarks in cyberspace. Once the domain name is registered, the owner will have the same rights as a trademark owner, that is, the domain name right. However, it should be pointed out that there are some substantial differences between trademarks and domain names. For example, a domain name is unique worldwide and represents only one user, while an identical or similar trademark may be used in different countries, on different categories of goods, by different people, at the same time. A domain name is international, while a trademark is regional: the holder of a trademark can enjoy relevant rights only in the country in which the trademark is registered. Unlike trademarks, domain names cannot be licensed; they can only be transferred. In addition, domain names must follow the principle of "register first." Without registration, domain names may not be used in cyberspace. Trademarks may be established through "register first," "use first," or a compromise between the two.[44]

Domain name registration

In China, the MIIT is in charge of the administration of Internet domain names. With the authorization of the MIIT, the CNNIC has the responsibility, as China's domain name registry, to operate and administer the ".cn" country-code top-level domain and Chinese domain name system.[45] Therefore, in order to provide domain name registration services, one must obtain a certificate from the CNNIC and also get approval from the MIIT.

Under the *Administrative Measure for Internet Domain Names in China*, a party must meet the following requirements in order to engage in domain name registration services: be a legal person or a legal institution established in accordance with the law; have a registered capital of not less than 1 million yuan; have established a domain name registration service system within China; have technicians and customer service personnel dedicated to domain name registration services; have a reputation for providing or have the ability to provide long-term service to clients; have a business development plan and a relevant technical plan; have proper facilities for safeguarding network and information security; and have a proper domain name registration service withdrawal mechanism. In addition, the CNNIC *Implementing Rules of Domain Name Registration* stipulates that, in the process of providing domain name registration services, service providers are prohibited from: providing domain name registration services in the name of government agencies, other enterprises or institutions, or any social organizations; registering domain names with false information to take up domain name resources in disguised form; providing domain name registration services by means of unfair competition, e.g., misleading or threatening clients; rejecting the applications of the domain name holders for domain name transfer codes or charging holders for transfer applications; and disclosing the registration-related information of clients that infringes the legitimate rights and interests of clients, or using such information to obtain illegitimate interests.

Taking into account the possible conflict between domain names and trademarks, trade names, or geographical names, the *Interim Administrative Measures on the Registration of Internet Domains* establishes a series of restrictions on domain name registration. It stipulates that without the approval of relevant state organs, no one should use "China,"

"Chinese," "cn," "national," or other similar words as a domain name; with the approval of relevant local governments, no one should use the full or abbreviated names of administrative districts at or above the county level; in addition, no one should use the names of other countries or regions, foreign places, and international organizations known to the public; the names of industries; the generic names of goods; the names of enterprises or trademarks that have been registered in China; and names that may cause harm to the public interest.

One may submit an application for domain name registration by registering online, by e-mail, or in writing, and should sign the domain name registration agreements with the domain name registration service providers. A person who applies for domain name registration should be solely responsible for the domain name that they select, making sure that the domain name of their choice does not damage any third party's interests. In case of any changes to the registration information, the domain name holder should apply to the registrars to change the registration information within 30 days after the changes take place. In cases of domain name transfer, the domain name holder should submit the application form for domain name transfer and identification documents that either bear the official seals of the organization or that have been notarized to the registrars.

Domain name disputes

As discussed above, domain names can be regarded as a company's trademark in cyberspace. Since domain names have distinctive features and a high commercial value, the number of domain name disputes has increased rapidly over the past decade. In Chinese judicial practice, there are mainly three forms of domain name dispute, i.e., cybersquatting, reverse cybersquatting, and disputes caused by similarities among domain names.

Cybersquatting refers to "the practice of registering a trademark as a domain name with the intent of profiting from it by selling it, usually to the trademark holder. As long as the cybersquatter holds the domain name, the trademark holder cannot register its own trademark as a domain name" (Cases 5.9 and 5.10). The cybersquatter thus violates the basic right of the trademark holder to use his trademark.[46]

It is observed that, because of their high commercial value, well-known trademarks have become the worst-hit areas in cybersquatting and also the focus of judicial protection in China (Case 5.11 and Case 5.12).

Cases 5.9 and 5.10   Two cases of cybersquatting

A typical case occurred in the United States, where Panavision sued Toeppen for trademark infringement.[47] Toeppen registered the domain name www.panavision.com and then offered to sell it to Panavision for $13,000. After review, the court determined that, by having offered the domain for sale, the defendant had shown his intent to use the mark in commerce. The court further remarked that a domain name carried the reputation of a trademark, and the defendant's conduct diluted the plaintiff's mark.

In the case of *Cummins Inc.* v. *Chongqing Machinery Co.*, the defendant registered the domain name www.cummins.com.cn in order to promote its own products, which were similar to the plaintiff's.[48] Similarly, the court determined that the defendant's conduct constituted a trademark infringement; it issued a restraining order to the defendant, prohibiting him from using the domain name.

Case 5.11   *Procter & Gamble Co.* v. *Beijing Tiandi Co.*: the extension of trademark rights to domain names[49]

In *Procter & Gamble Co.* v. *Beijing Tiandi Co.*, the court held that the trademark rights of famous trademarks should extend to domain names. The court remarked that "Tide" was a well-known trademark, which was owned by the plaintiff; by adopting "tide" as its domain name, the defendant had diluted the trademark, caused confusion among consumers about the source of the product, and prevented the plaintiff from registering a domain name in the most concise way. The court decided that the defendant had infringed on the exclusive right of the plaintiff and that the action also constituted unfair competition.

Case 5.12 *E. I. Du Pont de Nemours & Co.* v. *Beijing Guowang Information Ltd.*: protection of a well-known mark[50]

In *E. I. Du Pont de Nemours & Co.* v. *Beijing Guowang Information Ltd.*, the plaintiff was the owner of the DuPont trademark but the defendant had registered dupont.com.cn as a domain name. The court held that "DuPont" was a well-known mark, which should enjoy a higher level of protection than an ordinary mark. The defendant had no justified reason for registering a domain name that was similar to the DuPont mark, and such registration could cause confusion among the public. Therefore, the court ruled that the defendant's trademark constituted an infringement and unfair competition.

Reverse cybersquatting refers to the situation whereby, in bad faith, a person registers another person's domain name as his own trademark. In China, many famous domain names have renowned Chinese names. For example, China's largest port site, www.sina.com.cn, is often referred to as 新浪; another influential site, www.163.com, is often called 网易. These Chinese names may not match the enterprise names of the domain name owners. As a result, people may attempt to register these famous Chinese names as their enterprise names, thus causing trademark infringement disputes (Case 5.13).

Case 5.13 Chinese enterprise names and trademark infringement[51]

In May 1997, Suzhou Yilong Electronic Ltd. (Yilong) applied for the registration of the 雅虎 mark; Yahoo! Inc., an American Internet company, put forward an objection, claiming that the 雅虎 mark was the Chinese transliteration of its enterprise name. However, China's trademark regulator, the SAIC, approved Yilong's application. The SAIC held that Yahoo! Inc. had registered only the Yahoo! mark in China; it had not registered the 雅虎 mark, so it should not enjoy the exclusive right to use an unregistered mark. Furthermore, the goods and services provided by Yilong under the 雅虎 mark were different from those provided by Yahoo! Inc. in terms of their functions and distribution channels, so that the registration of the 雅虎 mark by Yilong would not cause confusion among consumers. It is argued that the SAIC merely stuck to China's trademark law and failed to give full consideration to the protection of a company's domain name.

Reverse cybersquatting may also be reflected in trademark abuse, where the trademark owner improperly uses its position to threaten or file a lawsuit against someone who is not infringing when registering a domain name. In fact, in such cases a company is attempting to exercise control over a trademark beyond that legally offered by trademark law (Case 5.14).

Case 5.14 *Shijiazhuang Fulande Co. v. Beijing Mitian Jiaye Ltd.*: protecting domain name right from expansion of the scope of trademark right[52]

In the case of *Shijiazhuang Fulande Co. v. Beijing Mitian Jiaye Ltd.*, the plaintiff, who had registered the PDA trademark in 1997, sued the defendant, who had registered the domain name pda.com.cn in 1998, for trademark infringement. The court held that PDA was a commodity mark, and the registration of the PDA mark as a domain name by the defendant should not be regarded as using the trademark on identical or similar commodities. The court recognized that the defendant was using the PDA mark on its website, but the goods and services promoted on the website were not owned by the defendant. In other words, the defendant was using PDA as a service mark, while the plaintiff was using it as a commodity mark. The court decided that since the plaintiff could not prove that the PDA mark was a well-known mark, the defendant's conduct did not constitute trademark infringement. In this case, the court made its decision mainly to prevent the plaintiff from expanding the legal scope of trademark right, and thus damaging the rights of domain name owners.

Domain names disputes may also be caused by *similarity among domain names*. Someone may register a domain name that is similar to a well-known one, in order to obtain illegitimate benefits. Such practices may have a negative impact on the registrant of the well-known domain name (Cases 5.15 and 5.16).

It is observed, however, that two parties that provide different goods or services may have identical or similar trademarks. If they both intend to register their identical or similar marks as their domain names, it is probable that the domain names of their choice may be identical or similar. In this case, there will be both a coexistence of and a conflict between legitimate rights.

Cases 5.15 and 5.16   Registration of similar domain names

Someone registered the domain name www.goqq.com, which was similar to China's renowned website www.qq.com, in order to engage in the business of transferring and selling QQ accounts.[53] This caused many consumers to mistakenly think that the former site had been established by Tencent Co., the owner of the second site, and trademark infringement thus occurred.

Another example involved a newspaper called *Urban Express*, which registered the domain name www.19floor.net in 2001.[54] After several years of operation, this domain name earned a good reputation among Internet users. In 2005, a person named Wang Linyang registered the domain name www.19floor.com. The name, website columns, and page layout were all similar to those of *Urban Express*. This also led to a domain name dispute.

Solutions to domain name disputes

At present, China mainly uses two methods to resolve the above-described domain name disputes: one is to resort to law, particularly trademark law and unfair competition law; the other is to resort to a ruling by the CNNIC, a semi-governmental administrative agency responsible for Internet affairs in China.

The legal model

In the legal model, China mainly adopts the law against trademark infringement and the law against unfair competition to resolve domain name disputes. Under the *2001 Interpretation of the Supreme People's Court on the Application of Laws in the Trial of Civil Disputes over Domain Names of Computer Network* (hereinafter referred to as the *SPC Interpretation on Domain Names*), a court shall find a defendant's action of registration or use of a domain name to be an infringement or unfair competition if each of the following criteria is satisfied: the rights and interests that the plaintiff claims are legal; the defendant's domain name or the main part of the domain name constitutes a copy, imitation, translation, or transliteration of a well-known trademark of the plaintiff, or is the same as or sufficiently similar to the plaintiff's registered trademark or domain name that the concerned public would be misled; the defendant has neither rights nor interests in the domain name or its main part, nor reasonable grounds to register and/or use the domain name; and the defendant's registration or use of the domain name has malice. Furthermore, the *SPC Interpretation on Domain Names* provides specific guidelines about what constitutes malice in the registration or use of a domain name. It states that a court should convict a defendant of malicious action if he is proved to have registered another's well-known trademark as a domain name for commercial purposes; to have registered or used a domain name that is the same as or similar to the plaintiff's registered trademark or domain name for commercial purposes, and for the purposes of deliberate confusion with the plaintiff's products, services, or websites in order to mislead Internet users into visiting his own website or another website; to have made efforts to sell, lease, or transfer the domain name in other ways at a high price to obtain unfair gain; and to have not used or prepared to use the domain name after registration, but to have intentionally hindered the plaintiff's registration. However, if the defendant produces evidence that the domain name he owns has gained certain fame before the lawsuit and can be distinguished from the plaintiff's registered trademark or domain name, or if there are other circumstances that prove he did not act in bad faith, the court may convict the defendant of a non-malicious action. This provision is designed to balance the interests of the involved parties, and paves the way for the establishment of laws against reverse cybersquatting.

It has been recognized that there are some differences between the right to domain names and the right to trademarks or fair competition; and due to these differences, the current legal model is sometimes found to be insufficient to protect the rights or interests of domain name holders. For example, where a tort involving domain names is established, the court can only require the defendant to stop infringement and make compensation; it cannot determine the owner of the domain name at issue. In this sense, the court cannot fully protect the legal rights of the domain name holder. Therefore, with reference to the ICANN in the United States,[55] China has established a non-profit organization, namely the China Internet Network and Information Center (CNNIC), to help solve various domain name disputes.

The CNNIC model

Founded in 1997 according to relevant laws, the CNNIC is an organization responsible for the registration and administration of .cn national domain names. With reference to the practice of the ICANN, it has since promulgated a series of rules and regulations for resolving domain name disputes. The most important rule is the *CNNIC Domain Name Dispute Resolution Policy*, which was enacted in 2002 and revised in 2006. It should be noted that these rules are applicable only to .cn domain names and Chinese domain names that are administered by the CNNIC.

Under the *CNNIC Domain Name Dispute Resolution Policy*, a complaint against a registered domain name can be established if any of the following situations is involved: the disputed domain name is identical with or confusingly similar to the complainant's name or mark in which the complainant enjoys legal rights or interests; the disputed domain name holder has no right or legitimate interest in respect of the domain name or major part of the domain name; or the disputed domain name holder has registered or has been using the domain name in bad faith. Like the above-mentioned judicial interpretation on domain name disputes, this CNNIC resolution policy also specifies the situations in which the registration or use of a domain name is regarded as malicious.

These situations include: the purpose for registering or acquiring the domain name is to sell, rent, or transfer the domain name registration to the complainant, who is the owner of the name or mark, or to a competitor of that complainant, and to obtain unjustified benefits; the disputed domain name holder frequently registers domain names in order to prevent the owners of names or marks from using those names or marks as domain names; or the disputed domain name holder has registered or acquired the domain name for the purpose of damaging the complainant's reputation, interrupting the complainant's normal business activities, or creating confusion about the complainant's name or mark among the public. However, a party can demonstrate that it is entitled to the rights and interests of the disputed domain name if any of the following circumstances is verified: before receiving any notice of the dispute, the party used or intended to use the domain name for the purpose of offering goods or services with good faith; the party as an individual or an organization has been widely known to the public by the domain name, even if it has not obtained the trademark or service mark rights; or the fair or non-commercial use of the domain name by the party neither purports to mislead or divert consumers for commercial gains, nor does it tarnish the trademark or service mark at issue. These rules can thus be used by the domain name registrant as a defense against allegations of trademark infringement.

Any party who considers that a domain name registered by others conflicts with its legal rights and interests may file a complaint with a dispute resolution service provider. Upon acceptance of the complaint, the dispute resolution service provider should form a panel, which is often composed of one or three experts on the Internet and relevant legal affairs. The providers of domain name dispute resolution services should provide lists of the names of online experts for plaintiffs and defendants to choose from. The panel is expected to abide by the principles of independence and impartiality, and render a decision on the dispute within 14 days from the date of the appointment of the panel.

It should be pointed out that, although the CNNIC imitates the ICANN model to some extent, it also has its own characteristics. For example, the CNNIC rules are not merely applicable to conflicts between domain names and trademarks; they have been extended to the conflict between domain names and other names or logos enjoying legal rights, such as business names and personal names.[56] In addition, the CNNIC model has received legislative recognition and support, which is not the case with ICANN. Under the *Administrative Measure for Internet*

Domain Names in China, the administrative authority for domain name registration such as the CNNIC can designate an independent organization to resolve domain name disputes. The decisions made by such an organization should apply only to changes in the information on the holders of disputed domain names. If the decision of a domain name dispute resolution organization is not in accord with a legally effective ruling made by a court or an arbitration institution, the ruling of the court or the arbitration institution should prevail. This provision not only lends legal support to the CNNIC resolution model, but also defines its relationship to the courts or arbitration bodies (Case 5.17).

Case 5.17 *Royal Canin* v. *Liu Weize*: a dispute resolved by judicial proceedings and CNNIC[57]

In the case of *Royal Canin* v. *Liu Weize*, involving trademark infringement and unfair competition, both judicial proceedings and the CNNIC resolution model were used. In August 1997, plaintiff Royal Canin, a French pet foods company, registered the Royal Canin trademark and related figures with China's Trademark Office; in 2002, it established two subsidiary companies in China; in 2004, it registered the domain name www.royal-canin.com.cn, which had not been put into use. The official websites of the French company included www.royal-canin.com and www.royal-canin.cn. In 2006, defendant Liu Weize registered the domain name www.royalcanin.cn to answer various questions encountered by users in the use of Royal Canin's dog food. At the top of the home page, the website carried the following statement in a red font: "Please distinguish this site from the Chinese website of Royal Canin; if you want to visit the official website of French Royal Canin, please login to www.royal-canin.com or www.royal-canin.cn."

In August 2006, the plaintiff appealed to a domain name disputes resolution center in China, claiming that the defendant did not enjoy any legitimate rights to the domain name www.royalcanin.cn and had registered that domain name in bad faith. The plaintiff requested the defendant to transfer the involved

---

domain name to Royal Canin. The request was rejected by the domain name disputes resolution center. On the basis of equal consultation, the two parties then signed an agreement on the transfer of the domain name. The defendant did not go through the domain name transferring procedure, however. The plaintiff therefore filed a case at a court, requiring the defendant to stop infringement, cancel the registration of the involved domain name, make an apology to the plaintiff, and bear all costs of litigation.

The first-trial court held that the registration and use of the domain name at issue by the defendant were in bad faith; the defendant did not enjoy the rights to and interests in the main part of the domain name "royalcanin," and had no justifiable reasons for registering or using the domain name. Besides, the main part of the domain name was similar to the enterprise name, trademark, and domain names of the plaintiff, thus causing confusion among consumers. The court decided that the defendant's conduct constituted unfair competition and the plaintiff's claim was supported. Objecting to the decision of the first-trial court, defendant Liu Weize appealed to a higher court. After investigation, the second-trial court ruled that the use of the involved domain name by Liu Weize would not cause confusion among the public; also, Liu Weize was not using the domain name to engage in commercial activities, and the agreement that he had reached with Royal Canin on the sale of the domain name was insufficient to prove that he had purported to obtain improper benefits, so that his conduct should not be regarded as malicious. The final verdict rejected all claims by Royal Canin.

Patents

A patent is a property right granted by a government to an inventor. Specifically, a patent gives the inventor the right to exclude others from making, using, offering for sale, or selling his invention throughout the country or importing his invention into the country for a limited period of time, in exchange for the public disclosure of the invention. As an important type of intellectual property, patent is recognized and protected by Chinese law. The PRC *Patent Law* was adopted in 1984, and amended for the first time in 1992 and for the second time in 2008. In addition, China also promulgated the *Implementation Regulation of the Patent Law* in 1985. The main purpose of patent legislation is to protect the legitimate interests of patent holders, encourage inventions and creations, foster the spreading and application of inventions and creations, and promote technological improvement and economic/social progress. During the past decade, the rapid development of Internet technology has had a significant impact on China's patent system. This section first discusses some basic concepts of patent rights, including the subject and object of patent, the conditions for patent licenses, and patent protection. It then explores the application of patent law to the Internet. The section has a particular focus on the patentability of computer codes and Internet business models.

Patent basics

The subject and object of patent

The subject of a patent is a person who enjoys the protection of patent law and also undertakes corresponding obligations. It includes an "inventor" and "creator," which refers to a person who has made creative contributions to the substantive features of an invention/creation. A person who engages only in organizational work, provides facilities for making use of material and technical means, or takes part in other auxiliary functions during the course of accomplishing the invention/creation is not considered to be an inventor or a creator. Under the *Patent Law* there are two types of invention/creation: service invention/creation and non-service invention/creation. Service invention/creation refers to an invention/creation that is made by a person in execution of the tasks of the entity to which he belongs, or that is made by him mainly through the use of material and technical means provided by that entity. For a service invention/creation, the right to apply for a patent belongs to the entity. After the application is approved, the entity becomes the patentee. For a non-service invention/creation, the right to apply for a patent belongs to the inventor or creator. After the application is approved, the inventor or creator becomes the patentee. Where a non-service invention/creation is completed by two or more inventors and creators, all of these people are considered as co-inventors or co-creators. The right to apply for and possess a patent belongs to all creators and inventors. The right to apply for a patent and the patent right may be assigned. Where the right to apply for a patent is assigned and the application for that patent is then approved, the assignee becomes the patentee. After the assignment of the right to apply for a patent and the patent right, however, the assignee cannot become the creator/inventor, and the creator/inventor does not lose his personal rights.

The object of patent refers to the invention/creation that is entitled to patent rights according to patent law. In China, the object of patent includes inventions, utility models, and designs. Inventions refers to new technical solutions put forward for a product, method, or the improvement thereof. An invention must be a technical solution; it results from the application of the laws of nature to specific technical problems, not being the laws of nature itself. Therefore, an invention is usually achieved through intellectual activities within natural science. An achievement in literature, arts, and social sciences does not constitute an invention recognized by patent law, and thus is not subject to patent protection. Inventions can be divided into inventions of products and inventions of methods. Inventions of products refers to the invention of new products and new substances, such as new materials, utensils, equipment, and machinery. Inventions of methods refers to the invention of new methods and procedures that are applied to solving specific technical problems, such as new manufacturing methods, new processing methods, and new methods for product use. Inventions can be either original or improving. An improving invention is to improve existing products or methods through substantive new technical solutions. For example, an incandescent lamp whose quality and life have been improved significantly may be the object of a patent under improving invention. In short, inventions are technical solutions that produce new products or methods.

Utility models refers to new practical technology solutions for a product's form, structure, or the combination thereof. In China, a patent for utility models protects only those products that are manufactured by industrial methods and that take up space. Unprocessed and natural products and all related methods, such as manufacturing methods, processing methods, communication methods, and methods of use, do not come under the protection of the utility models patent. In addition, a patent for utility models focuses on the product's form, structure, or the combination thereof, that is, such a patent concerns a new technical solution for the product's external form, internal structure, or the combination thereof. A new design that alters the form, pattern, color, or the combination thereof for aesthetic purposes is not a technical solution as required by the utility models patent.

Designs refers to new designs for a product's shape, pattern, or their combination, and the combination of color with shape or pattern which is aesthetically pleasing and industrially applicable. Under China's *Patent Examination Guidelines*, the carrier of a design must be a product. Handicrafts, agricultural products, livestock products, and natural products cannot be the carriers of a design since they cannot be produced repeatedly. Specifically, what may constitute a design includes: the shape of a product; the pattern of a product; the shape and pattern of a product; the shape and color of a product; the pattern and color of a product; and the shape, pattern, and color of a product. In addition, a design may be used in industry and manufactured in batches.

The grant of patent right

Inventions cannot be automatically granted patent rights; instead, the relevant party must file an application with the patents administrative organ. In accordance with the *Patent Law*, an invention must meet two basic requirements to be granted patent right: it cannot violate state laws, social morality, or public interest; and it cannot be completed on the basis of genetic resources, the acquisition or use of which breaches the stipulations of related laws and regulations. In addition to meeting these two basic requirements, any invention for which a patent may be granted must satisfy three substantial requirements, namely, novelty, inventiveness, and practical applicability.

Novelty means that the invention or utility has neither existed nor been publicized before the filing date of the patent application. Therefore, an invention or utility model that has novelty is neither a prior art nor described in an application that was filed by any other person before its date of filing and published on or after its date of filing. The term "prior art" mainly refers to an invention or utility model that has been publicly disclosed in publications in the country or abroad, or has been publicly used or made known to the public by any other means in the country, before the filing date of the application.

Inventiveness means that, as compared with existing technology, the invention has prominent substantive features and represents notable progress. The term "existing technology" refers to technology that has been disclosed through publication in the country and abroad or has been known to the public in the country by any means. The term "prominent substantive features" means that the invention is non-obvious to a person skilled in the art.[58] If such a person can achieve the invention simply through logical analysis, deduction, generalization, or limited experimentation on the basis of existing technology, the invention is obvious and thus possesses no prominent substantive features. The term "notable progress" means that, compared to existing technology, the invention can produce an advantageous technical effect, such as overcoming the defects and deficiencies of existing technology, providing a different technical solution to solve a certain technical problem, and representing a certain new trend in technical development.

Practical applicability means that the invention or utility model can be made or used and can bring positive results. In other words, the invention for which a patent may be granted must be practical rather than purely theoretical. If it is a product, it must be able to be made industrially and solve a technical problem; if it is a method, it must be able to be used industrially and solve a technical problem. In addition, the invention must be able to generate positive economic or social effects, such as increasing the quantity of products, improving product quality, adding more functions to a product, saving energy or resources, and preventing environmental pollution. Only when a patent application for a product or a method satisfies such conditions can a patent be granted.

The acquisition of patent rights should not only meet the above-mentioned basic and substantive requirements, but also follow the procedures provided by patent law, including the initiation of a patent application, preliminary examination, substantive examination, and approval of the grant of patent. After a patent is granted, its validity is limited. For an invention, the duration of patent right is 20 years; for a utility model or a design, it is 10 years. The patentee should pay an annual fee beginning from the year in which the patent is granted.

The protection of patent right

Patent protection is an integral part of the patent law. To effectively protect a patent, the *Patent Law* first clarifies how to determine the scope of patent protection, that is, the scope of protection of the patent right for an invention or utility model should be determined by the terms of the claims, which can be interpreted through the description and the appended drawings; the scope of protection of the patent right for a design should be determined by the product's design, as shown in the drawings or photographs, a brief description of which can be used to explain the patentable design of the product. Based on these provisions,

China's patent law and related regulations define three forms of patent infringement, including direct patent infringement, indirect patent infringement, and passing off a patent.

Direct patent infringement refers to the act of exploiting a patent without the permission of the patentee. The act of "exploiting a patent" mainly includes making, using, offering to sell, selling, or importing the patented product; using the patented process; using, offering to use, selling, or importing the product directly obtained by the patented process; or making, selling, or importing the product incorporating its patented design, for production or commercial purposes. As long as such an act is conducted without the authorization of the patentee, it constitutes direct infringement.

Under the *Patent Law*, the patentee has the exclusive right to exploit his patented products or methods. This does not mean that only the patentee can exploit the patent, however. The *Patent Law* also provides that, with the permission of the patentee, any individual or entity other than the patentee may exploit the patented products or methods. In certain circumstances, a patent may be exploited without the permission of the patentee. For instance, where a national emergency or any extraordinary state affair occurs, the Patent Office may grant a compulsory license to exploit a patent for invention or utility model.[59]

Indirect patent infringement refers to the situation whereby the offender intentionally induces, incites, or helps others to directly infringe on a patent, although his action does not directly constitute patent infringement. The common forms of indirect infringement include: without the permission of the patentee, selling the components of the patented product, selling the molds specifically designed to use the patented product, selling the equipment specifically designed to exploit the patented methods, or assigning the patented technology. In Chinese judicial practice, these acts are usually handled as joint infringement, and the offender will bear corresponding civil liability.

Passing off a patent involves two forms of illegal act. The first form is to pass the patent to another person, which includes the following acts: without permission, marking the patent number of another person on the product produced or sold by himself, or on the package of that product; without permission, using the patent number of another person in the contract, advertisement, or other promotional materials; and forging or altering the patent certificate, patent documents, or patent application documents of another person.[60] The second form is to pass off an unpatented product as a patented product or to pass off an unpatented method as a patented method.[61] Examples include producing or selling an unpatented product marked with a patent mark; after a patent right has been declared invalid, continuing to mark a patent mark on the product produced or sold by himself; declaring an unpatented technology in the contract, advertisement, or other promotional materials to be a patented technology; and forging or altering the patent certificate, patent documents, or patent application documents.[62]

Where a patent infringement dispute occurs, the involved parties may settle it themselves through consultation. If the parties are reluctant to settle the dispute through consultation or the consultation fails to result in an agreement, the parties may resort to a court or request the relevant authority to handle the matter. Where a person passes off a patent, he will be required by the relevant authority to correct his action, in addition to bearing civil liability. If the infringement constitutes a crime, he may be prosecuted for criminal liability.

It should be noted that in China's patent protection system, none of the following is viewed as an infringement of the patent right: (a) where, after the sale of a patented product that was made or imported by the patentee or with the authorization of the patentee, or that was directly obtained through the use of the patented process, any other person uses, offers to sell, or sells that product; (b) where, before the filing date of the patent application, any person who has already made the identical product, used the identical process, or made necessary preparations for its making or use, continues to make or use it within the original scope only; (c) where any foreign transportation vehicle which temporarily passes through China's territory uses the patent in its devices and installations according to relevant agreements; (d) where any person uses the patent solely for the purposes of scientific research and experimentation; (e) where any person uses, manufactures, applies, or imports patented drugs or medical devices for the purpose of providing information to the authority handling patent applications; and (f) where a person uses or sells a patented product without knowing that it was made and sold without the authorization of the patentee, while being able to prove that he has obtained the product from legitimate distribution channels.[63] These are the situations in which patent infringement may be exempted. If the perpetrator is unable to prove such a situation, his action shall be deemed illegal.

Patenting computer software

As indicated earlier, the essence of the patent system is to provide legal protection for invention/creation, encourage scientific and technological development, and promote economic and social progress. Thus, with the rapid development of Internet technology, to offer patent protection for Internet-related inventions has become the focus of the development of patent law. In China and some other countries, a hot topic is whether or not computer software should be included within the scope of patent protection.

Computer software usually refers to computer programs and related documentation. Computer programs refers to the coded instructional sequences which can be operated on information processing equipment such as computers for the purpose of obtaining certain results.[64] Computer programs include source code programs and object code programs. The source code text and the object code text of a piece of software should be seen as one work. Documentation refers to the materials and diagrams which are written in natural or formal language and used to describe the content, components, design, functions, testing results, and method of use of a computer program. Examples of documentation include explanations for program design, flow charts, and user manuals.

As an intellectual achievement, computer software is protected in China by intellectual property law. However, there are different views and practices with regard to the choice of the mode of protection. According to the *Regulations on the Protection of Computer Software* published in 2001, computer software comes under the category of copyright protection. It is argued that using copyright law to protect computer software has the following three advantages. First, computer software is creative and replicable, which are features of the object of copyright protection. Moreover, infringements of computer software are mainly presented by the illegal copying of computer software and the disseminating and selling of the copies; these kinds of action are prohibited by Chinese copyright law. Second, under Chinese copyright law, copyright can be obtained automatically. Therefore, any computer software, after its completion, may obtain the protection of copyright law without going through such procedures as application and approval. Third, it is easier to obtain protection from international treaties. International intellectual property agreements such as the *Berne Convention* and the *Universal Copyright Convention* often include computer software within the scope of copyright protection. Abiding by these treaties is conducive to obtaining international protection for Chinese computer software.[65]

It is well recognized, however, that there are some problems with copyright protection for computer software. First, the copyright law protects only the expression of a thought rather than the thought itself. For computer software, the most valuable aspect is its inner thought. Once the thought has been disclosed, professionals can develop similar software in different ways. Second, the copyright law doesn't prohibit others from using the work; but the value of computer software lies in its use. The copyright protection available to computer software is obviously insufficient. Third, the copyright law aims at encouraging the development of literature and art, but the purpose of protection for software is to promote industrial development. In other words, the development of software relates to its practical function, rather than to satisfying people's spiritual needs. In particular, it is difficult to apply the protection of the author's personal rights in the copyright law to computer programmers, since a patent for software usually goes to the company rather than to the company's programmers.

Given the deficiencies of the copyright protection model, many countries have attempted to adopt contract law, trade secrets acts, and anti-unfair competition law for the protection of computer software. Since questions remain, however, these models have failed to become mainstream solutions. After a comprehensive weighing up of the pros and cons, the patent protection mode for software has been confirmed in many countries. In the case of *Diamond* v. *Diehr* in the 1980s, the U.S. Supreme Court determined that the execution of a physical process controlled by running a computer program is patentable. The Court reiterated its earlier rulings that mathematical formulas in the abstract are not eligible for patent protection, but it held that the mere presence of a software element does not make an otherwise patent-eligible machine or process unpatentable. If the invention as a whole meets the requirements of patentability, it then can be patented, even if it includes software components. This case was a turning point in the course of software protection. Since then, the United States has gradually applied patent protection to computer software, and this practice has been followed by the international community.

Commentators note that patent protection for software has many advantages. For example, patent law protects creative thinking, which is precisely the most valuable part of computer software. Patent protection is exclusive: once a patent has been granted, other similar inventions are no longer protected and used. This is crucial for computer programmers in protecting their software designs and technical methods. In addition, the acquisition of a patent is premised on making the technical proposal known to the public. Making the software source code known to the public can effectively avoid the repeated development of the software. Moreover, the protection of a patent is effective for only 20 years, which is much shorter than the 50 years of copyright protection, but closer to the economic life of computer software.

However, the patent protection model for software is not without its questions. Under patent law, for example, the mathematical formulas created by intellectual activity cannot receive patents; but computer programmers mainly use mathematical methods. In other words, computer codes cannot be the object of patent law. In addition, a patent must possess novelty, inventiveness, and practical applicability; and because of its technical characteristics, most software can hardly meet the former two requirements. Moreover, the review cycle of an application for a patent is relatively long, but the economic life of software is very short. The best-selling time of software would have passed before the application review was completed. This may not conform to the interests of software developers. Finally, patent law requires the patentee to publicize his invention, including the software design. This makes it easy to imitate and copy computer programs; and accordingly, software developers find it difficult to protect their software by means of patents.[66]

Currently, computer software is explicitly included within the scope of protection of Chinese copyright law, but it is not excluded from the protection of Chinese patent law. The *Patent Examination Guide* released by the State Intellectual Property Office in 2010 provides that an invention application relating to computer software can be the subject matter of patent protection if it constitutes a technical solution. This involves computer software that is designed to perform control over an industrial process or a measurement/test process, to process external data, or to improve the internal performance of a computer system. If an invention application involves the execution of any of these software programs, it can be viewed as dealing with technical problems, using technical means, and being able to obtain technical effects, and is thus subject to patent protection. In addition, the *Guide* states that if the method for encoding Chinese characters is integrated with a special keyboard so that it works as a method for inputting Chinese characters into a computer system or for a computer to process Chinese character information, such a method is also subject to patent protection. It can be seen that China has adopted a more open software patent protection system, which is consistent with the trend of international development. In judicial practice, however, China has not rejected software protection by means of other laws. Through the use of different laws, China has tried to achieve a balance between protecting the interests of software developers and preserving the public interest.

Patenting Internet business methods

Business methods are mainly concerned with the use of computer software and hardware for achieving business purposes. Business method patents are a type of patent which claim and disclose new methods of doing business. In judicial practice, business method patents not only share common characteristics with computer software but also possess special features that originate from the combination of computer technology with business activities.[67] As in the case of software patent protection, the United States is also the pioneer and advocate of patenting business methods. In 1996, the U.S. Patent and Trademark Office revised the Examination Guidelines for Computer-Related Inventions, stressing that the examination of business methods should be treated equally to other technical methods. In 1998, the U.S. Court of Appeals for the Federal Circuit ruled in the case of State Street Bank that business methods were patentable. This case opened the door for the subsequent patent applications of a variety of business methods. Following the United States, Japan, the European Union and other countries also began to adopt patent protection of business methods.

Chinese patent law and related laws have not included specific provisions for business methods, but there has been a dispute about the patentability of business methods. One important issue concerns whether business methods should be viewed as the rules and methods of intellectual activities. Intellectual activities refers to a person's thinking activities that produce abstract results through reasoning, analysis, and judgment. The rules and methods of intellectual activities are those rules and methods governing a person's thinking, expression, judgment, and memorization; they do not use technical means, nor do they solve any technical problem or produce any technical effect. Since the rules and methods of intellectual activities do not constitute technical solutions, they are not granted patent rights. In China, business methods had long been viewed as rules and methods of intellectual activities, and so they did not fall within the scope of patent protection.[68] By 2006, China's State Intellectual Property Office had revised the *Patent Examination Guide*, making it possible to patent business methods in some circumstances. According to the revised *Guide*, if a claim relates only to the rules or methods of intellectual activities, it should not be granted patent rights; if a claim contains not only the rules or methods of intellectual activities but also technical features, then the claim as a whole is not a rule or method of intellectual activities, and the possibility of obtaining patent rights should not be ruled out. This means that if business methods not only concern the rules and methods of intellectual activities but also include certain technical solutions, then they may be granted patent protection.

Regarding the patentability of business methods, another important issue is whether business methods should be viewed as technical solutions. By tradition, business methods have been considered as the rules and methods of business activities rather than as technical solutions.[69] In accordance with the revised *Patent Examination Guide*, a technical solution is an aggregation of technical means that apply the laws of nature to solve a technical problem; where a solution does not adopt technical means to solve a technical problem and thereby does not achieve a technical effect, it is not qualified to receive patent protection; where a solution is essentially about solving a technical problem through the use of technical means, it should not be excluded from patent protection. Therefore, if a business method has no relation to computer technology, largely deals with commercial activity rather than technical problems, and mainly obtains business results rather than technical effects, it can then be treated as a rule or method of intellectual activities and thereby cannot be the object of patent protection. To judge whether a business method is a technical solution, three criteria for technical solutions can be used, namely, novelty, inventiveness, and practical applicability. If an Internet business method meets these three elements, it is patentable.

At present, patent applications relating to business methods lie mainly in the two areas of financial services and electronic commerce (Case 5.18).

In the area of electronic commerce, business method patents may relate to online advertising, buying, auctions, and payments. Since payment is integral to all aspects of e-commerce activities, online payment has become one crucial area of patent applications. Based on an analysis of patenting documents, China's patent applications for online payment so far have involved the following areas: payment methods for Internet content; Internet service charging methods; payment by voice methods for e-commerce; immediate payment methods; payment methods for communication services; pre-payment methods for online shopping; mobile payment methods based on image analysis; payment methods

---

Case 5.18 Citibank: applications to patent business methods

With regard to financial services, a famous case concerns Citibank, a major international bank headquartered in the United States. Since 1992, Citibank has submitted more than 20 patent applications to China's Intellectual Property Office, 2 of which have received approval. One was "the electronic money system," which was approved in 2002.[70] It was an integrated processing system which covered e-money issuance, payment, and settlement, the substitution of other payment instruments (such as currency, checks, and bank cards), and accounting management. Another patented business method was "the computer system for data management and related methods of operating the said system," which was approved in 2003.[71] This patent application was a kind of computer system and method by which a bank might trade securities on behalf of its clients.

---

based on communication terminals; bank card-based payment methods; and authentication methods for safe online payment.[72]

Patentable business methods are not limited to financial services and e-commerce. With the development of Internet technology, more and more business methods may be able to obtain patent protection. However, some commentators argue that the expansion of business method patents may affect the balance mechanism of the existing patent system, so that reasonable restrictions on such expansion should be made. There are also some commentators who hold that, since China's local enterprises lag far behind large foreign enterprises in terms of business management, and the patenting of business methods may be more conducive for foreign companies, it is currently inappropriate to draft business methods directly into the patent law.[73] In spite of this, it can be safely concluded that, with China's Internet industry and its market economic system becoming more mature, a more effective business method patent system will be established in the future.

Notes

1. WIPO (2011) "What Is Intellectual Property?" retrieved May 12, 2011 from http://www.wipo.int/about-ip/en/.
2. Merriam-Webster Dictionary, "Copyright," retrieved June 20, 2011 from http://www.merriam-webster.com/dictionary/copyright.
3. John D. Zelezny (2011) *Communication Law: Liberties, Restraints, and the Modern Media*, 6th edition, Wadsworth: Cengage Learning, p. 320.
4. See the *Legal Explanation on the Copyright Law*, which can be accessed at http://www.npc.gov.cn/npc/flsyywd/minshang/node_2200.htm.
5. Yongzheng Wei (2006) *Lectures on Journalism and Communication Law*, 2nd edition, Beijing, China: Renmin University of China Press.
6. Yongzheng Wei (2006) *Lectures on Journalism and Communication Law*, 2nd edition, Beijing, China: Renmin University of China Press.
7. See the *Provisions on the Implementation of the PRC Copyright Law*.
8. See the *Legal Explanation on the Copyright Law*, which can be accessed at http://www.npc.gov.cn/npc/flsyywd/minshang/node_2200.htm.
9. See the *Provisions on the Implementation of the Copyright Law*.
10. See Article 16 of the *Copyright Law* of the PRC.
11. See Jun Qian (2009) "On Online Copyright Protection," retrieved October 12, 2010 from http://www.pkulaw.cn/fulltext_form.aspx?db=art&gid=335591330.
12. See Article 24 of the *Copyright Law* of the PRC.
13. Yongzheng Wei (2006) *Lectures on Journalism and Communication Law*, 2nd edition, Beijing, China: Renmin University of China Press.
14. Yongzheng Wei (2006) *Lectures on Journalism and Communication Law*, 2nd edition, Beijing, China: Renmin University of China Press, p. 343.
15. The source of the case: Haidian People's Court of Beijing Civil Verdict Haidian Intellectual Property Division First Trial Case No. 21 (1999).
16. The source of the case: the Criminal Verdict on the Case of Wang Antao Violating Copyright, *The Communiqué of Supreme People's Court* 1999 (5).
17. The source of the case: Haidian People's Court of Beijing Civil Verdict Haidian Civil Division First Trial Case No. 18 (1999).
18. See Article 2 of the *Regulations on the Protection of the Right to Online Dissemination of Information*.
19. The case can be accessed at http://china.findlaw.cn/falvchangshi/sunhaipeichang/wangluo/anli/29475.html.
20. See Article 4(1) of the *Regulations on the Protection of the Right to Online Dissemination of Information*.
21. See Article 4(2) of the *Regulations on the Protection of the Right to Online Dissemination of Information*.
22. See Article 12 of the *Regulations on the Protection of the Right to Online Dissemination of Information*.
23. See Article 4(3) of the *Regulations on the Protection of the Right to Online Dissemination of Information*.
24. See Article 5 of the *Regulations on the Protection of the Right to Online Dissemination of Information*.

25. See the *Legal Explanation on the Regulation on the Protection of the Right to Online Dissemination of Information*, which can be accessed at http://china.findlaw.cn/chanquan/zhuzuoquanfa/zzqlw/8453.html.

26. Yongzheng Wei (2006) *Lectures on Journalism and Communication Law*, 2nd edition, Beijing, China: Renmin University of China Press, p. 348.

27. Among 12 cases of fair use listed in the *Copyright Law* of the PRC, personal use, free performances, imitation of calligraphy or painting, etc. are not applicable to the Internet and thus are excluded from the *Regulations on the Protection of the Right to Online Dissemination of Information*.

28. See Articles 6 and 7 of the *Regulations on the Protection of the Right to Online Dissemination of Information*.

29. Yongzheng Wei (2006) *Lectures on Journalism and Communication Law*, 2nd edition, Beijing, China: Renmin University of China Press.

30. See Jun Qian (2009) "On Online Copyright Protection," retrieved October 12, 2010 from http://www.pkulaw.cn/fulltext_form.aspx?db=art&gid=335591330.

31. See the *Legal Explanation on the Regulations on the Protection of the Right to Online Dissemination of Information*, which can be accessed at http://china.findlaw.cn/chanquan/zhuzuoquanfa/zzqlw/8453.html.

32. See the *Legal Explanation on the Regulations on the Protection of the Right to Online Dissemination of Information*, which can be accessed at http://china.findlaw.cn/chanquan/zhuzuoquanfa/zzqlw/8453.html.

33. See the *Legal Explanation on the Regulations on the Protection of the Right to Online Dissemination of Information*, which can be accessed at http://china.findlaw.cn/chanquan/zhuzuoquanfa/zzqlw/8453.html.

34. See the *Legal Explanation on the Regulations on the Protection of the Right to Online Dissemination of Information*, which can be accessed at http://china.findlaw.cn/chanquan/zhuzuoquanfa/zzqlw/8453.html.

35. The source of the case: Haidian People's Court of Beijing Civil Verdict Haidian Intellectual Property Division First Trial Case No. 57 (1999).

36. See *The Communiqué of the Supreme People's Court* 2001 (5).

37. The source of the case: Beijing No. 1 Immediate People's Court Civil Verdict Beijing No. 1 Immediate Civil Division First Trial Case No. 8995 (2005).

38. See Article 1 of the *Trademark Law* of the PRC.

39. See Article 10 of the *Trademark Law* of the PRC.

40. See Article 31 of the *Trademark Law* of the PRC.

41. See Shaozhang Li (2008) "Trademark Infringement," in Huang Ping (ed.) *Tort Law*, Beijing: China University of Political Science and Law Press.

42. The source of the case: Shanghai No. 2 Immediate People's Court Civil Verdict Shanghai No. 2 Immediate Civil Division 5 First Trial Case No. 147 (2007).

43. See Article 3(1) of the *Administrative Measures on Internet Domain Names in China*, which can be accessed at http://www.cnnic.cn/html/Dir/2004/11/25/2592.htm.

44. It should be noted that different countries or regions have different rules in this regard.

45. There are currently two types of top-level domain, namely, the generic top-level domain name and the country/region code top-level domain name. China's country code top-level domain name is .cn. The system of Chinese domain name registration largely involves the administration of domain names registered under .cn.

46. Monica Kilian (2000) "Cybersquatting and Trademark Infringement," *Murdoch University Electronic Journal of Law* 7(3), retrieved July 30, 2011 from http://www.murdoch.edu.au/elaw/issues/v7n3/kilian73.html.

47. The source of the case: Panavision International v. Toeppen, United States Court of Appeals for the Ninth Circuit 1998, 141 F.3d 1316.

48. The source of the case: Beijing High People's Court Civil Verdict Beijing High Civil Division Final Trial Case No. 859 (2002).

49. The source of the case: Beijing High People's Court Civil Verdict Beijing High Civil Division Final Trial Case No. 286 (2002).

50. The source of the case: Beijing No. 1 Immediate People's Court Civil Verdict Beijing No. 1 Immediate Intellectual Property Division First Trial Case No. 11 (2000).

51. The case is adapted from Chunbao Yang (2001) "A Study on Several Legal Issues Concerning Domain Names and Relevant Management," Master's thesis, East China University of Political Science and Law.

52. The source of the case: Beijing No. 1 Immediate People's Court Civil Verdict Beijing No. 1 Immediate Intellectual Property Division First Trial Case No. 48 (1999).

53. See Licong Chen (2009) "Perfecting the Legal Protection for Domain Names," retrieved July 12, 2011 from http://www.pkulaw.cn/fulltext_form. aspx?db=art&gid=335596481.

54. The source of the case: Zhejiang High People's Court Civil Verdict Zhejiang High Civil Division 3 Final Trial Case No. 286 (2008).

55. Founded in the United States in 1998, the Internet Corporation for Assigned Names and Numbers (ICANN) is a non-profit organization that is responsible for managing the IP address spaces and assignment of address blocks to regional Internet registries, for maintaining registries of IP identifiers, and for the management of the top-level domain name space.

56. See Zhibin Yi (2002) "The Mandatory Administrative Proceeding on Domain Name Disputes and Related Legal Value," retrieved August 1, 2011 from http://www.pkulaw.cn/fulltext_form.aspx?db=art&gid=335566349.

57. The source of the case: Beijing High People's Court Civil Verdict Beijing High Civil Division Final Trial Case No. 1157 (2008).

58. "The person skilled in art" in the *Patent Law* of the PRC refers to a fictional person who is presumed to be aware of all the common technical knowledge, to have access to all the existing technologies, and to have the capability to apply all the routine experimental measures in the involved technical field.

59. Article 14 and Article 48–58 of the *Patent Law* of the PRC stipulate a set of circumstances and procedures in which a patent may be exploited without the authorization of the patentee for the purpose of protecting the public interest.

60. See Article 84 of the *Rules for the Implementation of the Patent Law* of the PRC.

61. It should be pointed out that this act is illegal but may not be regarded as an infringement in China.

62. See Article 85 of the *Rules for the Implementation of the Patent Law* of the PRC.

63. See Article 69–70 of the *Patent Law* of the PRC.

64. Computer programs also include those symbolic instructional sequences or numeric language sequences that can be automatically converted into coded instructional sequences.

65. See Guangtao Deng (2006) "On the Intellectual Property Protection for Computer Software," retrieved September 11, 2011 from http://vip. chinalawinfo.com/newlaw2002/slc/slc.asp?db=art&gid=335577275; Jin Lei (2006) "On the Patent Protection Model for Computer Software," retrieved September 10, 2011 from http://article.chinalawinfo.com/Article_Detail.asp?ArticleID=35248.

66. See Guangtao Deng (2006) "On the Intellectual Property Protection for Computer Software," retrieved May 11, 2011 from http://vip.chinalawinfo. com/newlaw2002/slc/slc.asp?db=art&gid=335577275; Jin Lei (2006) "On the Patent Protection Model for Computer Software," retrieved May 10, 2011 from http://article.chinalawinfo.com/Article_Detail. asp?ArticleID=35248.

67. See the *Examination Principles on the Patent Application for Inventions Related to Business Methods (Tentative)* promulgated in 2004 by the State Intellectual Property Office.

68. See Song Beibei (2007) "On the Issue of the Patentability of Business Methods," *Auditing and Finance*, 3.

69. See Beibei Song (2007) "On the Issue of the Patentability of Business Methods," *Auditing and Finance*, 3.

70. It was reported that this patent automatically became invalid in 2006, since it had long lacked maintenance.

71. It was reported that this patent was announced invalid by the State Intellectual Property Office in May 2009.

72. See Yanliang Wei (2007) "How to Profit from the Patents for Online Payment Methods," retrieved August 10, 2011 from http://article. chinalawinfo.com/Article_Detail.asp?ArticleID=36476.

73. See Xiaoqing Feng (2010) "On Business Method Patents," retrieved May 1, 2011 from http://www.civillaw.com.cn/article/default.asp?id=49307.

Appendix:
Constitution of the People's
Republic of China[1]

(Adopted at the Fifth Session of the Fifth National People's Congress and promulgated for implementation by the Announcement of the National People's Congress on December 4, 1982.

Amended in accordance with the Amendments to the Constitution of the People's Republic of China adopted respectively at the First Session of the Seventh National People's Congress on April 12, 1988, the First Session of the Eighth National People's Congress on March 29, 1993, the Second Session of the Ninth National People's Congress on March 15, 1999 and the Second Session of the Tenth National People's Congress on March 14, 2004.)

Contents

Section 5 The Local People's Congresses and Local People's Governments at Various Levels

Section 6 The Organs of Self-Government of National Autonomous Areas

Section 7 The People's Courts and the People's Procuratorates

Chapter IV The National Flag, the National Anthem, the National Emblem and the Capital

Preamble

China is a country with one of the longest histories in the world. The people of all of China's nationalities have jointly created a culture of grandeur and have a glorious revolutionary tradition.

After 1840, feudal China was gradually turned into a semi-colonial and semi-feudal country. The Chinese people waged many successive heroic struggles for national independence and liberation and for democracy and freedom.

Great and earthshaking historical changes have taken place in China in the 20th century.

The Revolution of 1911, led by Dr. Sun Yat-sen, abolished the feudal monarchy and gave birth to the Republic of China. But the historic mission of the Chinese people to overthrow imperialism and feudalism remained unaccomplished.

After waging protracted and arduous struggles, armed and otherwise, along a zigzag course, the Chinese people of all nationalities led by the Communist Party of China with Chairman Mao Zedong as its leader ultimately, in 1949, overthrew the rule of imperialism, feudalism and bureaucrat-capitalism, won a great victory in the New-Democratic Revolution and founded the People's Republic of China. Since then the Chinese people have taken control of state power and become masters of the country.

After the founding of the People's Republic, China gradually achieved its transition from a New-Democratic to a socialist society. The socialist transformation of the private ownership of the means of production has been completed, the system of exploitation of man by man abolished and the socialist system established. The people's democratic dictatorship led by the working class and based on the alliance of workers and peasants, which is in essence the dictatorship of the proletariat, has been consolidated and developed. The Chinese people and the Chinese People's Liberation Army have defeated imperialist and hegemonist aggression, sabotage and armed provocations and have thereby safeguarded China's national independence and security and strengthened its national defense. Major successes have been achieved in economic development. An independent and relatively comprehensive socialist system of industry has basically been established. There has been a marked increase in agricultural production. Significant advances have been made in educational, scientific and cultural undertakings, while education in socialist ideology has produced noteworthy results. The life of the people has improved considerably.

The victory in China's New-Democratic Revolution and the successes in its socialist cause have been achieved by the Chinese people of all nationalities, under the leadership of the Communist Party of China and the guidance of Marxism-Leninism and Mao Zedong Thought, by upholding truth, correcting errors and surmounting numerous difficulties and hardships. China will be in the primary stage of socialism for a long time to come. The basic task of the nation is to concentrate its effort on socialist modernization along the road of Chinese-style socialism. Under the leadership of the Communist Party of China and the guidance of Marxism-Leninism, Mao Zedong Thought, Deng Xiaoping Theory and the important thought of Three Represents, the Chinese people of all nationalities will continue to adhere to the people's democratic dictatorship and the socialist road, persevere in reform and opening to the outside world, steadily improve socialist institutions, develop the socialist market economy, develop socialist democracy, improve the socialist legal system and work hard and self-reliantly to modernize the country's industry, agriculture, national defense and science and technology step by step and promote the coordinated development of the material, political and spiritual civilizations, to turn China into a socialist country that is prosperous, powerful, democratic and culturally advanced.

The exploiting classes as such have been abolished in our country. However, class struggle will continue to exist within certain bounds for a long time to come. The Chinese people must fight against those forces and elements, both at home and abroad, that are hostile to China's socialist system and try to undermine it.

Taiwan is part of the sacred territory of the People's Republic of China. It is the inviolable duty of all Chinese people, including our compatriots in Taiwan, to accomplish the great task of reunifying the motherland.

In building socialism it is essential to rely on workers, peasants and intellectuals and to unite all forces that can be united. In the long years of revolution and construction, there has been formed under the leadership of the Communist Party of China a broad patriotic united front which is composed of the democratic parties and people's organizations and which embraces all socialist working people, all builders of socialism, all patriots who support socialism, and all patriots who stand for the reunification of the motherland. This united front will continue to be consolidated and developed. The Chinese People's Political Consultative Conference, a broadly based representative organization of the united front which has played a significant historical role, will play a still more important role in the country's political and social life, in promoting friendship with other countries and in the struggle for socialist modernization and for the reunification and unity of the country. The system of the multi-party cooperation and political consultation led by the Communist Party of China will exist and develop for a long time to come.

The People's Republic of China is a unitary multi-national State created jointly by the people of all its nationalities. Socialist relations of equality, unity and mutual assistance have been established among the nationalities and will continue to be strengthened. In the struggle to safeguard the unity of the nationalities, it is necessary to combat big-nation chauvinism, mainly Han chauvinism, and to combat local national chauvinism. The State will do its utmost to promote the common prosperity of all the nationalities.

China's achievements in revolution and construction are inseparable from the support of the people of the world. The future of China is closely linked to the future of the world. China consistently carries out an independent foreign policy and adheres to the five principles of mutual respect for sovereignty and territorial integrity, mutual non-aggression, non-interference in each other's internal affairs, equality and mutual benefit, and peaceful coexistence in developing diplomatic relations and economic and cultural exchanges with other countries. China consistently opposes imperialism, hegemonism and colonialism, works to strengthen unity with the people of other countries, supports the oppressed nations and the developing countries in their just struggle to win and preserve national independence and develop their national economies, and strives to safeguard world peace and promote the cause of human progress.

This Constitution, in legal form, affirms the achievements of the struggles of the Chinese people of all nationalities and defines the basic system and basic tasks of the State; it is the fundamental law of the State and has supreme legal authority. The people of all nationalities, all State organs, the armed forces, all political parties and public organizations and all enterprises and institutions in the country must take the Constitution as the basic standard of conduct, and they have the duty to uphold the dignity of the Constitution and ensure its implementation.

Chapter I General Principles

Article 1 The People's Republic of China is a socialist state under the people's democratic dictatorship led by the working class and based on the alliance of workers and peasants.

The socialist system is the basic system of the People's Republic of China. Disruption of the socialist system by any organization or individual is prohibited.

Article 2 All power in the People's Republic of China belongs to the people.

The National People's Congress and the local people's congresses at various levels are the organs through which the people exercise state power.

The people administer State affairs and manage economic and cultural undertakings and social affairs through various channels and in various ways in accordance with the provisions of law.

Article 3 The State organs of the People's Republic of China apply the principle of democratic centralism.

The National People's Congress and the local people's congresses at various levels are constituted through democratic elections. They are responsible to the people and subject to their supervision.

All administrative, judicial and procuratorial organs of the State are created by the people's congresses to which they are responsible and by which they are supervised.

The division of functions and powers between the central and local State organs is guided by the principle of giving full scope to the initiative and enthusiasm of the local authorities under the unified leadership of the central authorities.

Article 4 All nationalities in the People's Republic of China are equal. The State protects the lawful rights and interests of the minority nationalities and upholds and develops a relationship of equality, unity and mutual assistance among all of China's nationalities. Discrimination against and oppression of any nationality are prohibited; any act which undermines the unity of the nationalities or instigates division is prohibited.

The State assists areas inhabited by minority nationalities in accelerating their economic and cultural development according to the characteristics and needs of the various minority nationalities.

Regional autonomy is practiced in areas where people of minority nationalities live in concentrated communities; in these areas organs of self-government are established to exercise the power of autonomy. All national autonomous areas are integral parts of the People's Republic of China.

All nationalities have the freedom to use and develop their own spoken and written languages and to preserve or reform their own folkways and customs.

Article 5 The People's Republic of China governs the country according to law and makes it a socialist country under rule of law.

The State upholds the uniformity and dignity of the socialist legal system.

No laws or administrative or local regulations may contravene the Constitution.

All State organs, the armed forces, all political parties and public organizations and all enterprises and institutions must abide by the Constitution and other laws. All acts in violation of the Constitution or other laws must be investigated.

No organization or individual is privileged to be beyond the Constitution or other laws.

Article 6 The basis of the socialist economic system of the People's Republic of China is socialist public ownership of the means of production, namely, ownership by the whole people and collective ownership by the working people. The system of socialist public ownership supersedes the system of exploitation of man by man; it applies the principle of "from each according to his ability, to each according to his work".

In the primary stage of socialism, the State upholds the basic economic system in which the public ownership is dominant and diverse forms of ownership develop side by side and keeps to the distribution system in which distribution according to work is dominant and diverse modes of distribution coexist.

Article 7 The State-owned economy, namely, the socialist economy under ownership by the whole people, is the leading force in the national economy. The State ensures the consolidation and growth of the State-owned economy.

Article 8 The rural collective economic organizations apply the dual operation system characterized by the combination of centralized operation with decentralized operation on the basis of operation by households under a contract. In rural areas, all forms of cooperative economy, such as producers', supply and marketing, credit and consumers' cooperatives, belong to the sector of socialist economy under collective ownership by the working people. Working people who are members of rural economic collectives have the right, within the limits prescribed by law, to farm plots of cropland and hilly land allotted for their private use, engage in household sideline production and raise privately owned livestock.

The various forms of cooperative economy in cities and towns, such as those in the handicraft, industrial, building, transport, commercial and service trades, all belong to the sector of socialist economy under collective ownership by the working people.

The State protects the lawful rights and interests of the urban and rural economic collectives and encourages, guides and helps the growth of the collective economy.

Article 9 All mineral resources, waters, forests, mountains, grasslands, unreclaimed land, beaches and other natural resources are owned by the State, that is, by the whole people, with the exception of the forests, mountains, grasslands, unreclaimed land and beaches that are owned by collectives as prescribed by law.

The State ensures the rational use of natural resources and protects rare animals and plants. Appropriation or damaging of natural resources by any organization or individual by whatever means is prohibited.

Article 10 Land in the cities is owned by the State.

Land in the rural and suburban areas is owned by collectives except for those portions which belong to the State as prescribed by law; house sites and privately farmed plots of cropland and hilly land are also owned by collectives.

The State may, in the public interest and in accordance with law, expropriate or requisition land for its use and make compensation for the land expropriated or requisitioned.

No organization or individual may appropriate, buy, sell or otherwise engage in the transfer of land by unlawful means. The right to the use of land may be transferred according to law.

All organizations and individuals using land must ensure its rational use.

Article 11 The non-public sectors of the economy such as the individual and private sectors of the economy, operating within the limits prescribed by law, constitute an important component of the socialist market economy.

The State protects the lawful rights and interests of the non-public sectors of the economy such as the individual and private sectors of the economy. The State encourages, supports and guides the development of the non-public sectors of the economy and, in accordance with law, exercises supervision and control over the non-public sectors of the economy.

Article 12 Socialist public property is inviolable.

The State protects socialist public property. Appropriation or damaging of State or collective property by any organization or individual by whatever means is prohibited.

Article 13 Citizens' lawful private property is inviolable.

The State, in accordance with law, protects the rights of citizens to private property and to its inheritance.

The State may, in the public interest and in accordance with law, expropriate or requisition private property for its use and make compensation for the private property expropriated or requisitioned.

Article 14 The State continuously raises labor productivity, improves economic results and develops the productive forces by enhancing the enthusiasm of the working people, raising the level of their technical skill, disseminating advanced science and technology, improving the systems of economic administration and enterprise operation and management, instituting the socialist system of responsibility in various forms and improving the organization of work.

The State practices strict economy and combats waste.

The State properly apportions accumulation and consumption, concerns itself with the interests of the collective and the individual as well as of the State and, on the basis of expanded production, gradually improves the material and cultural life of the people.

The State establishes a sound social security system compatible with the level of economic development.

Article 15 The State practices socialist market economy.

The State strengthens economic legislation, improves macro-regulation and control.

The State prohibits in accordance with law any organization or individual from disturbing the socio-economic order.

Article 16 State-owned enterprises have decision-making power with regard to their operation within the limits prescribed by law.

State-owned enterprises practice democratic management through congresses of workers and staff and in other ways in accordance with law.

Article 17 Collective economic organizations have decision-making power in conducting independent economic activities, on condition that they abide by the relevant laws.

Collective economic organizations practice democratic management and, in accordance with law, elect or remove their managerial personnel and decide on major issues concerning operation and management.

Article 18 The People's Republic of China permits foreign enterprises, other foreign economic organizations and individual foreigners to invest in China and to enter into various forms of economic cooperation with Chinese enterprises and other Chinese economic organizations in accordance with the provisions of the laws of the People's Republic of China.

All foreign enterprises, other foreign economic organizations as well as Chinese–foreign joint ventures within Chinese territory shall abide by the laws of the People's Republic of China. Their lawful rights and interests are protected by the laws of the People's Republic of China.

Article 19 The State undertakes the development of socialist education and works to raise the scientific and cultural level of the whole nation.

The State establishes and administers schools of various types, universalizes compulsory primary education and promotes secondary, vocational and higher education as well as pre-school education.

The State develops educational facilities in order to eliminate illiteracy and provide political, scientific, technical and professional education for workers, peasants, State functionaries and other working people. It encourages people to become educated through independent study.

The State encourages the collective economic organizations, State enterprises and institutions and other sectors of society to establish educational institutions of various types in accordance with law.

The State promotes the nationwide use of Putonghua [common speech based on Beijing pronunciation—Tr.].

Article 20 The State promotes the development of the natural and social sciences, disseminates knowledge of science and technology, and commends and rewards achievements in scientific research as well as technological innovations and inventions.

Article 21 The State develops medical and health services, promotes modern medicine and traditional Chinese medicine, encourages and supports the setting up of various medical and health facilities by the rural economic collectives, State enterprises and institutions and neighborhood organizations, and promotes health and sanitation activities of a mass character, all for the protection of the people's health.

The State develops physical culture and promotes mass sports activities to improve the people's physical fitness.

Article 22 The State promotes the development of art and literature, the press, radio and television broadcasting, publishing and distribution services, libraries, museums, cultural centers and other cultural undertakings that serve the people and socialism, and it sponsors mass cultural activities.

The State protects sites of scenic and historical interest, valuable cultural monuments and relics and other significant items of China's historical and cultural heritage.

Article 23 The State trains specialized personnel in all fields who serve socialism, expands the ranks of intellectuals and creates conditions to give full scope to their role in socialist modernization.

Article 24 The State strengthens the building of a socialist society with an advanced culture and ideology by promoting education in high ideals, ethics, general knowledge, discipline and the legal system, and by promoting the formulation and observance of rules of conduct and common pledges by various sections of the people in urban and rural areas.

The State advocates the civic virtues of love of the motherland, of the people, of labor, of science and of socialism. It conducts education among the people in patriotism and collectivism, in internationalism and communism and in dialectical and historical materialism, to combat capitalist, feudal and other decadent ideas.

Article 25 The State promotes family planning so that population growth may fit the plans for economic and social development.

Article 26 The State protects and improves the environment in which people live and the ecological environment. It prevents and controls pollution and other public hazards.

The State organizes and encourages afforestation and the protection of forests.

Article 27 All State organs carry out the principle of simple and efficient administration, the system of responsibility for work and the system of training functionaries and appraising their performance in order constantly to improve the quality of work and efficiency and combat bureaucratism.

All State organs and functionaries must rely on the support of the people, keep in close touch with them, heed their opinions and suggestions, accept their supervision and do their best to serve them.

Article 28 The State maintains public order and suppresses treasonable and other criminal activities that endanger State security; it penalizes criminal activities that endanger public security and disrupt the socialist economy as well as other criminal activities; and it punishes and reforms criminals.

Article 29 The armed forces of the People's Republic of China belong to the people. Their tasks are to strengthen national defense, resist aggression, defend the motherland, safeguard the people's peaceful labor, participate in national reconstruction and do their best to serve the people.

The State strengthens the revolutionization, modernization and regularization of the armed forces in order to increase national defense capability.

Article 30 The administrative division of the People's Republic of China is as follows:

(1) The country is divided into provinces, autonomous regions, and municipalities directly under the Central Government;

(2) Provinces and autonomous regions are divided into autonomous prefectures, counties, autonomous counties, and cities; and

(3) Counties and autonomous counties are divided into townships, nationality townships, and towns.

Municipalities directly under the Central Government and other large cities are divided into districts and counties. Autonomous prefectures are divided into counties, autonomous counties, and cities.

All autonomous regions, autonomous prefectures and autonomous counties are national autonomous areas.

Article 31 The State may establish special administrative regions when necessary. The systems to be instituted in special administrative regions shall be prescribed by law enacted by the National People's Congress in the light of specific conditions.

Article 32 The People's Republic of China protects the lawful rights and interests of foreigners within Chinese territory; foreigners on Chinese territory must abide by the laws of the People's Republic of China.

The People's Republic of China may grant asylum to foreigners who request it for political reasons.

Chapter II The Fundamental Rights and Duties of Citizens

Article 33 All persons holding the nationality of the People's Republic of China are citizens of the People's Republic of China.

All citizens of the People's Republic of China are equal before the law.

The State respects and preserves human rights.

Every citizen is entitled to the rights and at the same time must perform the duties prescribed by the Constitution and other laws.

Article 34 All citizens of the People's Republic of China who have reached the age of 18 have the right to vote and stand for election, regardless of ethnic status, race, sex, occupation, family background, religious belief, education, property status or length of residence, except persons deprived of political rights according to law.

Article 35 Citizens of the People's Republic of China enjoy freedom of speech, of the press, of assembly, of association, of procession and of demonstration.

Article 36 Citizens of the People's Republic of China enjoy freedom of religious belief.

No State organ, public organization or individual may compel citizens to believe in, or not to believe in, any religion; nor may they discriminate against citizens who believe in, or do not believe in, any religion.

The State protects normal religious activities. No one may make use of religion to engage in activities that disrupt public order, impair the health of citizens or interfere with the educational system of the State.

Religious bodies and religious affairs are not subject to any foreign domination.

Article 37 Freedom of the person of citizens of the People's Republic of China is inviolable.

No citizen may be arrested except with the approval or by decision of a people's procuratorate or by decision of a people's court, and arrests must be made by a public security organ.

Unlawful detention or deprivation or restriction of citizens' freedom of the person by other means is prohibited, and unlawful search of the person of citizens is prohibited.

Article 38 The personal dignity of citizens of the People's Republic of China is inviolable. Insult, libel, false accusation or false incrimination directed against citizens by any means is prohibited.

Article 39 The residences of citizens of the People's Republic of China are inviolable. Unlawful search of, or intrusion into, a citizen's residence is prohibited.

Article 40 Freedom and privacy of correspondence of citizens of the People's Republic of China are protected by law. No organization or individual may, on any ground, infringe upon citizens' freedom and privacy of correspondence, except in cases where, to meet the needs of State security or of criminal investigation, public security or procuratorial organs are permitted to censor correspondence in accordance with the procedures prescribed by law.

Article 41 Citizens of the People's Republic of China have the right to criticize and make suggestions regarding any State organ or functionary. Citizens have the right to make to relevant State organs complaints or charges against, or exposures of, any State organ or functionary for violation of law or dereliction of duty; but fabrication or distortion of facts for purposes of libel or false incrimination is prohibited.

The State organ concerned must, in a responsible manner and by ascertaining the facts, deal with the complaints, charges or exposures made by citizens. No one may suppress such complaints, charges and exposures or retaliate against the citizens making them.

Citizens who have suffered losses as a result of infringement of their civic rights by any State organ or functionary have the right to compensation in accordance with the provisions of law.

Article 42 Citizens of the People's Republic of China have the right as well as the duty to work.

Through various channels, the State creates conditions for employment, enhances occupational safety and health, improves working conditions and, on the basis of expanded production, increases remuneration for work and welfare benefits.

Work is a matter of honor for every citizen who is able to work. All working people in State-owned enterprises and in urban and rural economic collectives should approach their work as the masters of the country that they are. The State promotes socialist labor emulation, and commends and rewards model and advanced workers. The State encourages citizens to take part in voluntary labor.

The State provides necessary vocational training for citizens before they are employed.

Article 43 Working people in the People's Republic of China have the right to rest.

The State expands facilities for the rest and recuperation of the working people and prescribes working hours and vacations for workers and staff.

Article 44 The State applies the system of retirement for workers and staff members of enterprises and institutions and for functionaries of organs of State according to law. The livelihood of retired persons is ensured by the State and society.

Article 45 Citizens of the People's Republic of China have the right to material assistance from the State and society when they are old, ill or disabled. The State develops social insurance, social relief and medical and health services that are required for citizens to enjoy this right.

The State and society ensure the livelihood of disabled members of the armed forces, provide pensions to the families of martyrs and give preferential treatment to the families of military personnel.

The State and society help make arrangements for the work, livelihood and education of the blind, deaf-mutes and other handicapped citizens.

Article 46 Citizens of the People's Republic of China have the duty as well as the right to receive education.

The State promotes the all-round development of children and young people, morally, intellectually and physically.

Article 47 Citizens of the People's Republic of China have the freedom to engage in scientific research, literary and artistic creation and other cultural pursuits. The State encourages and assists creative endeavors conducive to the interests of the people that are made by citizens engaged in education, science, technology, literature, art and other cultural work.

Article 48 Women in the People's Republic of China enjoy equal rights with men in all spheres of life, in political, economic, cultural, social and family life.

The State protects the rights and interests of women, applies the principle of equal pay for equal work to men and women alike and trains and selects cadres from among women.

Article 49 Marriage, the family and mother and child are protected by the State.

Both husband and wife have the duty to practice family planning.

Parents have the duty to rear and educate their children who are minors, and children who have come of age have the duty to support and assist their parents.

Violation of the freedom of marriage is prohibited. Maltreatment of old people, women and children is prohibited.

Article 50 The People's Republic of China protects the legitimate rights and interests of Chinese nationals residing abroad and protects the lawful rights and interests of returned overseas Chinese and of the family members of Chinese nationals residing abroad.

Article 51 Citizens of the People's Republic of China, in exercising their freedoms and rights, may not infringe upon the interests of the State, of society or of the collective, or upon the lawful freedoms and rights of other citizens.

Article 52 It is the duty of citizens of the People's Republic of China to safeguard the unification of the country and the unity of all its nationalities.

Article 53 Citizens of the People's Republic of China must abide by the Constitution and other laws, keep State secrets, protect public property, observe labor discipline and public order and respect social ethics.

Article 54 It is the duty of citizens of the People's Republic of China to safeguard the security, honor and interests of the motherland; they must not commit acts detrimental to the security, honor and interests of the motherland.

Article 55 It is the sacred duty of every citizen of the People's Republic of China to defend the motherland and resist aggression.

It is the honorable duty of citizens of the People's Republic of China to perform military service and join the militia in accordance with law.

Article 56 It is the duty of citizens of the People's Republic of China to pay taxes in accordance with law.

Chapter III The Structure of the State

Section 1 The National People's Congress

Article 57 The National People's Congress of the People's Republic of China is the highest organ of state power. Its permanent body is the Standing Committee of the National People's Congress.

Article 58 The National People's Congress and its Standing Committee exercise the legislative power of the State.

Article 59 The National People's Congress is composed of deputies elected from the provinces, autonomous regions, municipalities directly under the Central Government, and special administrative regions, and of deputies elected from the armed forces. All the minority nationalities are entitled to appropriate representation.

Election of deputies to the National People's Congress is conducted by the Standing Committee of the National People's Congress.

The number of deputies to the National People's Congress and the procedure of their election are prescribed by law.

Article 60 The National People's Congress is elected for a term of five years.

The Standing Committee of the National People's Congress must ensure the completion of election of deputies to the succeeding National People's Congress two months prior to the expiration of the term of office of the current National People's Congress. Should extraordinary circumstances prevent such an election, it may be postponed and the term of office of the current National People's Congress extended by the decision of a vote of more than two-thirds of all those on the Standing Committee of the current National People's Congress. The election of deputies to the succeeding National People's Congress must be completed within one year after the termination of such extraordinary circumstances.

Article 61 The National People's Congress meets in session once a year and is convened by its Standing Committee. A session of the National People's Congress may be convened at any time the Standing Committee deems it necessary or when more than one-fifth of the deputies to the National People's Congress so propose.

When the National People's Congress meets, it elects a Presidium to conduct its session.

Article 62 The National People's Congress exercises the following functions and powers:

(1) to amend the Constitution;

(2) to supervise the enforcement of the Constitution;

(3) to enact and amend basic laws governing criminal offences, civil affairs, the State organs and other matters;

(4) to elect the President and the Vice-President of the People's Republic of China;

(5) to decide on the choice of the Premier of the State Council upon nomination by the President of the People's Republic of China, and on the choice of the Vice-Premiers, State Councilors, Ministers in charge of ministries or commissions, the Auditor-General and the Secretary-General of the State Council upon nomination by the Premier;

(6) to elect the Chairman of the Central Military Commission and, upon nomination by the Chairman, to decide on the choice of all other members of the Central Military Commission;

(7) to elect the President of the Supreme People's Court;

(8) to elect the Procurator-General of the Supreme People's Procuratorate;

(9) to examine and approve the plan for national economic and social development and the report on its implementation;

(10) to examine and approve the State budget and the report on its implementation;

(11) to alter or annul inappropriate decisions of the Standing Committee of the National People's Congress;

(12) to approve the establishment of provinces, autonomous regions, and municipalities directly under the Central Government;

(13) to decide on the establishment of special administrative regions and the systems to be instituted there;

(14) to decide on questions of war and peace; and

(15) to exercise such other functions and powers as the highest organ of state power should exercise.

Article 63 The National People's Congress has the power to remove from office the following persons:

(1) the President and the Vice-President of the People's Republic of China;

(2) the Premier, Vice-Premiers, State Councilors, Ministers in charge of ministries or commissions, the Auditor-General and the Secretary-General of the State Council;

(3) the Chairman of the Central Military Commission and other members of the Commission;

(4) the President of the Supreme People's Court; and

(5) the Procurator-General of the Supreme People's Procuratorate.

Article 64 Amendments to the Constitution are to be proposed by the Standing Committee of the National People's Congress or by more than one-fifth of the deputies to the National People's Congress and adopted by a vote of more than two-thirds of all the deputies to the Congress.

Laws and resolutions are to be adopted by a majority vote of all the deputies to the National People's Congress.

Article 65 The Standing Committee of the National People's Congress is composed of the following:

the Chairman;

the Vice-Chairmen;

the Secretary-General; and

the members.

Minority nationalities are entitled to appropriate representation on the Standing Committee of the National People's Congress.

The National People's Congress elects, and has the power to recall, members of its Standing Committee.

No one on the Standing Committee of the National People's Congress shall hold office in any of the administrative, judicial or procuratorial organs of the State.

Article 66 The Standing Committee of the National People's Congress is elected for the same term as the National People's Congress; it shall exercise its functions and powers until a new Standing Committee is elected by the succeeding National People's Congress.

The Chairman and Vice-Chairmen of the Standing Committee shall serve no more than two consecutive terms.

Article 67 The Standing Committee of the National People's Congress exercises the following functions and powers:

(1) to interpret the Constitution and supervise its enforcement;

(2) to enact and amend laws, with the exception of those which should be enacted by the National People's Congress;

(3) to partially supplement and amend, when the National People's Congress is not in session, laws enacted by the National People's Congress, provided that the basic principles of these laws are not contravened;

(4) to interpret laws;

(5) to review and approve, when the National People's Congress is not in session, partial adjustments to the plan for national economic and social development or to the State budget that prove necessary in the course of their implementation;

(6) to supervise the work of the State Council, the Central Military Commission, the Supreme People's Court and the Supreme People's Procuratorate;

(7) to annul those administrative regulations, decisions or orders of the State Council that contravene the Constitution or other laws;

(8) to annul those local regulations or decisions of the organs of state power of provinces, autonomous regions, and municipalities directly under the Central Government that contravene the Constitution, other laws or administrative regulations;

(9) to decide, when the National People's Congress is not in session, on the choice of Ministers in charge of ministries or commissions, the Auditor-General or the Secretary-General of the State Council upon nomination by the Premier of the State Council;

(10) to decide, when the National People's Congress is not in session, on the choice of other members of the Central Military Commission upon nomination by the Chairman of the Commission;

(11) to appoint or remove, at the recommendation of the President of the Supreme People's Court, the Vice-Presidents and Judges of the Supreme People's Court, members of its Judicial Committee and the President of the Military Court;

(12) to appoint or remove, at the recommendation of the Procurator-General of the Supreme People's Procuratorate, the Deputy Procurators-General and procurators of the Supreme People's Procuratorate, members of its Procuratorial Committee and the Chief Procurator of the Military Procuratorate, and to approve the appointment or removal of the chief procurators of the people's procuratorates of provinces, autonomous regions, and municipalities directly under the Central Government;

(13) to decide on the appointment or recall of plenipotentiary representatives abroad;

(14) to decide on the ratification or abrogation of treaties and important agreements concluded with foreign states;

(15) to institute systems of titles and ranks for military and diplomatic personnel and of other specific titles and ranks;

(16) to institute State medals and titles of honor and decide on their conferment;

(17) to decide on the granting of special pardons;

(18) to decide, when the National People's Congress is not in session, on the proclamation of a state of war in the event of an armed attack on the country or in fulfillment of international treaty obligations concerning common defense against aggression;

(19) to decide on general or partial mobilization;

(20) to decide on entering into the state of emergency throughout the country or in particular provinces, autonomous regions, or municipalities directly under the Central Government; and

(21) to exercise such other functions and powers as the National People's Congress may assign to it.

Article 68 The Chairman of the Standing Committee of the National People's Congress directs the work of the Standing Committee and convenes its meetings. The Vice-Chairmen and the Secretary-General assist the Chairman in his work.

The Chairman, the Vice-Chairmen and the Secretary-General constitute the Council of Chairmen which handles the important day-to-day work of the Standing Committee of the National People's Congress.

Article 69 The Standing Committee of the National People's Congress is responsible to the National People's Congress and reports on its work to the Congress.

Article 70 The National People's Congress establishes a Nationalities Committee, a Law Committee, a Finance and Economic Committee, an Education, Science, Culture and Public Health Committee, a Foreign Affairs Committee, an Overseas Chinese Committee and such other special committees as are necessary. These special committees work under the direction of the Standing Committee of the National People's Congress when the Congress is not in session.

The special committees examine, discuss and draw up relevant bills and draft resolutions under the direction of the National People's Congress and its Standing Committee.

Article 71 The National People's Congress and its Standing Committee may, when they deem it necessary, appoint committees of inquiry into specific questions and adopt relevant resolutions in the light of their reports.

All organs of State, public organizations and citizens concerned are obliged to furnish the necessary information to the committees of inquiry when they conduct investigations.

Article 72 Deputies to the National People's Congress and members of its Standing Committee have the right, in accordance with procedures prescribed by law, to submit bills and proposals within the scope of the respective functions and powers of the National People's Congress and its Standing Committee.

Article 73 Deputies to the National People's Congress and members of the Standing Committee have the right, during the sessions of the Congress and the meetings of the Committee, to address questions, in accordance with procedures prescribed by law, to the State Council or the ministries and commissions under the State Council, which must answer the questions in a responsible manner.

Article 74 No deputy to the National People's Congress may be arrested or placed on criminal trial without the consent of the Presidium of the current session of the National People's Congress or, when the National People's Congress is not in session, without the consent of its Standing Committee.

Article 75 Deputies to the National People's Congress may not be held legally liable for their speeches or votes at its meetings.

Article 76 Deputies to the National People's Congress must play an exemplary role in abiding by the Constitution and other laws and keeping State secrets and, in public activities, production and other work, assist in the enforcement of the Constitution and other laws.

Deputies to the National People's Congress should maintain close contact with the units which elected them and with the people, heed and convey the opinions and demands of the people and work hard to serve them.

Article 77 Deputies to the National People's Congress are subject to supervision by the units which elected them. The electoral units have the power, through procedures prescribed by law, to recall deputies they elected.

Article 78 The organization and working procedures of the National People's Congress and its Standing Committee are prescribed by law.

Section 2 The President of the People's Republic of China

Article 79 The President and Vice-President of the People's Republic of China are elected by the National People's Congress.

Citizens of the People's Republic of China who have the right to vote and to stand for election and who have reached the age of 45 are eligible for election as President or Vice-President of the People's Republic of China.

The term of office of the President and Vice-President of the People's Republic of China is the same as that of the National People's Congress, and they shall serve no more than two consecutive terms.

Article 80 The President of the People's Republic of China, in pursuance of the decisions of the National People's Congress and its Standing Committee, promulgates statutes, appoints or removes the Premier, Vice-Premiers, State Councilors, Ministers in charge of ministries or commissions, the Auditor-General and the Secretary-General of the State Council; confers State medals and titles of honor; issues orders of special pardons; proclaims entering of the state of emergency; proclaims a state of war; and issues mobilization orders.

Article 81 The President of the People's Republic of China, on behalf of the People's Republic of China, engages in activities involving State affairs and receives foreign diplomatic representatives and, in pursuance of the decisions of the Standing Committee of the National People's Congress, appoints or recalls plenipotentiary representatives abroad, and ratifies or abrogates treaties and important agreements concluded with foreign states.

Article 82 The Vice-President of the People's Republic of China assists the President in his work.

The Vice-President of the People's Republic of China may exercise such functions and powers of the President as the President may entrust to him.

Article 83 The President and Vice-President of the People's Republic of China exercise their functions and powers until the new President and Vice-President elected by the succeeding National People's Congress assume office.

Article 84 In the event that the office of the President of the People's Republic of China falls vacant, the Vice-President succeeds to the office of the President.

In the event that the office of the Vice-President of the People's Republic of China falls vacant, the National People's Congress shall elect a new Vice-President to fill the vacancy.

In the event that the offices of both the President and the Vice-President of the People's Republic of China fall vacant, the National People's Congress shall elect a new President and a new Vice-President. Prior to such election, the Chairman of the Standing Committee of the National People's Congress shall temporarily act as the President of the People's Republic of China.

Section 3 The State Council

Article 85 The State Council, that is, the Central People's Government, of the People's Republic of China is the executive body of the highest organ of state power; it is the highest organ of State administration.

Article 86 The State Council is composed of the following:

the Premier;

the Vice-Premiers;

the State Councilors;

the Ministers in charge of ministries;

the Ministers in charge of commissions;

the Auditor-General; and

the Secretary-General.

The Premier assumes overall responsibility for the work of the State Council. The ministers assume overall responsibility for the work of the ministries and commissions.

The organization of the State Council is prescribed by law.

Article 87 The term of office of the State Council is the same as that of the National People's Congress.

The Premier, Vice-Premiers and State Councilors shall serve no more than two consecutive terms.

Article 88 The Premier directs the work of the State Council. The Vice-Premiers and State Councilors assist the Premier in his work.

Executive meetings of the State Council are to be attended by the Premier, the Vice-Premiers, the State Councilors and the Secretary-General of the State Council.

The Premier convenes and presides over the executive meetings and plenary meetings of the State Council.

Article 89 The State Council exercises the following functions and powers:

(1) to adopt administrative measures, enact administrative regulations and issue decisions and orders in accordance with the Constitution and other laws;

(2) to submit proposals to the National People's Congress or its Standing Committee;

(3) to formulate the tasks and responsibilities of the ministries and commissions of the State Council, to exercise unified leadership over the work of the ministries and commissions and to direct all other administrative work of a national character that does not fall within the jurisdiction of the ministries and commissions;

(4) to exercise unified leadership over the work of local organs of State administration at various levels throughout the country, and to formulate the detailed division of functions and powers between the Central Government and the organs of State administration of provinces, autonomous regions, and municipalities directly under the Central Government;

(5) to draw up and implement the plan for national economic and social development and the State budget;

(6) to direct and administer economic affairs and urban and rural development;

(7) to direct and administer the affairs of education, science, culture, public health, physical culture and family planning;

(8) to direct and administer civil affairs, public security, judicial administration, supervision and other related matters;

(9) to conduct foreign affairs and conclude treaties and agreements with foreign states;

(10) to direct and administer the building of national defense;

(11) to direct and administer affairs concerning the nationalities and to safeguard the equal rights of minority nationalities and the right to autonomy of the national autonomous areas;

(12) to protect the legitimate rights and interests of Chinese nationals residing abroad and protect the lawful rights and interests of returned overseas Chinese and of the family members of Chinese nationals residing abroad;

(13) to alter or annul inappropriate orders, directives and regulations issued by the ministries or commissions;

(14) to alter or annul inappropriate decisions and orders issued by local organs of State administration at various levels;

(15) to approve the geographic division of provinces, autonomous regions, and municipalities directly under the Central Government, and to approve the establishment and geographic division of autonomous prefectures, counties, autonomous counties, and cities;

(16) in accordance with the provisions of law, to decide on entering into the state of emergency in parts of provinces, autonomous regions, and municipalities directly under the Central Government;

(17) to examine and decide on the size of administrative organs and, in accordance with the provisions of law, to appoint or remove administrative officials, train them, appraise their performance and reward or punish them; and

(18) to exercise such other functions and powers as the National People's Congress or its Standing Committee may assign to it.

Article 90 Ministers in charge of the ministries or commissions of the State Council are responsible for the work of their respective departments and they convene and preside over ministerial meetings or general and executive meetings of the commissions to discuss and decide on major issues in the work of their respective departments.

The ministries and commissions issue orders, directives and regulations within the jurisdiction of their respective departments and in accordance with law and the administrative regulations, decisions and orders issued by the State Council.

Article 91 The State Council establishes an auditing body to supervise through auditing the revenue and expenditure of all departments under the State Council and of the local governments at various levels, and the revenue and expenditure of all financial and monetary organizations, enterprises and institutions of the State.

Under the direction of the Premier of the State Council and in accordance with the provisions of law, the auditing body independently exercises its power of supervision through auditing, subject to no interference by any other administrative organ or any public organization or individual.

Article 92 The State Council is responsible and reports on its work to the National People's Congress or, when the National People's Congress is not in session, to its Standing Committee.

Section 4 The Central Military Commission

Article 93 The Central Military Commission of the People's Republic of China directs the armed forces of the country.

The Central Military Commission is composed of the following:

the Chairman;

the Vice-Chairmen; and

the members.

The Chairman assumes overall responsibility for the work of the Central Military Commission.

The term of office of the Central Military Commission is the same as that of the National People's Congress.

Article 94 The Chairman of the Central Military Commission is responsible to the National People's Congress and its Standing Committee.

Section 5 The Local People's Congresses and Local People's Government at Various Levels

Article 95 People's congresses and people's governments are established in provinces, municipalities directly under the Central Government, counties, cities, municipal districts, townships, nationality townships, and towns.

The organization of local people's congresses and local people's governments at various levels is prescribed by law.

Organs of self-government are established in autonomous regions, autonomous prefectures and autonomous counties. The organization and working procedures of organs of self-government are prescribed by law in accordance with the basic principles laid down in Sections 5 and 6 of Chapter III of the Constitution.

Article 96 Local people's congresses at various levels are local organs of state power.

Local people's congresses at or above the county level establish standing committees.

Article 97 Deputies to the people's congresses of provinces, municipalities directly under the Central Government and cities divided into districts are elected by the people's congresses at the next lower level; deputies to the people's congresses of counties, cities not divided into districts, municipal districts, townships, nationality townships, and towns are elected directly by their constituencies.

The number of deputies to local people's congresses at various levels and the manner of their election are prescribed by law.

Article 98 The term of office of the local people's congresses at various levels is five years.

Article 99 Local people's congresses at various levels ensure the observance and implementation of the Constitution and other laws and the administrative regulations in their respective administrative areas. Within the limits of their authority as prescribed by law, they adopt and issue resolutions and examine and decide on plans for local economic and cultural development and for the development of public services.

Local people's congresses at or above the county level shall examine and approve the plans for economic and social development and the budgets of their respective administrative areas and examine and approve the reports on their implementation. They have the power to alter or annul inappropriate decisions of their own standing committees.

The people's congresses of nationality townships may, within the limits of their authority as prescribed by law, take specific measures suited to the characteristics of the nationalities concerned.

Article 100 The people's congresses of provinces, and municipalities directly under the Central Government, and their standing committees may adopt local regulations, which must not contravene the Constitution and other laws and administrative regulations, and they shall report such local regulations to the Standing Committee of the National People's Congress for the record.

Article 101 Local people's congresses at their respective levels elect and have the power to recall governors and deputy governors, or mayors and deputy mayors, or heads and deputy heads of counties, districts, townships and towns.

Local people's congresses at or above the county level elect, and have the power to recall, presidents of people's courts and chief procurators of people's procuratorates at the corresponding level. The election or recall of chief procurators of people's procuratorates shall be reported to the chief procurators of the people's procuratorates at the next higher level for submission to the standing committees of the people's congresses at the corresponding level for approval.

Article 102 Deputies to the people's congresses of provinces, municipalities directly under the Central Government and cities divided into districts are subject to supervision by the units which elected them; deputies to the people's congresses of counties, cities not divided into districts, municipal districts, townships, nationality townships, and towns are subject to supervision by their constituencies.

The units and constituencies which elect deputies to local people's congresses at various levels have the power to recall the deputies according to procedures prescribed by law.

Article 103 The standing committee of a local people's congress at or above the county level is composed of a chairman, vice-chairmen and members, and is responsible and reports on its work to the people's congress at the corresponding level.

A local people's congress at or above the county level elects, and has the power to recall, members of its standing committee.

No one on the standing committee of a local people's congress at or above the county level shall hold office in State administrative, judicial and procuratorial organs.

Article 104 The standing committee of a local people's congress at or above the county level discusses and decides on major issues in all fields of work in its administrative area; supervises the work of the people's government, people's court and people's procuratorate at the corresponding level; annuls inappropriate decisions and orders of the people's government at the corresponding level; annuls inappropriate resolutions of the people's congress at the next lower level; decides on the appointment or removal of functionaries of State organs within the limits of its authority as prescribed by law; and, when the people's congress at the corresponding level is not in session, recalls individual deputies to the people's congress at the next higher level and elects individual deputies to fill vacancies in that people's congress.

Article 105 Local people's governments at various levels are the executive bodies of local organs of state power as well as the local organs of State administration at the corresponding levels.

Governors, mayors and heads of counties, districts, townships and towns assume overall responsibility for local people's governments at various levels.

Article 106 The term of office of local people's governments at various levels is the same as that of the people's congresses at the corresponding levels.

Article 107 Local people's governments at or above the county level, within the limits of their authority as prescribed by law, conduct administrative work concerning the economy, education, science, culture, public health, physical culture, urban and rural development, finance, civil affairs, public security, nationalities affairs, judicial administration, supervision and family planning in their respective administrative areas; issue decisions and orders; appoint or remove administrative functionaries, train them, appraise their performance and reward or punish them.

People's governments of townships, nationality townships, and towns execute the resolutions of the people's congresses at the corresponding levels as well as the decisions and orders of the State administrative organs at the next higher level and conduct administrative work in their respective administrative areas.

People's governments of provinces, and of municipalities directly under the Central Government decide on the establishment and geographic division of townships, nationality townships, and towns.

Article 108 Local people's governments at or above the county level direct the work of their subordinate departments and of people's governments at lower levels, and have the power to alter or annul inappropriate decisions of their subordinate departments and of the people's governments at lower levels.

Article 109 Auditing bodies are established by local people's governments at or above the county level. Local auditing bodies at various levels, independently and in accordance with the provisions of law, exercise their power of supervision through auditing and are responsible to the people's government at the corresponding level and to the auditing body at the next higher level.

Article 110 Local people's governments at various levels are responsible and report on their work to people's congresses at the corresponding levels. Local people's governments at or above the county level are responsible and report on their work to the standing committees of the people's congresses at the corresponding levels when the congresses are not in session.

Local people's governments at various levels are responsible and report on their work to the State administrative organs at the next higher level. Local people's governments at various levels throughout the country are State administrative organs under the unified leadership of the State Council and are subordinate to it.

Article 111 The residents' committees and villagers' committees established among urban and rural residents on the basis of their place of residence are mass organizations of self-management at the grass-roots level. The chairman, vice-chairmen and members of each residents' or villagers' committee are elected by the residents. The relationship between the residents' and villagers' committees and the grass-roots organs of state power is prescribed by law.

The residents' and villagers' committees establish sub-committees for people's mediation, public security, public health and other matters in order to manage public affairs and social services in their areas, mediate civil disputes, help maintain public order and convey residents' opinions and demands and make suggestions to the people's government.

Section 6 The Organs of Self-Government of National Autonomous Areas

Article 112 The organs of self-government of national autonomous areas are the people's congresses and people's governments of autonomous regions, autonomous prefectures and autonomous counties.

Article 113 In the people's congress of an autonomous region, autonomous prefecture or autonomous county, in addition to the deputies of the nationality exercising regional autonomy in the administrative area, the other nationalities inhabiting the area are also entitled to appropriate representation.

Among the chairman and vice-chairmen of the standing committee of the people's congress of an autonomous region, autonomous prefecture or autonomous county there shall be one or more citizens of the nationality or nationalities exercising regional autonomy in the area concerned.

Article 114 The chairman of an autonomous region, the prefect of an autonomous prefecture or the head of an autonomous county shall be a citizen of the nationality exercising regional autonomy in the area concerned.

Article 115 The organs of self-government of autonomous regions, autonomous prefectures and autonomous counties exercise the functions and powers of local organs of State as specified in Section 5 of Chapter III of the Constitution. At the same time, they exercise the power of autonomy within the limits of their authority as prescribed by the Constitution, the Law of the People's Republic of China on Regional National Autonomy and other laws and implement the laws and policies of the State in the light of the existing local situation.

Article 116 The people's congresses of national autonomous areas have the power to enact regulations on the exercise of autonomy and other separate regulations in the light of the political, economic and cultural characteristics of the nationality or nationalities in the areas concerned. The regulations on the exercise of autonomy and other separate regulations of autonomous regions shall be submitted to the Standing Committee of the National People's Congress for approval before they go into effect. Those of autonomous prefectures and counties shall be submitted to the standing committees of the people's congresses of provinces or autonomous regions for approval before they go into effect, and they shall be reported to the Standing Committee of the National People's Congress for the record.

Article 117 The organs of self-government of the national autonomous areas have the power of autonomy in administering the finances of their areas. All revenues accruing to the national autonomous areas under the financial system of the State shall be managed and used by the organs of self-government of those areas on their own.

Article 118 The organs of self-government of the national autonomous areas independently arrange for and administer local economic development under the guidance of State plans.

In exploiting natural resources and building enterprises in the national autonomous areas, the State shall give due consideration to the interests of those areas.

Article 119 The organs of self-government of the national autonomous areas independently administer educational, scientific, cultural, public health and physical culture affairs in their respective areas, protect and sift through the cultural heritage of the nationalities and work for a vigorous development of their cultures.

Article 120 The organs of self-government of the national autonomous areas may, according to the military system of the State and practical local needs and with the approval of the State Council, organize local public security forces for the maintenance of public order.

Article 121 In performing their functions, the organs of self-government of the national autonomous areas, in accordance with the provisions of the regulations on the exercise of autonomy in those areas, employ the spoken and written language or languages in common use in the locality.

Article 122 The State provides financial, material and technical assistance to the minority nationalities to help accelerate their economic and cultural development.

The State helps the national autonomous areas train large numbers of cadres at various levels and specialized personnel and skilled workers of various professions and trades from among the nationality or nationalities in those areas.

Section 7 The People's Courts and the People's Procuratorates

Article 123 The people's courts of the People's Republic of China are the judicial organs of the State.

Article 124 The People's Republic of China establishes the Supreme People's Court and the people's courts at various local levels, military courts and other special people's courts.

The term of office of the President of the Supreme People's Court is the same as that of the National People's Congress. The President shall serve no more than two consecutive terms.

The organization of the people's courts is prescribed by law.

Article 125 Except in special circumstances as specified by law, all cases in the people's courts are heard in public. The accused has the right to defense.

Article 126 The people's courts exercise judicial power independently, in accordance with the provisions of law, and not subject to interference by any administrative organ, public organization or individual.

Article 127 The Supreme People's Court is the highest judicial organ.

The Supreme People's Court supervises the administration of justice by the people's courts at various local levels and by the special people's courts. People's courts at higher levels supervise the administration of justice by those at lower levels.

Article 128 The Supreme People's Court is responsible to the National People's Congress and its Standing Committee. Local people's courts at various levels are responsible to the organs of state power which created them.

Article 129 The people's procuratorates of the People's Republic of China are State organs for legal supervision.

Article 130 The People's Republic of China establishes the Supreme People's Procuratorate and the people's procuratorates at various local levels, military procuratorates and other special people's procuratorates.

The term of office of the Procurator-General of the Supreme People's Procuratorate is the same as that of the National People's Congress; the Procurator-General shall serve no more than two consecutive terms.

The organization of the people's procuratorates is prescribed by law.

Article 131 The people's procuratorates exercise procuratorial power independently, in accordance with the provisions of law, and not subject to interference by any administrative organ, public organization or individual.

Article 132 The Supreme People's Procuratorate is the highest procuratorial organ.

The Supreme People's Procuratorate directs the work of the people's procuratorates at various local levels and of the special people's procuratorates. People's procuratorates at higher levels direct the work of those at lower levels.

Article 133 The Supreme People's Procuratorate is responsible to the National People's Congress and its Standing Committee. People's procuratorates at various local levels are responsible to the organs of state power which created them and to the people's procuratorates at higher levels.

Article 134 Citizens of all China's nationalities have the right to use their native spoken and written languages in court proceedings. The people's courts and people's procuratorates should provide translation for any party to the court proceedings who is not familiar with the spoken or written languages commonly used in the locality.

In an area where people of a minority nationality live in a concentrated community or where a number of nationalities live together, court hearings should be conducted in the language or languages commonly used in the locality; indictments, judgments, notices and other documents should be written, according to actual needs, in the language or languages commonly used in the locality.

Article 135 The people's courts, the people's procuratorates and the public security organs shall, in handling criminal cases, divide their functions, each taking responsibility for its own work, and they shall coordinate their efforts and check each other to ensure the correct and effective enforcement of law.

Chapter IV The National Flag, the National Anthem, the National Emblem and the Capital

Article 136 The national flag of the People's Republic of China is a red flag with five stars.

The national anthem of the People's Republic of China is the March of the Volunteers.

Article 137 The national emblem of the People's Republic of China consists of an image of Tian'anmen in its center illuminated by five stars and encircled by ears of grain and a cogwheel.

Article 138 The capital of the People's Republic of China is Beijing.

Note

1. This English translation is available on the official website of the National People's Congress of China, http://www.npc.gov.cn/englishnpc/Law/2007-12/05/content_1381903.htm.

Index